No Use

No Use

Nuclear Weapons and U.S. National Security

Thomas M. Nichols

PENN

UNIVERSITY OF PENNSYLVANIA PRESS

PHILADELPHIA

A volume in the Haney Foundation Series, established in 1961
with the generous support of Dr. John Louis Haney.

Published by
University of Pennsylvania Press
Philadelphia, Pennsylvania 19104-4112
www.upenn.edu/pennpress

Printed in the United States of America on acid-free paper
10 9 8 7 6 5 4 3 2 1

Library of Congress Cataloging-in-Publication Data
Nichols, Thomas M.
   No use : nuclear weapons and U.S. national security / Thomas M. Nichols.—
1st ed.
      p. cm.— (Haney Foundation series)
   Includes bibliographical references and index.
   ISBN 978-0-8122-4566-0 (hardcover : alk. paper)
   1. Nuclear weapons—Government policy—United States. 2. National
security—United States. 3. United States—Military policy. 4. Nuclear
disarmament—United States. 5. Security, International. I. Title. II. Series: Haney
Foundation series.
   UA23.N5495 2014
   355.0''170973—dc23
                                                          2013026524

For my father, Nick James Nichols,
who saw the beginning of the nuclear age,
and my daughter, Hope Virginia Nichols,
who I hope will see its end

General Black: We're talking about the wrong subject. We've got to stop war, not limit it.

Professor Groteschele: That is not up to us, General Black.

Black: We're the ones who know most about it.

General Stark: You're a soldier, Blackie. You carry out policy. You don't make it.

Black: Don't kid yourself, Stark. The way we say a war can be fought *is* making policy. If we say we can fight a limited war with nuclear weapons, we let everyone off the hook. It's what they want to hear. We can just keep on doing what we're doing, and nobody really gets hurt.

Groteschele: Are you advocating disarmament, General Black?

Black [pauses]: I don't know.

—*Fail-Safe* (1964)

Contents

Although writing a book about the meaning of nuclear weapons has been in the back of my mind for years, I always hesitated about starting the project. A fair part of that reticence reflected the fact that much of what follows here could not have been written even a decade ago: not only did I think differently then about nuclear weapons during the Cold War and its immediate aftermath, but there was much that we simply did not yet know (and still do not know) about the making of nuclear policies in the United States and the former Soviet Union. Nonetheless, I knew that the issues in this book have been coloring many of the other problems I've studied over the years. Whether writing about Soviet civil-military politics as I did at the start of my career, or considering the advent of a new international age of preventive war as I did in my most recent work, the use of nuclear weapons and the possibility of nuclear war were constant companions to the questions I was investigating.

Paradoxically, I nonetheless avoided writing specifically about nuclear weapons for quite some time, because the implications of their use are so complicated and immense that they tend to swamp all other conclusions about anything else. The new reality, for example, that the United States and other nations now think much more permissively about preventive war—that is, attacking other nations far in advance of an actual threat—logically raises the question of whether anyone would use nuclear weapons in such preventive attacks. But to focus on that possibility in the larger discussion of preventive war risks placing the momentous but slight possibility of nuclear use at the center of what should be a larger discussion about the use of any kind of force. Once we start to think about nuclear bombs going off, it gets a little harder to think about anything else.

I also shied away from a project on nuclear weapons because I did not want my work to be overly influenced by my own experiences coming of age in the shadow of global nuclear war. (Whether I've succeeded will be up to the reader, of course.) As I've written elsewhere, I grew up in an Air Force town that was home to a major Strategic Air Command nuclear bomber base. Like many communities that hosted the American nuclear deterrent, we didn't like to think much about the weapons that were sitting up the road at the base, but we knew they were there and what that meant for us in the event of a war. The Cold War did not end until I was thirty, and until then I had never known anything but a world that was, at least to me, defined by the standoff with the USSR and kept at peace only by the protective shield of American nuclear power. While I was somewhat more comfortable writing about nuclear history, as I did in the late 1990s, I am not certain that I could have written about the future of nuclear weapons while I was still so close to their past.

As the twentieth anniversary of the 1989 fall of the Berlin Wall approached, however, I finally decided to study and write about nuclear weapons directly rather than by implication. I presumed that I knew my way around these issues, and that my thinking was mostly settled. At the least, I felt reasonably well equipped to tackle modern nuclear strategy: I had spent years studying the Soviet Union and Russia, worked in both the private and public sector on both nuclear and conventional military issues, and taught strategy and national security affairs in a military institution.

As I began writing the book, I quickly realized I was mistaken. First, I found that any approach to the study of nuclear issues required relearning the history of the Cold War. Although I had experienced it and had to some extent participated in it, like many other scholars of international relations I felt swamped by the revelations and new knowledge that became available only after the Cold War's end. These new histories showed how deeply the Soviets and the Americans were plagued by irresolvable questions about the role of nuclear arms, and more important, how both were ruled by an almost paralyzing fear of nuclear conflict. It is one thing to guess at these findings, which might have been predictable or intuitive on a human level, but it is another to see them in the actual documents and memoirs from the Cold War era.

Second, and more unsettling, I found that many of my own previous beliefs about the utility of nuclear force fell apart on closer examination. I realized that a great deal of what I thought I *knew* about nuclear deterrence actually reflected what I *assumed* about nuclear deterrence. Much of my thinking about nuclear arms rested on my familiarity with the Soviet Union and my subjective judgment about what would deter the Soviet leadership from resorting to war. My beliefs about deterrence—like all beliefs about deterrence—were based on my best guess about the nature of the enemy. This is not to say that I believed in any actual need for the tens of thousands of nuclear weapons stockpiled during the Cold War, but rather only that I accepted that the Soviet Union, for whatever mad reasons, could only be deterred from taking great risks by the presence of a large nuclear arsenal massed against it. The goal was to make the Kremlin afraid to court war, and if it took 20,000 warheads to do it, such was the price of keeping the peace during the Cold War.

I cannot know now whether I was right or wrong to believe this. I think I was correct, in a general way, to regard the Soviet regime in its day as mildly psychotic: delusional, paranoid, prone in unpredictable measure both to fits of great fear and sweeping overconfidence, and obsessed with totems of power, including the near-worship of nuclear weapons, in a way that made no sense to a normal person. I also had to accept as well the unfortunate reality that the American national security bureaucracy had become inured to dealing with ghastly amounts of nuclear firepower. It is clearer to me now that the grinding business of maintaining a nuclear deterrent took on a life of its own far earlier than I and many others wanted to believe. Within a decade of their discovery, nuclear weapons were an industry and an intellectual endeavor that escaped control in both East and West. We live with that legacy today, and it is a far more durable one than I expected to find.

Nuclear weapons are a routine part of the lives of the great powers. Concepts and weapons created during a different time, and which could only be rationalized by the supreme needs of national survival, continue to define the international security environment. As I write this, the last U.S. troops have returned from a war ostensibly launched to prevent Iraq from acquiring nuclear weapons and other weapons of mass destruction. Even larger conflicts potentially loom with North Korea and Iran over the same issue. The United States and its allies, so far, are still investing their hopes in nuclear deterrence. What was once a desperate expedient forced upon the West by the accidental and brief existence of the Soviet Union is now a virtually unquestionable cornerstone of American national security policy.

I am neither an antinuclear activist nor a sanguine theorist of nuclear employment. I do not think a goal of zero nuclear weapons can be reached in my lifetime, but neither do I believe that nuclear weapons can solve any of the new problems America faces in the twenty-first century. If I am certain of anything, it is only that I know that we can do better in our thinking about nuclear weapons than we have since 1945, and so rather than provide only criticism, this book is my attempt to contribute to a more constructive rethinking of nuclear weapons and of their role in both American and international security.

Books can take a long time to write, especially when events (and the author's mind) keep changing, and they are never written alone. This study is no exception, and it would have been impossible to complete without the help of many people and institutions.

I am indebted to the International Security Program and the Project on Managing the Atom at the Belfer Center for Science and International Affairs at Harvard University's John F. Kennedy School of Government. During my three years as a Fellow at the Kennedy School, I was fortunate to receive the advice and input of a diverse group of colleagues with expertise in nuclear issues ranging from proliferation policy to nuclear engineering. My time at the Belfer Center was a good reminder that even in midcareer, scholars can—and should—learn something new. I would especially like to thank Managing the Atom's executive director, Martin Malin, for his friendship and advice, and the International Security Program (ISP) board and its director, Steven Miller, for the willingness to host me for an extended stay. I also wish to thank Susan Lynch at ISP for all of her assistance during my time there.

An early draft of the concepts in this study, and particularly on the problems of nuclear war with small states, was presented in Zurich at a conference on the history of proliferation held by the Center for Security Studies at the Swiss Federal Institute of Technology. I later presented parts of the research to colleagues at the Czech Institute of International Relations in Prague and the Polish Institute of International Affairs in Warsaw. I thank all of these organizations for their invitations to discuss my work with them and for their comments.

Much of the discussion in the book regarding ethical and moral problems in nuclear strategy is the result of issues I have studied as a senior associate of the Carnegie Council on Ethics and International Affairs in New York City. My association with the council encouraged me to include those issues in my curriculum at Harvard Extension and in the classrooms of the Naval War College, and I wish to thank the council and its president,

Joel Rosenthal, for my affiliation with the council during the writing of this study.

I was fortunate to have a great deal of feedback on earlier drafts of this book and the concepts in it from many of my colleagues at the U.S. Naval War College, including David Burbach, Col. Steve Charbonneau USAF, Tom Fedyszyn, Steve Fought, Nick Gvosdev, Joan Johnson-Freese, Mackubin Owens, John Schindler, Andrew Stigler, and Dana Struckman. I want to extend special thanks to my friend and colleague, Lt. Col. Mike Waters USAF, who not only read significant portions of the manuscript, but had to put up with the civilian guy across the office constantly peppering him with questions. Finally, I would also like to thank the provost, Ambassador Mary Ann Peters, for her strong support of faculty research at the Naval War College.

I owe thanks as well to many friends and colleagues at other institutions for their help and comments, including Matthew Bunn, William Burr, Elbridge Colby, Jeffrey Lewis, Kier Lieber, Jeffrey Mccausland, Andrew Newman, T. V. Paul, Andrew Ross, Gary Schaub, Steve Sternheimer, and James Wilson. I would also like to thank the anonymous reviewers for the University of Pennsylvania Press. As always, the conclusions of this study are those of the author alone. They do not represent the views of any of the people who provided comments or the institutions who provided assistance with the project, nor of the United States Government or of any other organizations with which I have been affiliated.

For many years, I have had the privilege of teaching at the Harvard Extension and Summer Schools. I am grateful to my students in my classes there on nuclear weapons and international security who participated in lively debates with me about many of the ideas in the book during its writing. Both Harvard Extension and the Naval War College have student research programs that also made it possible for me to work with many talented research assistants and graduate students, and I wish to thank Tim Clarke, Dan Feldman, Ahmed Hassan, Amy Hull, Michael Miner, David Nicholson, Joshua Sheehan, and Chris Thomas for their help.

Bill Finan, my editor at the University of Pennsylvania Press, was a source of constant support and wise advice for this book from conception to publication. Bill and I worked on my previous book as well, and once again I have not only benefited from his steady editorial hand (which I know I've put to the test over the years) but also from his friendship, optimism, and encouragement.

This book is dedicated to my father, Nick James Nichols, and to my daughter, Hope Virginia Nichols. My father was one of America's dwindling number of World War II veterans, and although he passed away as the book was nearing completion, we had many conversations about its subject. He was stationed in California as a private in the U.S. Army in early 1945, and while the first nuclear bomb may well have saved his life, he never believed that anyone would ever be crazy or evil enough to fight an all-out nuclear war. He had a confidence and peace of mind about this that I envied during the Cold War, but his wisdom seems to have been borne out, at least where the Americans and the Russians are concerned. My daughter, born in Moscow long after the Cold War's end, is too young to know what all the fuss was about. I hope that when she reads some of these pages in later years, she will wonder exactly the same thing.

Why Nuclear Weapons Still Matter

> We endorse setting the goal of a world free of nuclear weapons and working
> energetically on the actions required to achieve that goal.
> —George Shultz, William Perry, Henry Kissinger, and Sam Nunn, 2007

> As long as nuclear weapons exist, the United States will maintain safe,
> secure, and effective nuclear forces, including deployed and stockpiled
> nuclear weapons, highly capable nuclear delivery systems and command
> and control capabilities, and the physical infrastructure and the expert
> personnel needed to sustain them.
> —U.S. Nuclear Posture Review, 2010

Isn't Nuclear War Yesterday's Problem?

The Soviet flag was lowered over the Kremlin for the last time on Christmas
Day 1991. That evening, U.S. President George H. W. Bush addressed the
American people and assured them that the long nuclear nightmare of the
Cold War had finally come to an end. "For over 40 years," Bush said, "the
United States led the West in the struggle against communism and the
threat it posed to our most precious values. This struggle shaped the lives
of all Americans. It forced all nations to live under the specter of nuclear
destruction."

That confrontation, the president declared, "is now over."[1]

And so it was. For a brief period at the close of the twentieth century,
it seemed as if the nuclear anxieties of the Cold War could finally be put

aside. Both the United States and the new Russian Federation began to dismantle their nuclear weapons, target them away from each other, and to corral and secure what was left of the former Soviet Union's nuclear arsenal. Nuclear war receded into the recent past as yesterday's worry, no longer relevant in a world released from the constant tension of the longstanding Soviet-American nuclear confrontation.

Prominent Cold Warriors in the United States and Europe, and even some in Russia, have since advocated deep reductions in nuclear arms. Many have supported the goal of reaching "global zero," the complete eradication of nuclear weapons. In 2008, a bipartisan group that included former National Security Advisor and Secretary of State Henry Kissinger, former Secretary of State George Shultz, former Senator Sam Nunn, and former Secretary of Defense William Perry (sometimes collectively called the "Gang of Four") issued a now-famous open letter in which they called for a world free of nuclear weapons.[2] For a time, this message of nuclear abolition resonated widely and attracted considerable attention among both policy elites and ordinary citizens, and a collection of senior officials and top military commanders from several countries soon joined these statesmen in rejecting the foundations of the strategic doctrines they helped to create. In 2009, U.S. President Barack Obama formally committed the United States to the objective of the complete eradication of nuclear arms in a speech in Prague, a goal he reaffirmed in an official review of U.S. nuclear policies in 2010.

But the moment passed quickly. In May 2011, Shultz, Perry, Kissinger, and Nunn hosted a meeting in London later described by former Australian foreign minister Gareth Evans as "featuring a worldwide cast of some 30 former foreign and defense ministers, generals, and ambassadors who share their concern and commitment" to nuclear disarmament. None of these officials, however, were still in their former positions of power. "Our average age was over 65," Evans noted ruefully, and the limits of their effectiveness were neatly described at the conference by former British Defense Minister Des Browne: "People who used to be something really want to tackle this issue. The trouble is that those who are something don't."[3] As President Obama began his second term in office, his administration retained and reaffirmed previous Cold War concepts, strategies and forces. Today, more than 20,000 nuclear weapons remain around the world, with some 5,000 of those operational and ready for war, and many arms control advocates are concerned that the window for further reductions, at least for some time to come, has closed.[4]

Despite this slowing momentum, the U.S. and its allies deserve credit for at least trying to reduce their dependence on nuclear arms. (Great Britain has seriously considered the question of whether it needs a nuclear deterrent at all.)[5] Other nations, however, are trying to reach their own nuclear moment. North Korea, with a tiny arsenal (and a new leader assuming power in 2012 while still so young he would not have been allowed to be a member of the U.S. Senate) has made explicit nuclear threats against its neighbors and the United States. In late 2012, North Korea finally succeeded in testing a three-stage missile—the precursor to an intercontinental-range attack capability—by launching a satellite into space.[6] A few months later, the North Korean regime issued a cascade of nuclear threats that were extreme even by Pyongyang's typically extreme level of rhetoric, provoking an ongoing crisis with the United States and South Korea whose outcome is still uncertain.[7] Meanwhile, Iran's mullahs remain unswerving in their determination to join the nuclear club, and even backward Myanmar has been caught toying with nuclear weapons technology.[8]

Russia and China are long-standing members of the nuclear club, and strategic nuclear weapons remain central to their respective defense strategies, in part to compensate for the limited reach and power of their conventional forces. The Chinese appear to have made a decision, at least for the near future, to sustain a small but increasingly modern nuclear force.[9] The Russians, however, remain stubbornly committed to their insistence on the right to maintain a large and varied nuclear arsenal—and to use it if necessary. Senior Russian military officers bluntly admit that this position is driven not only by a firm belief in traditional nuclear deterrence, but by the hope that nuclear weapons can compensate for the poor overall state of the Russian military. "The nuclear status of Russia," according to the commander of Russia's nuclear forces, "will remain in the foreseeable future, until scientific and technical progress or a change in the nature of international relations eliminates the deterring role of nuclear weapons."[10]

The Indians and the Pakistanis, locked in their own regional nuclear arms race, continue to rely on nuclear weapons as the core of their national defenses. Israeli nuclear strategy is likely predicated on similar concerns about national survival, although the size of the Israeli arsenal remains unknown and unacknowledged. The Israeli nuclear program has long been one of the world's worst-kept secrets, as part of a careful game meant to induce uncertainty and caution in Israel's enemies (and to avoid international inspection and pressure for disarmament).

The United States, for its part, has for more than forty years maintained a public commitment to nuclear disarmament in one form or another, while simultaneously asserting the right to possess and use nuclear weapons in any number of scenarios. The end of the Cold War allowed the Americans and the Russians to slash their nuclear inventories, but these were reductions from unimaginably huge levels. From a high of over 30,000 weapons in the late 1960s, the United States as of 2013 has more than 4,000 warheads, and many more in storage awaiting destruction. Fewer than 2,000 are deployed, a number that will drop to 1,550 in coming years as the result of "New START," ratified by the U.S. Senate in the last days of 2010 and the Russian parliament shortly thereafter. Despite this step forward, thousands of nuclear arms, representing many millions of tons of destructive power, will remain in place on both sides. As U.S. Senator Lamar Alexander (R-TN) said during the ratification debate, he was willing to vote for the treaty because it left America with "enough nuclear warheads to blow anyone to kingdom come."[11]

While we will return to New START in later chapters, it is worth noting that the difficulties and anxieties surrounding the treaty's ratification were themselves testimony to the centrality of nuclear weapons to U.S. security thinking. The debate was mired in partisan politics, to be sure, but treaty opponents issued bitter warnings that even modest nuclear reductions would endanger U.S. national security—at a time when the United States is all but supreme as a military power and the North Atlantic Treaty Organization (NATO) is the dominant alliance from Anchorage to Istanbul and beyond.[12] There is no denying that strategic nuclear weapons are today the only means capable of ending the American system of government and the United States itself in minutes; as the Pentagon's advisory body, the Defense Science Board, noted in 2008, "no threat can put the nation's existence at risk as quickly and as chillingly as nuclear weapons."[13]

Nonetheless, achieving a small additional reduction should not have proved so contentious, especially after the major, and sometimes unilateral, U.S. arms reductions of the early 1990s. It is clear that most U.S. political leaders and many in the other established nuclear nations see significant possibilities for nuclear reductions and lowering the danger of nuclear conflict. It is just as evident, however, that the Americans and others continue, as a matter of national policy, to invest an immense amount of faith in nuclear weapons. Meanwhile, rogue states and would-be great powers pursue nuclear programs as shortcuts to what they hope will be more security and greater prestige.

Why is it so difficult for the major powers, and the United States in particular, to break the nuclear addiction, and what role should nuclear weapons play in America's national security? These are the central questions of this book.

Nuclear Doctrine and American Security Strategy

Nuclear weapons are different from other instruments of war. Not only is their power beyond imagination, but also they are still the first and only weapons capable of eradicating human civilization. Historical analogies fail us, because none exist.

Every country that possesses nuclear weapons has had to wrestle with questions about the political and military utility of their arsenal—in effect, about what nuclear weapons *mean*. The answers to these questions are expressed in each nation's overarching beliefs and assumptions about nuclear arms and their purpose, which in turn guide nuclear strategy, planning, and forces. This collection of informal beliefs and formal policies constitute nuclear doctrine, a word that appropriately suggests an almost theological set of assumptions about why nuclear weapons exist and how they should be used. (This is not "doctrine" as the U.S. military often uses the term, which only describes particular guidance for combat and weaponry of various types.) These concepts, at least in theory, provide the foundation for building strategy, in which large-scale military assets such as nuclear weapons are employed to achieve the goals of national policy.

Once the objects of intense study and detailed analysis, nuclear doctrine and strategy have eroded into disarray both among civilian thinkers and government nuclear strategists, whose numbers are dwindling. The U.S. Chairman of the Joint Chiefs of Staff, Admiral Michael Mullen, noted in 2010 that the experts who once worked through these problems are now largely gone: "We have not worked very hard to find [their] replacements. We don't have anybody in our military that does that anymore. It's as if we all breathed a collective sigh of relief when the Soviet Union collapsed and said to ourselves, 'Well, I guess we don't need to worry about that anymore.' We were dead wrong."[14] The careful analysis and comparison of nuclear arsenals has become, in arms control thinker Michael Krepon's words, "the province of an aging, shrinking demographic."[15] Even in senior American military educational institutions such as the U.S. Air Force's Air War College or the U.S. Naval War College, the study of nuclear strategy fell by the wayside almost before the first stones of the Berlin Wall were cleared away.

As a result, Cold War–era precepts about nuclear weapons have continued to dominate national security policy and nuclear strategies by default. The doctrines of the Cold War continue to lock the United States, Russia, and others into outdated thinking about nuclear weapons, especially the tenacious, unshakeable belief that nuclear force is integral to the national security of any major power. This was a reflexive article of truth for most leaders during the Cold War, as well as for the generation of thinkers and policymakers whose formative experiences were forged in the tense later years of the Soviet-American struggle.

Former U.S. Secretary of State George Shultz, for example, decades later recalled the incredulity of the British prime minister when U.S. President Ronald Reagan and Soviet President Mikhail Gorbachev broached the topic of eliminating the world's nuclear weapons during their 1986 summit in Iceland:

> When I came back to Washington from Reykjavik I was more or less summoned to the British ambassador's residence. And Prime Minister Margaret Thatcher "hand-bagged" me. That is, you know, she carried that little stiff handbag, and she whacked me. She said, "George, how can you sit there and allow the president to agree to a world free of nuclear weapons?" I said, "But Margaret, he's the president." She said, "Yes, but you're supposed to be the one holding his feet on the ground." "But Margaret, I agreed with him," I said.
>
> Her reaction was typical. I think people were enamored of the idea of deterrence through nuclear weapons. . . . The idea of a world free of nuclear weapons would not have gone down well in Washington and among our allies in 1986. . . . I don't think the world was ready for it.[16]

The world, apparently, is still not ready for it. Assumptions about the utility of nuclear force and the strength of nuclear deterrence continue to echo through the entire security architecture of the nuclear-armed nations.

In the United States, the stubborn adherence to the idea that nuclear weapons have broad political as well as military utility is a construct that continues to have a powerful effect on choices about weapons, the formulation of strategies, and the daily conduct of U.S. diplomacy, especially with NATO and the Russian Federation. In the early 1990s, U.S. Air Force General George Butler found himself taken aback by the breadth and staying power of these beliefs when he called for phasing out the U.S. nuclear arsenal in the wake of the Soviet collapse. He was "dismayed," he later wrote, "that even among more serious commentators, the lessons of 50 years at the nuclear brink can still be so grievously misread; that the assertions and assumptions underpinning an era of desperate threats and risks prevail unchallenged; that a handful of nations cling to the impossible notion that the power of nuclear weapons is so immense their use can be threatened with impunity, yet their proliferation contained."[17]

In 1999, almost a decade after the end of the Cold War, a group of scholars at the Brookings Institution noted that U.S. thinking about the role of nuclear arms continued to adhere to the belief that the "targeting and declaratory doctrines developed during the [Cold War], which emphasize early and large attacks against nuclear forces and permit the first use of nuclear weapons [are] valuable in deterring threats to U.S. interests."[18] Ten years after the Brookings report, a joint working group of scientists and policy analysts found that "U.S. nuclear strategy and policy continued to lack a coherent and compelling rationale."[19] And when the Obama administration released its own review of nuclear doctrine in 2010, critics almost immediately derided it as little more than a continuation of tradition rather than anything substantively new.[20]

Of course, it could be argued with some justice that American thinking about nuclear weapons was never all that clear-headed in the first place. To be sure, U.S. planners and their Soviet counterparts worked hard on these issues. They came up with elaborate, highly detailed scenarios for various kinds of nuclear conflict, all of which were predicated on optimistic assumptions about how nuclear conflicts could be fought, controlled, and terminated despite the vast damage and widespread chaos that would characterize even a modest nuclear exchange.

These efforts consumed immense human and material resources, but never produced useful answers. As Lawrence Freedman noted in a landmark study of nuclear strategy written in the early 1980s: "The question of what happens if deterrence fails is vital for the intellectual cohesion and credibility of nuclear strategy. . . . No operational nuclear strategy has yet to be devised that does not carry an enormous risk of degenerating into a bloody contest of resolve or a furious exchange of devastating and crippling blows against the political and economic centers of the industrialized world."[21] If U.S. nuclear strategy seemed complicated and fantastic during the Cold War, in part it was because there was an opposing Soviet superpower whose own nuclear doctrine was clearly defined and no less intricate. Soviet planning provided a constant spur to thinking, creative or otherwise, about American nuclear forces and what purpose they were supposed to serve.

Today, all that is left of the Soviet nuclear superpower is a faded Russian successor that can barely contend with problems on its own borders. Russia's nuclear forces, while still a notional danger, lack the ideological and imperial purposes that made the Soviet arsenal such a deadly threat. With the Soviet Union gone, the United States is left with a massive nuclear complex that was designed to fight, and if possible survive, a global nuclear war with a similarly armed superpower. Deprived of its original logic, U.S. doctrine has since lost whatever internal coherence it might have had, and cannot provide guidance for answers to nuclear threats that are evolving and changing. Reforming U.S. nuclear doctrine is the key not only to the reform of U.S. national security policy, but also to the continued reduction of nuclear arsenals and the prevention of the wider spread of nuclear weaponry.

A less alarmist view might be to ask why there should be any serious concern about nuclear doctrine in the United States or in any other of the major powers. The United States, Russia, Britain, France, and China have already adopted clear views on the role of nuclear weapons, with all-out nuclear war among them deterred by the promise of assured destruction, and smaller strikes by regional proliferators deterred by the considerable nuclear muscle of the bigger nations. Whether by accident or design, the outcome is the same: steep reductions in the world's arsenals have obviated the complicated nuclear warfighting scenarios of the past.

Where the smaller nuclear powers are concerned, presumably they will replicate the successful Soviet-American experience. ("Success" in this sense is measured by more than a half century in which there was no use of nuclear weapons.) Why not assume that the Indians and the Pakistanis, and perhaps the Israelis and the Iranians, will be deterred by the thought of even a small nuclear war? These relative newcomers to the nuclear game may well be developing strategies for regional conflict and thinking through the implications of localized exchanges of nuclear weapons, but that does not mean that they are willing to risk war with each other any more than the superpowers were.

Moreover, with the twin boons of the end of the Cold War and the advent of globalization, the Russians, Americans, Chinese, and almost everyone else should now rest assured that they are safer in a less ideologically charged, more transparent, and more interconnected world. The arcane intricacies of brinkmanship have been displaced by attempts to get to, or stay at, lower numbers of nuclear weapons, and maybe even achieve the grail of "zero" in a more tranquil future. Scholar John Mueller, for one, has dismissed the idea that nuclear arms were ever all that important; in 1988 he predicted that the "nuclear arms competition may eventually come under control not so much out of conscious design as out of atrophy born of boredom."[22] In the years since the end of the Cold War, he has continued to maintain that the fixation on nuclear threats is misguided and wasteful.[23]

Unfortunately, the real world stubbornly refuses to conform to such optimistic expectations. Even if we accept the arguable proposition that something like the classical model of nuclear deterrence will operate among the established nuclear powers and prevent all-out nuclear war, simply to leave it at that is to seize upon the least likely threat and declare the nuclear issue solved. Scholar Paul Bracken has for many years pointed out that the stability of deterrence between the United States and the Soviet Union will be no guide to the future, a warning he issued again in late 2012: "Back in the Cold War, it's my view that there was never a time when either side seriously considered a calculated strike on the other. All of them had plans—and you could find colonels and one-star generals who thought about these things—but at the top of the government, both sides backed down. That's not going to be true in the case of North Korea. It's not going to be true in South Asia with Pakistan and India, nor is it going to be true in the Middle East."[24] In other words, to say that traditional notions of deterrence, or even the much-debated nuclear "taboo"—if one actually exists—will likely govern great power relations is not to say very much, and may not be all that accurate.[25] Even analysts who continue to insist on the utility of nuclear deterrent threats accept that the outcome of the Cold War may have had more to do with luck than design.[26]

Russian and U.S. nuclear inventories have been reduced since the late 1980s. But all of the nuclear-armed powers retain a single-minded focus on nuclear deterrence, and they continue to modernize their arsenals. Worse, fears of rogue nuclear programs and nuclear terrorism have fueled confusion and overreaction in Washington and elsewhere. As arms control analyst Hans Kristensen wrote in 2007, "it is as if the uncertainty and unpredictability of the post-Cold War world have clouded strategic deterrence thinking and caused planners to incorporate all capabilities, just to be safe, into every potential scenario."[27]

These nuclear war plans, while smaller and less complicated than in the past, remain confused and convoluted. For example, U.S. and Russian war games since the Cold War have envisioned firing very small numbers of strategic nuclear missiles, as though this would contain or settle a major conflict among Russia, the United States, or China. A Russian war game in 1999 assumed a bizarre NATO attempt to grab the Russian enclave of Kaliningrad in the Baltic, and concluded with Russian nuclear strikes—two in Western Europe, two in North America itself—that led not to retaliation, but to the "aggressor" desisting from its designs on Russian real estate.[28] A decade later, another Russian exercise simulated a nuclear response against Poland, likely as a show of displeasure over U.S. missile defense plans in Europe.[29]

The Americans have generally been more sensible, but not by much. In late 2006, the U.S. military ran an exercise called "Vigilant Shield," in which a conflict with "Nemazee," "Ruebek," and "Churya" (that is, North Korea, Russia, and China) somehow led to a nuclear attack on the Pentagon and a government bunker in Maryland. Miraculously, only 6,000 people were killed when these hypothetical nuclear weapons detonated within sight of the White House and the Washington Mall, but the Americans finally prevailed with just a handful of U.S. strategic nuclear launches against targets in Eurasia. No reason was given for the attack on the U.S. capital region or why it was not followed by more strikes, although the likely reason is that a larger attack, requiring a larger response, would have complicated the tidy assumptions of the game designers.[30] All of this prompted journalist and Pentagon critic William Arkin to note that two of the core assumptions in the game were obviously that "nuclear warfare can break out for no particular reason at any particular time," and that "small nuclear weapons, while bad, don't really kill that many people."[31]

Removing nuclear weapons from their pride of place will require a fundamental change in the way Americans and others think about their security. Efforts to change the Cold War nuclear paradigm will encounter significant political, ideological, and bureaucratic obstacles, because reducing the importance of nuclear weapons will involve remaking American security strategy as a whole.

A major obstacle to this kind of reform is that the relatively nonviolent outcome of the Cold War has had a lasting effect on thinking about war and peace well past the fall of the Soviet Union. As the saying goes, "nothing succeeds like success," and policymakers and their bureaucracies understandably tend to want to stay with what they think worked and thus repeat their previous successes. They therefore defend long-standing concepts and programs that over time become almost impossible to challenge. As defense scholars Janne Nolan and James Holmes pointed out in an autopsy of repeated failures to change U.S. nuclear strategies, "career officials are capable of mounting a devastating defense against initiatives put forth by political appointees. . . . As a country, [the United States] has never had a real debate about how much deterrence is enough."[32] The strategic rationales of the Cold War are more difficult to defend today, but reams of papers, slides, and studies protect the nuclear bureaucracy like an intellectual Maginot Line.

This intellectual stagnation is especially unfortunate now that the moral dimension of nuclear use is more complicated than ever. The mutual Soviet-American stranglehold, in which nuclear deterrence and retaliation were coupled to national survival itself, obviated much of the discussion about the morality of nuclear weapons. Even during the worst periods of tension with the USSR, however, Western leaders and their advisors wondered about the moral acceptability of inflicting massive and indiscriminate casualties on an enemy once all is lost, and whether an existential threat was worth an equally existential response. Today, large-scale nuclear war is highly unlikely, and nuclear use against a smaller power will therefore be a discretionary option rather than a desperate necessity. Without a threat to American civilization itself, nuclear weapons are now more an instrument of choice rather than necessity, and this has led many men and women who were once the chief advocates of nuclear deterrence to argue for abandoning outdated concepts of nuclear combat and dismantling the weapons that serve them.

In the end, only the United States, with its fortunate geopolitical advantages, its unique position of international leadership, and its huge qualitative edge in nuclear matters (to say nothing of other technologies) can meaningfully lead any kind of change in global norms about the purpose and meaning of nuclear arms. This will require difficult and politically unpopular choices, material sacrifice, steadfast diplomacy, and the courage to assert America's confidence in its ability to lead and protect the international order without nuclear threats. But the creation of a post-nuclear age will not happen without a fundamental rejection both of beliefs about nuclear weapons and ideas about what constitutes "national security" in the twenty-first century.

Overview

Concepts about nuclear weapons, rather than the weapons themselves, are central to the problem of security in a nuclear world. Consequently, this book is about the current state of U.S. nuclear doctrine and strategy, the effects of American thinking about nuclear weapons on international security, and the various ways that the United States might reduce the overall threat of nuclear weapons to the international community. This book is not about nuclear technology, nor is it meant to present a comprehensive history of the Cold War or the nuclear arms race. Those books and articles have already been written over the past three decades, as seminal contributions by Robert Jervis, Lawrence Freedman, John Newhouse, and others, and they are works to which this one owes a clear intellectual debt.

Instead, this study is aimed at reducing the centrality of nuclear weapons in U.S. security strategy in the twenty-first century. Of course, it is impossible to understand the current nuclear situation without understanding the intellectual and physical legacy of the Cold War. The U.S. missiles that stand on alert at this moment were designed and built in the 1960s, and were the result of a series of strategic debates and decisions that now seem like ancient history to students and specialists alike. We live in a world that was shaped by the Cold War, and engaging current policies about nuclear weapons means unavoidably engaging the thought and work that laid their foundations decades ago. Accordingly, the next chapter of this book will present an overview of U.S. nuclear strategy from the end of World War II to the end of the Cold War.

Chapter 2 recounts the disarray and confusion that settled over U.S. nuclear doctrine after the Soviet collapse. Three times since the Cold War, the United States has tried to engage in a full review of its nuclear doctrine. Each time, these efforts failed to move U.S. nuclear thinking beyond formulations that represented an amalgam of outdated intellectual constructs and stubborn rationalizations for existing weapons systems. These missed opportunities repeatedly produced cautious documents that served, in the main, to reaffirm the status quo and defend the right to use nuclear weapons.

Eastern and Western planners alike were obsessed by an arms race that was dominated by numbers and capabilities, and so they routinely contemplated thousands of nuclear strikes during a world war. Whether even the most courageous or iron-willed leaders would have been able to make some sort of sense out of a situation that would likely have degenerated into uncontrollable global chaos within minutes was a question uneasily subordinated to the all-encompassing task of deterrence. With the Cold War gone, however, so is the need to arm for protracted nuclear war, and Chapter 3 argues for reforming U.S. nuclear doctrine around the concept of "minimum deterrence," the notion that even the largest nuclear powers can be deterred by the threat of only a very few strategic nuclear strikes.

Minimum deterrence is increasingly growing into official policy in the major nuclear powers, and is already the foundation of nuclear defense in Britain, France, and the People's Republic of China. Still, a U.S. doctrine of minimum deterrence needs to be given greater coherence and more explicit recognition if it is to enhance the international stability required both for further nuclear reductions and a lasting nuclear peace. The United States remains the leader of the wealthiest and most powerful military alliance in human history, and neither the United States nor NATO faces any severe nuclear danger. While Russia has the ability to destroy the United States and its European allies, and China could inflict grievous damage to Eurasia and North America, there is no threat remotely like that posed by the former Soviet Union in the twenty-first century, nor is one likely to emerge over even the longest horizon, and there is no reason to continue to act, speak, and spend as if there were.

If nightmares are measured not by their intensity but by their likelihood, then the most terrifying scenario is a nuclear crisis with a small nation. After the Soviet implosion, the United States found itself a superpower able to destroy the Earth itself but paralyzed in the face of lesser threats. Chapter 4 will examine this problem of small nuclear powers, a far more complicated dilemma than it might appear—and more than U.S. policymakers have been willing to admit.

The United States has long relied on the policy of "ambiguity," in which Washington has intentionally left unclear how it might respond to a chemical or biological attack, or perhaps to the use only of a single nuclear weapon, by a small nation. This lack of clarity leaves the door open for nuclear use, but without forcing the Americans to make threats that could come back to haunt them if those threats have to be fulfilled. Meanwhile, rogue regimes and their leaders are ostensibly deterred by their uncertainty about the consequences of their actions. But is any threat to use nuclear weapons against small states in crowded regions either credible or morally defensible? It is one thing to contemplate a strike on the Soviet Union during World War III in a desperate bid for survival; it is another entirely to contemplate the massive, and perhaps grossly disproportionate, dislocation and havoc that would be created by engaging in nuclear strikes in small, densely populated areas such as East Asia or the Middle East.

Simple promises of nuclear retaliation against small aggressors are too facile. In a large-scale exchange with a peer, the need for action is immediate and the later consequences are a distant consideration in the heat of a fight for national survival. Smaller nations, however, cannot threaten the U.S. system of government or the American state, and the decision to use nuclear weapons, except in dire cases of preemption of additional nuclear strikes, will turn heavily on the proportionality and cost of the consequences. Chapter 5 will consider the costs of nuclear responses and the alternative of conventional retaliation. If nuclear proliferation is to be stopped, the United States and its allies—and, one might argue, the Russians as well—are going to have to devote more thought to how rogues and their clients can be deterred or their arsenals destroyed without resorting to nuclear force.

The final chapter will consider the price of the proposals for nuclear peace put forward in this study. These costs, both financial and political, will be considerable, but not insurmountable. The most wrenching questions, however, will not be over dollars and weapons, but diplomacy, sacrifice, and self-image. Will the American people and their representatives be willing to become more pacifist and more warlike at the same time? On the one hand, ending the nuclear addiction means not only divesting the United States of large numbers of nuclear weapons, but ending almost seventy years of reliance on the absolute power of nuclear arms. On the other hand, it means that the United States must be ready to make good on real threats of military force—and accept the casualties it will produce among our own soldiers—against countries and groups that refuse to overcome their nuclear obsessions.

False Choices

Since the collapse of the USSR, questions over the future of nuclear weapons and their role in U.S. national security have been plagued by false choices. Nuclear pacifism or nuclear aggression? Missile defenses, or surrender to nuclear blackmail? Abolition of nuclear weapons, or uncontrolled proliferation? We no longer face the choice of "Red or dead"; indeed, even during the Cold War this was an artificial dichotomy in a world where the main question was, or should have been, how to avoid a nuclear war, no matter how it originated.[33] But that does not mean the years of difficult choices are now over.

The underlying questions about nuclear force have remained much the same since 1945. What is the actual political role of nuclear weapons? Do they have any military utility? Can a moral allowance be made for the use of weapons that can kill thousands, even millions, and eradicate entire cities in an instant? During the Cold War, the danger of Armageddon competed with the question of national survival. The deterrent threat of mass killing did not represent the moral high ground or the nobler heritages of either Russian or American civilization. But as horrible as it was, nuclear deterrence was the unavoidable result of the intense struggle that emerged from the ruins of World War II.

Today, the world is less dangerous, but that reality has had little effect on thinking about the role of nuclear weapons in the national security policies of the United States and other nations. Global nuclear war, which seemed so possible only a quarter century ago, is now so remote a possibility that it seems almost pointless to try to imagine how it could occur. And yet, the former superpowers still plan for it. U.S. Ambassador to NATO Ivo Daalder and former Defense Department official Jan Lodal noted in 2008 that the United States "still has a nuclear force posture that, even with fewer nuclear weapons, retains all of the essential characteristics it had during the Cold War."[34] As of 2011, New START now limits the United States and Russia to 1,550 warheads, nested on each side in a Cold War triad of land-based missiles, bomber aircraft, and submarine-launched weapons. Counting weapons in storage, this number represents more than a two-thirds decline in the stockpile of nuclear devices since the height of the Cold War. Both sides, however, remain in their Cold War postures, and each retains enough nuclear capacity to destroy every major city in the Northern Hemisphere, and with them Western civilization itself.

The false binary choices of the Cold War should be behind us, but the systems and strategies of the Cold War remain. How did we come to this state of affairs? We explore the history of U.S. nuclear strategy and its enduring legacy in the next chapter.

Chapter 1

Nuclear Strategy, 1950–1990: The Search for Meaning

> *Senator Glenn.* I got lost in what is credible and not credible. This whole thing gets so incredible when you think about wiping out whole nations.
> *Secretary Brown.* That is why we sound a little crazy when we talk about it.
> —Defense Secretary Harold Brown and Senator John Glenn during U.S. Senate hearings, 1980

"Weapons in Search of a Doctrine"

Nuclear weapons, as Henry Kissinger often remarked during the Cold War, are weapons continually in search of a doctrine. The history of the evolution of nuclear strategy in the United States, as in the other nuclear powers, is a story of the ongoing attempt to find political meaning and military relevance in weapons so destructive that they defeat traditional notions about strategy and the use of force in international affairs. As early as 1946, the American strategic thinker Bernard Brodie wrote that nuclear weapons represented the "end of strategy," since any attempt at strategic reasoning collapsed in the face of the twin facts that nuclear weapons existed and were unimaginably powerful.[1] The question that arose after the first detonation of a nuclear bomb in the summer of 1945 remains today: What do nuclear weapons actually *do*?

Nearly seven decades later, there is still no American consensus on this question. Scholars, security analysts, civilian policymakers, and military leaders all continue to be divided over whether nuclear arms exist to *fight* wars, or to *prevent* wars—or whether the readiness to fight increases or decreases the likelihood of having to fight at all. In 1984, Robert Jervis, echoing Brodie, charged that a "rational strategy for the employment of nuclear weapons is a contradiction in terms. The enormous destructive power of these weapons creates insoluble problems," and thus the history of nuclear strategy "has been a series of attempts to find a way out of this predicament and return to the simpler, more comforting pre-nuclear world."[2] Other strategists during the Cold War rejected this kind of thinking as defeatism; Colin Gray wrote in a 1979 reflection on Brodie's work that even in the most terrifying circumstances, there is still "a role for strategy—that is, for the sensible, politically directed application of military power in thermonuclear war."[3]

Those debates continue to the present day, but they cannot be understood without examining the Cold War efforts that preceded them. The world-destroying strategies conjured by the professional strategists, "the Wizards of Armageddon," in Fred Kaplan's famous phrase, are largely relics of the past, relegated to history by the generations who lived through the Cold War and regarded as curiosities by younger generations who did not.[4] Nonetheless, the theories that animated the work of the Cold War strategists remain at the foundation of current thinking about nuclear issues.

The 1950s: "At Times and Places of Our Own Choosing"

For the first few years after the nuclear attacks on Hiroshima and Nagasaki, the United States did not have a nuclear "strategy" so much as it had a nuclear "problem." American leaders had difficulty comprehending the enormity of their new super-weapon; while they saw the devastation visited upon Hiroshima and Nagasaki, these were relatively small, one-sided attacks that were retribution for a surprise attack, four years of war, and hundreds of thousands of U.S. casualties. The first two nuclear bombs, Fat Man and Little Boy, inflicted a huge amount of destruction in moments, but the damage was still comparable to the ruin inflicted in slow-motion over weeks of relentless firebombing, and both of the afflicted Japanese cities still stand today.

Within years of Japan's defeat, however, nuclear delivery systems became more reliable and nuclear bombs became vastly more powerful. In short order, nuclear attack was no longer even remotely comparable to a strategic bombing campaign. Instead, policymakers had to think about the instant and complete destruction of dozens of major cities from long distances, a horrifying concept never before encountered in the study or practice of war.

The essence of the American problem in this first decade after World War II was that unarguable nuclear superiority did not seem to buy very much security, especially in Europe. The newly formed North Atlantic Treaty Organization faced the conventional superiority of a Communist coalition that stretched from the Baltic Sea to the Bering Strait. Worse, the Western nuclear arsenal (Britain's first bomb was detonated in 1952) did not seem to imbue the Soviet Union with any greater sense of caution: nuclear weapons did not thwart Soviet leader Josef Stalin's gambles in Berlin, nor did they prevent the invasion of South Korea. The Americans and their allies, as Lawrence Freedman later wrote, felt they were "being forced into fighting the [Cold War] and would have to fight any future hot war according to ground rules laid down by the communists."[5] Years later, revelations from Soviet archives and interviews of former Soviet policymakers would show that the Soviets were in fact acutely conscious of the danger of war and particularly of nuclear war.[6] But Stalin himself, bolstered by the crushing victory over the Nazis and the acquisition of a new European empire, was nonetheless willing to run significant risks even in the face of a nuclear near-monopoly.[7]

The U.S. solution at the time was the strategy of "Massive Retaliation," first described in a 1953 U.S. National Security Council paper and enunciated publicly a year later in more detail by Secretary of State John Foster Dulles. President Dwight Eisenhower's initial "New Look" at strategy affirmed that nuclear weapons would be essential to repulse a Soviet attack on the U.S. and NATO. Dulles went farther, and warned that the utility of nuclear arms extended beyond the battlefield: they could even act as a general strategic deterrent. That is, a U.S. nuclear attack on a grand scale—"Massive Retaliation"—against the USSR or its allies would henceforth be the price for any kind of Soviet or Communist-sponsored aggression, anywhere in the world.

No longer would the Americans try to match the USSR man for man and pound for pound. Instead, Washington would try to exploit its nuclear superiority by using it to deter Soviet aggression. Moscow was put on notice that any major offenses (however they might be defined) by the USSR or its proxies against the Western allies would result in the United States exercising its "great capacity to retaliate, instantly, by means and at places of [America's] choosing."[8]

The Americans really had little choice at the time. Even with mass conscription or huge increases in defense spending, there was no way to fight the Communist bloc on its own terms. Outmanned and outgunned, the West had no hope of protecting every possible corner of the earth from a hemispheric Sino-Soviet alliance. Korea, where Western arms had restored the status quo only by a whisker, was proof enough of that. Allowing the East to dictate the terms of every engagement would be disastrous. "If the enemy," Dulles said in 1954, "could pick his time and his place and method of warfare—and if our policy was to remain the traditional one of meeting aggression by direct and local opposition—then we needed to be ready to fight in the Arctic and the tropics, in Asia, in the Near East and in Europe; by sea, by land, by air; by old weapons and by new weapons."[9] Massive Retaliation was an asymmetric solution to this asymmetric dilemma, with nuclear weapons threatened as the dire punishment that Western conventional forces could not guarantee.

As a concept, Massive Retaliation was simplicity itself. As an actual strategy, however, it lacked clarity and credibility. The most obvious and logical question centered on the nuclear threshold. What might trigger U.S. retaliation? An invasion of Europe, certainly, but beyond that? Aggression in Indochina? Soviet abuse of its own allies? Proxy warfare conducted by a third power? Massive Retaliation was a hammer, not a scalpel, and it could not be tailored for anything much less than a direct, punishing attack on the Soviet Union. The Americans themselves were not sure where the nuclear lines were drawn, as there were simply too many scenarios to contemplate. It is one thing to induce uncertainty in the opponent; it is another entirely to *share* that uncertainty. (As we will see in Chapter 4, the United States replicated this mistake four decades later in trying to gain political leverage from its nuclear arsenal against rogue states after the Cold War.)

The true Achilles' heel of the whole strategy, however, was that it rested on the inherently unsustainable condition of U.S. nuclear superiority. Massive Retaliation, a deeply flawed concept from the outset, could only last until the USSR developed the ability to retaliate in kind. Soviet leaders accordingly developed a missile-centric doctrine focused on a swift and secure retaliatory capability. In 1960, the USSR established the Strategic Rocket Forces, described by the Soviet defense minister at the time as "unquestionably the main service of the Armed Forces."[10] America's threats of nuclear punishment after 1960 would now have to be made in the teeth of an inevitable Soviet nuclear response, and Soviet-era authors themselves accurately described Massive Retaliation as defunct by 1960.

Massive Retaliation, never fully conceptualized and never executed, in short order became obsolete in the face of new Soviet capabilities. In the end, "Massive Retaliation" was less a strategy than an expression of desperation, and it could not last into the missile age.

The 1960s and the Rise of the Strategists

As the Soviet arsenal grew in both size and capability, U.S. leaders tried to salvage some sense of purpose for their own rapidly increasing nuclear stockpile. The American capacity to destroy the USSR with impunity was out of reach by the time President John F. Kennedy took office in 1960; he was told bluntly (and correctly) by his military advisors that even if the United States launched everything it had at every possible Soviet, Chinese, and Eastern European target, some portion of the Soviet arsenal was certain to survive and inflict horrifying amounts of damage on North America.[11] Accordingly, nuclear strategy became a more evenly matched, two-sided game between the United States and the Soviet Union.

U.S. Secretary of Defense Robert McNamara was determined in this period to wrest control of nuclear issues away from the military, whose approach to nuclear strategy consisted largely of making operational plans to match weapons to targets.[12] Nuclear targeting was no small enterprise in itself; by the mid-1970s, U.S. nuclear war planners had marked 40,000 potential targets for nuclear destruction in the Soviet bloc.[13] But targeting is not the same thing as "strategy," and McNamara wanted decisions over nuclear issues vested in a growing class of civilian defense analysts and policy intellectuals. This set the stage for the rise of the U.S. nuclear strategists, who would generate the many scenarios and strategies that dominated American nuclear thinking well into the 1980s.

Military control of nuclear strategy was undesirable, but the arrival of the civilian strategists was no less problematic. Soon, the nuclear enterprise represented the worst of both worlds, with both military officers and civilian analysts melded into a single community of nuclear experts. To be sure, the Americans (and others) needed to develop greater expertise on nuclear questions, but the unique tribe of defense specialists that emerged in the

1960s soon developed their own language, culture, and customs, which contributed to a growing gulf between theory and policy.

The dispassionate analysis of the use of nuclear weapons, for example, required a new vocabulary, a kind of nuclear Newspeak. Expressions such as "launch on warning" and "counterforce" entered the lexicon, and terms such as "collateral damage" took on significantly amplified meaning. As Kaplan put it, the strategists "performed their calculations and spoke in their strange and esoteric tongues because to do otherwise would be to recognize, all too clearly and constantly, the ghastliness of their contemplations."[14] Much like taking a person through the classic stages of grief, thinkers such as Herman Kahn insisted that Americans had to move past denial and anger, and reach acceptance of the nuclear age. This process entailed calmly thinking through horrific scenarios in which millions of people would die and entire nations would be pulverized.[15] Kahn and other strategists pressed U.S. policymakers to think about the question posed in academic articles and quickly satirized in pop culture landmarks such as *Dr. Strangelove*: do we prefer 20 million dead or 100 million dead?

As soulless or amoral as it might appear, this kind of strategic theorizing served the necessary purpose of allowing ordinary human beings to think about extraordinary situations. Just as euphemism and scientific language assist medical doctors and other professionals in studying their specializations even as they wrestle with the heartbreaking suffering and eventual death of their charges—"pain management" and "end-of-life issues," as they are now gently called—so too did the detached and clinical language of the new strategists enable the contemplation of conflicts of a scale that would dwarf all the wars ever fought in human history.

There was, however, both a moral and an intellectual corrosiveness to this increasingly professionalized approach to nuclear strategy. It may have been necessary to "think about the unthinkable," but soon what was once unthinkable became an ordinary part of U.S. and Soviet national security policies. Military officers and civilian bureaucrats routinized the work of nuclear war planning, often in isolation from the rest of the defense community. This insularity, as Kaplan later wrote, allowed the nuclear theologians to avoid the reality that their efforts always led back to the same dead-end:

In the absence of any reality that was congenial to their abstract theorizing, the strategists in power treated the theory as if it *were* reality. For those mired in thinking about it all day, every day, in the corridors of officialdom, nuclear strategy had become the stuff of a living dreamworld. This mixture of habit, inertia, analytical convenience and fantasy was fueled by a peculiar logic as well. It was, after all, only rational to try to keep a nuclear war limited if one ever broke out. . . . Yet over the years, despite endless studies, nobody could find any options that seemed practical or made sense. [emphasis original][16]

Much like the aridity that came to characterize too much of the social sciences after they embraced "scientific" approaches in the 1970s, so too did the analysis of nuclear strategy quickly become distanced from what policymakers could reasonably comprehend. Looking back at the various briefings and scenarios for war presented to U.S. leaders, Senator Sam Nunn later said: "You can sit around and read all the analytical stuff in the world, but once we start firing battlefield nuclear weapons, I don't think anybody knew."[17] The theorists could pontificate and the war gamers could run their exercises, but as the numbers of weapons grew, the mathematics of nuclear war soon defied the imagination, just as the choices involved challenged the limits of moral reasoning.[18]

Both superpowers accelerated their acquisition of nuclear arms at re-markable rates. The United States alone managed to construct more than 30,000 weapons by 1967, only twenty-two years after the first nuclear test. The Soviet arsenal, too, was growing almost geometrically, and both sides soon commanded a host of delivery options that ranged from artillery shells to multiple-warhead ballistic missiles based on land and under the sea.

At these levels of numbers, what use were nuclear threats? Ironically, since every scenario for a major exchange led down the same path of anni-hilation, the U.S. and Soviet heartlands were now *safer* from direct assault, since neither side could chance a first strike. The sneak attack scenario feared in the 1950s—the so-called "BOOB," or "bolt out of the blue," attack—was no longer possible: a first-strike could neither disarm the vic-tim nor save the attacker. The much greater complication, with North America itself now vulnerable to Soviet weapons, was not whether the United States could defend itself, but whether the Americans would risk nuclear war for their allies in NATO.

The attempt to protect one group of nations with the nuclear weapons of another is the problem of "extended deterrence." To kill in self-defense, or in defense of the family or group, is a common human instinct. Dying for others requires overcoming the instinct for self-preservation with altruism and a notion of a greater good. It may well be, as the New Testament teaches, that there is no greater love than that "a man lay down his life for his friends," but U.S. leaders realized early on in the Cold War that to risk the lives of entire nations and the peace of the world itself on behalf of others was a more complicated proposition, especially after the two world wars had taught humanity a bloody lesson in what the defense of alliances could mean. The Soviets might not doubt that the Americans would make a brave last stand and use nuclear weapons to protect the North American homeland. But could the United States make an equally credible nuclear threat on behalf of their friends in Europe?

The United States was in a painful bind. Washington could hardly back away from a nuclear guarantee for NATO without seeing the Alliance crumble, first politically and then militarily, under the Soviet conventional threat. There was no alternative to defending Europe, but in the face of Soviet conventional superiority, the defense of Europe was impossible without keeping nuclear weapons in play.

When the United States held a nuclear monopoly, a strategy such as Massive Retaliation could more credibly threaten to punish the Kremlin for aggression against NATO. Holding the nuclear trump card lowered the cost to the Americans of making threats on Europe's behalf, not least because the consequences of any test of that resolve would fall almost entirely on the Soviet Union. But once the USSR obtained a secure retaliatory capability, that guarantee would now have to extend to the point of being willing to place the continental United States squarely in the Soviet nuclear crosshairs. Thus, extended deterrence was an immense gamble: it rested not on the intuitive understanding of self-defense, but increasingly on the imponderable question of whether a U.S. president would really risk trading Chicago for Bonn or New York for Paris.

Accordingly, the first order of business for U.S. strategists in the early 1960s was to scrap Massive Retaliation, ending its short tenure within only a few years of its announcement. Future U.S. presidents and their advisors would need more options to deal with a full spectrum of Soviet aggression other than the single choice of incinerating the USSR. A strategy such as Massive Retaliation could not serve the goals of extended deterrence, because it would require the Soviets to believe that an American president would be so steely—or so unhinged—that he would escalate directly from conventional hostilities in Europe to central nuclear war between the United States and the USSR. The key to strengthening the Western deterrent thus relied on showing the Soviet leaders that their American counterparts would, in effect, be left with no other way out but nuclear conflict. A new strategy would have to chart a path, one the Soviets could understand, that would credibly link a crisis to a catastrophe, and therefore induce caution in Moscow.

In order to establish the requirements for a more credible deterrent, Western thinkers began to explore the actual steps to nuclear war. In 1957, for example, Henry Kissinger published his seminal work, *Nuclear Weapons and Foreign Policy*, and the generation of strategists McNamara would later call upon were already working through these problems at research centers such as the RAND Corporation in California. It was at RAND that Herman Kahn first conceptualized the escalatory "ladder" described in his 1960 opus, *On Thermonuclear War*. Kahn's ladder was not a guide to nuclear war itself; rather, it was a detailed examination of various steps each side might take before finding themselves, willingly or not, propelled from a cold peace to complete destruction. Each rung of the ladder, such as "limited evacuation of cities" or "barely nuclear war," was a stop along the way toward the final step of "spasm" or "insensate" war.[19] Massive Retaliation was not credible because it was a threat to make an intentional leap from the lowest rungs of the ladder of escalation to the very highest. The challenge for U.S. policymakers trying to craft a new deterrent in its place, then, was to reduce the distance between each of these rungs by inserting realistic options that did not require momentous or even irrational decisions.

Shortly after arriving in Washington, the Kennedy administration set about trying to construct a more durable U.S. deterrent, both conceptually and materially. The first trial balloon from the Kennedy White House, however, was a hopelessly optimistic "no-cities" strategy, in which Washington and Moscow somehow would agree to refrain from targeting each other's civilian population centers. This proposal represented an American attempt to draw a distinction between "countervalue" attacks, which would strike a full range of social and political targets such as cities and government institutions, and "counterforce" attacks, which would be aimed only at military assets. The goal, at least in theory, was to enhance crisis stability by showing a willingness to discriminate between military targets and cities; presumably, an enemy would be more willing to tough it out and not attack during a tense period if assured that the other side had not targeted civilians and urban centers. At the least, an offer to limit targets might spur a similar pledge from the opponent and keep a nuclear exchange from raging out of control. Ideally, it would help avert war itself not only by sending a message of restraint to the Soviets, but by showing that the United States had come up with a real purpose for nuclear weapons besides the mindless killing of Soviet citizens.[20]

"No cities" was one of many attempts to place a rung on Kahn's ladder somewhere between the outbreak of conventional hostilities and total nuclear war. Like Massive Retaliation, however, it was inherently flawed. Indeed, it was a strategy that only a pure theorist could love, and it could not survive first contact with the real world, where its success would have to rely on the goodwill of a cooperative adversary in the midst of a possible holocaust. Even if both belligerents could reach some sort of prior agreement about conducting a nuclear war, a strategy of "city-avoidance" was doomed from the start by the fact that so many Soviet targets, and no small number of American assets, were located close to population centers. Were Moscow and Washington, the military nerve centers of their respective nations, to be spared? (And if they were slated to be destroyed, who would be left to negotiate a cease-fire or surrender on either side?) The sanctity of cities could never be guaranteed, and a promise not to hit them, or at least not to hit them in the first thirty minutes of the war, was not a promise worth making.

After a period of vigorous debate in the 1960s (during which the shock of the 1962 Cuban missile crisis nearly rendered the whole Soviet-American conflict moot), the United States and its allies in 1967 codified a strategy of "Flexible Response," which NATO described as "a flexible and balanced range of appropriate responses, *conventional and nuclear*, to all levels of aggression or threats of aggression" (emphasis added).[21] Here, the Americans and their allies tried to overcome the credibility problems inherent in "extended deterrence," and to link the defense of North America to the defense of the entire North Atlantic community. Rather than threaten discretionary retaliation at "times and places of our choosing" with the consequent killing of millions of civilians on both sides, U.S. and NATO strategists instead crafted a strategy of deliberate escalation backed by a wider menu of both conventional and nuclear military choices. Now, NATO would fight its way up the escalatory ladder, instead of jumping from the first rung to the last.

As before, the conventional defense of NATO in Europe had virtually no chance of succeeding against a Soviet invasion. That, of course, was the point: the United States and its allies might not resort to strategic nuclear attacks at the outset of the war, but if faced with a Soviet onslaught, they would have no choice but to escalate to tactical nuclear options on the battlefield. The first salvos would halt the Soviet advance, and then the burden either of defeat or escalation would shift to Moscow. Instead of the bluster of Massive Retaliation, the new approach in Flexible Response tried to convince the Soviets that escalation would happen practically by default. Nuclear use would no longer have to result from courageous or stoic American decisions, but would instead be driven by *Soviet* actions.

Flexible response relied on presenting the Kremlin with a paradox, in which the success of Warsaw Pact conventional forces on the battlefield would increase the chance that nuclear weapons would be used against them. Accordingly, U.S. nuclear weapons were intentionally placed in forward positions where they would be overrun by advancing Eastern forces. Henceforth, the Soviets would know that if war broke out in Europe, NATO commanders would be cornered, through no fault of their own, into having to use their nuclear arms or lose them once overwhelmed. Soviet leaders, at least in theory, would be presented with a storyline they could understand and believe, in which the first Soviet bullet fired in Europe would inexorably be tied to the last U.S. or British missile launched from the last silo or submarine. The Soviets would therefore understand that war would likely lead to consequences that neither side wanted but that neither could escape if a crisis were to spin out of control.

NATO's explicit rejection of "no first use," the pledge not to initiate the release of nuclear weapons, was central to this strategy. Logically, a promise not to escalate to nuclear force had to be rejected as a matter of doctrinal first principles: if the Soviet Union truly intended to menace Europe, NATO thinkers reasoned, a "no first use" pledge would be an open invitation to Moscow to try to keep the conflict at the conventional level, where the Soviet advantage was greatest. Instead, NATO's adoption of Flexible Response hammered home the point that the Americans and their allies were ready to drag the Soviets, rung by rung, up the escalatory ladder. A conventional war risked a battlefield nuclear war, and the tactical use of nuclear weapons risked theater nuclear war. At that point, the sunk costs of millions dead, the imminence of defeat, the panic of mass destruction, and the fog of war would all combine to make general nuclear war seem plausible and perhaps even probable. With Flexible Response, NATO was hoping to convince the leaders of the Kremlin that no matter how many men in the Red Army or missiles in the silos of the Strategic Rocket Forces, a war in Europe could not be won and to embark on such a mad enterprise would gain nothing while risking everything.

Parity and the Advent of Mutual Assured Destruction

In the mid-1960s, the Soviets began a major military buildup, including rapid increases in their nuclear forces.[22] By the end of the decade, the USSR would catch up to the Americans in strategic nuclear power, creating a situation of approximate nuclear equality, or "parity." While somewhat unequal in the numbers and distribution of their forces, by any standard each side now controlled roughly as much nuclear firepower as the other, and each could surely destroy the other under any circumstances. (Later in the decade, American secretaries of defense James Schlesinger and Harold Brown would use other terms such as "essential equivalence," but the idea was the same.) The mathematics of parity were unarguable, but the politics were less clear: what did it mean now that East and West were so closely matched?

In concrete terms, little had changed since the early 1960s. Nuclear war still meant appalling levels of damage to both sides, with no hope of anything like a meaningful "victory" for either East or West when it was over. The arrival of Soviet-American parity represented the crossing of a psychological borderline more than a change in the military balance, since it was achieved at numbers of weapons so high that any asymmetries were functionally meaningless. For many American strategists, parity meant the end of any further toying with the pretense of fighting, much less "winning," a nuclear war.

In fact, McNamara and his deputies in President Lyndon Johnson's administration had already decided by the late 1960s to take what they saw as a more direct and stabilizing approach, and to discard the question of victory entirely. Instead, the Americans sought to stress to the Soviets the unavoidable and permanent damage that both sides could do to each other. The Americans proposed, in effect, to enter into a mutual hostage arrangement with the Soviet Union, where each side would forego defenses, cap limits on strategic arms, and do their best to avoid all-out nuclear war. Any indication that either side felt it could survive a nuclear war, such as civil defense programs, would be considered provocative. Likewise, there would be no attempts to hide the size and readiness of retaliatory forces. The more each side understood about the reliability of the other's deterrent, the better. The Americans hoped that the Soviets would internalize and institutionalize the central fact of the superpower confrontations in the 1950s and 1960s that culminated in the Cuban scare: every crisis carried the risk of the extinction of both combatants.

The Soviets were not persuaded, or at least *pretended* they were not persuaded. The flinty Soviet marshals conceded only that victory, at best, would be defined not by a final crushing of the enemy such as the glorious Soviet entry into Berlin, but instead by the eventual long-term recovery of one system more rapidly than the other and the subsequent domination over whatever was left of the world. This position—echoed at times by some American politicians—remained the official Soviet line throughout the 1970s.[23] In both private and public diplomacy, however, Moscow acted with considerably more circumspection than its rhetoric might have suggested. In 1981, Soviet leader Leonid Brezhnev finally referred to the idea of nuclear victory as "dangerous madness," which was a hopeful sign. Later revelations, however, showed that Brezhnev's comments were actually part of an ongoing civil-military struggle at the highest levels of the Soviet regime over the issue of nuclear war.[24] Whether the Kremlin's high command really believed the USSR could win a nuclear war can never truly be known. It might have been a bluff to intimidate the Americans (who had more than a few generals and strategists with similar views themselves), or it may have represented an inability to think beyond the parallels with World War II that dominated Soviet military writings.[25]

Most American analysts were far less sanguine than the Soviet brass about the outcome of World War III, and believed that both sides would be destroyed in any sizable nuclear exchange. Initially, this new doctrine was called "assured destruction," and finally, by the wry acronym that its founders believed best described it: "MAD," or mutual assured destruction. Although MAD seemed like a simple idea in which the victim and the attacker both perish, it was actually far more complicated. Even its various proponents did not fully agree on what it meant, and there were competing notions of MAD during the Cold War that were not fully consistent with each other. Some accepted the possibility of limited nuclear use, while the most pristine version assumed that nuclear war inevitably meant total war and subsequent annihilation. In the end, however, even the Soviets had to bow to the reality that MAD itself was a *fact* rather than a *policy*, in the sense that the ability of both sides to destroy each other was empirically undeniable.[26]

More arguable is what that fact meant for actual policy. Proponents of MAD argued that to ignore the reality of mutual destruction was like trying to ignore the weather, which is always present and always the same for everyone. Opponents of MAD—many of them among the civilian and military national security elites both in the United States and USSR—rejected the helplessness and passivity implied in a doctrine of mutual destruction. They argued that even if MAD was a fact, it was self-defeating to admit it, and they rejected the idea of explicitly accepting a dangerous and delicately balanced nuclear standoff as at best counterintuitive, if not flatly ridiculous.[27]

As far as McNamara and the MAD advocates were concerned, Soviet and American arsenals had reached such staggering levels of quantity and destructive quality that mutual destruction was inescapable. The American public, however, was understandably skeptical about a strategy whose most prominent feature was to leave the United States open to attack. MAD, at least to some critics, sounded like a retreat in the face of the new and improved Soviet nuclear arsenal. Some of those critics were members of Congress, and McNamara consequently found himself having to reassure concerned legislators on Capitol Hill that the United States could still kill most of the Soviet population if necessary. "I think we could all agree," he said in testimony before the Senate in early 1967, "that if [the Soviets] struck first we are going to target our weapons against their society and destroy 120 million of them."[28]

The emergence of MAD as an explicit concept did not end the nuclear debate in either the United States or the Soviet Union. Rather, strategists on both sides intensified their search for ways out of the mutual destruction cage by trying to find more discriminating and thus supposedly more credible military uses for nuclear weapons. Opponents of a pure deterrence strategy, especially among the senior U.S. military leadership, argued that the only way to deter a nuclear war was to appear ready to fight one. Thus, as Kaplan notes, McNamara "talked Assured Destruction," but "the actual targeting strategy" created by the U.S. military remained counterforce, and the Secretary's attempts to use a doctrine of assured destruction as a means of "beating back the excessive demands of the military and [Joint Chiefs]" failed in the face of the Pentagon's insistence on being able to fight a global nuclear war.[29] (Two critics of this approach later sarcastically referred to these warfighting requirements as a strategy of "Nuclear Utilization Target Selection"—that is, "NUTS" as opposed to "MAD.")[30]

This inherent tension between targeting and doctrine continues in U.S. nuclear strategy to the present day. Although America's nuclear doctrine during the Cold War was termed "assured destruction," its nuclear forces were designed and postured for both a counterforce war as well as retaliatory strikes. Military logic demanded that the most pressing targets for U.S. strategic forces should be the same type of enemy nuclear forces, followed by other military targets, energy and industrial infrastructure, and finally, population. This ordering of strikes was meant to communicate to the enemy that in the event of nuclear war, the United States would act like a rational military power and seek first and foremost to protect itself (while sparing innocent civilians as much as possible), and then proceed to strip the enemy of its ability to fight, its ability to govern, its ability to recover, and finally, its ability to exist at all. The paradox, of course, was that a readiness to proceed along so orderly a path of escalation also ran the risk of signaling that that the United States did not fear "assured" destruction and was willing to fight a nuclear conflict—thus theoretically giving the enemy an incentive to abandon further efforts at deterrence, and instead to strike first and hope for the best.

The advocates of MAD had the better argument about nuclear targeting, not only because of the destructive power of nuclear weapons, but because of the continual problem of "co-location," meaning the proximity of military targets to nonmilitary areas. This is not a dilemma specific to nuclear war, of course: imprecise conventional bombers in World War II could not avoid devastating the areas around military targets placed in or near cities. Likewise, there was no way the nuclear counterforce scenario could really discriminate between military and civilian targets in any meaningful way—or at least not in a way that would allow the enemy to distinguish a limited strike from an all-out attack.

While there might be some hypothetical chance of limiting the use of nuclear arms on the battlefield, or even in the theater of war, those limits would almost certainly evaporate minutes into a strategic exchange. An attack meant only to cripple U.S. land-based missiles, for example, would require several hundred, if not thousands of warheads. Such a strike would be so large that the destruction would be indistinguishable from an attempt at national obliteration, especially in the midst of the kind of chaos which would surround a U.S. president in the few moments left for deliberation over how to respond. No matter what either side wanted or intended, the terrible imperative of MAD would quickly assert itself once such an exchange was under way

The search for a silver bullet that could solve this dilemma and allow a longer interval of nuclear warfighting (and thus ostensibly limit the conflict early) inevitably led both sides to think about missile defenses. By the mid-1960s, land- and sea-based intercontinental ballistic missiles (ICBMs) constituted the main Soviet and American deterrent forces, and once the superpowers could destroy each other in a matter of minutes, the urge to find a way out of that paralyzing reality was sure to follow. The idea of a national missile defense capable of destroying nuclear-armed, long-range ballistic missiles in flight was a natural extension of the Cold War arms race.[31]

The discussion about missile defenses in the 1960s was more important as a conceptual exercise rather than as practical effort. Missile defenses of any kind are complicated and difficult to construct even in the twenty-first century, but national defenses were virtually impossible in the era before the development of more advanced technologies. Supercomputers with only a fraction of the speed and computing power of a modern notebook or laptop computer cost millions of dollars each in the 1960s and 1970s. (Consider, for example, that the recently retired U.S. space shuttle at first carried less computing power aboard than people take for granted in their mobile phones today.) Moreover, "defenses" in the 1960s were not precise weapons that could cleanly eliminate incoming strikes and thus save large, soft targets such as cities. Rather, they were blunt instruments that relied on exploding nuclear weapons—some as large as five *megatons*—high in the atmosphere to wipe out the armada of warheads falling onto North America from space.

The Americans concluded early on that there was no way these systems could defend anything but the most hardened targets such as missile silos, and even those stood little chance of survival under most circumstances. But as Kaplan later observed, "once a few billion dollars are spent on any weapons program, the chance of stopping it from going into production is practically nil."[32] The Soviets, of course, had enough weapons to overwhelm any such defense easily, and could always build more. This early Cold War missile defense enterprise finally ended up resting on a half-hearted rationale based on stopping a putative (and at the time, nonexistent) Chinese ballistic threat. The idea was too seductive to abandon completely, but too impractical to defend with any semblance of technological seriousness. One of McNamara's deputies casually asked him if he really wanted to make the case that the United States needed a defense against a future ICBM threat from Asia: "China bomb, Bob?" McNamara muttered in reply: "What else am I going to blame it on?"[33] Eventually, the whole idea was shelved, at least for the time being.

American strategists in the late 1960s, under Lyndon Johnson and then President Richard Nixon, continued the quest to find political meaning in a strategic nuclear exchange even as they increasingly doubted whether such meaning existed. The Soviets, for their part, as disciples of both Clausewitz and Lenin, continued to insist, at least publicly, that even nuclear war would have a political character and that a meaningful victory was possible. This Soviet obstinacy was a challenge for the Americans, because a stable deterrent relationship requires that both sides have some sort of common understanding of the threat and of what each has at stake. The Americans hoped that an East-West agreement not to engage in mutual hemispheric suicide implied a more lasting foundation for cooperation and understanding between Moscow and Washington. The Soviets, however, had agreed to no such thing and were having none of it, choosing instead to regard the strategic nuclear standoff as a license to engage in various kinds of mischief so long as they avoided the risk of general war.[34]

MAD might have been an unarguable fact in terms of describing a strategic nuclear stalemate, but as a policy it was far more contentious. Supporters of an assured destruction doctrine would claim that all MAD was ever supposed to do was to prevent a global disaster, and that by the mid-1970s it was performing that task admirably. Critics countered that the concept had done little more than self-deter the United States from confronting an increasingly aggressive Soviet Union, and had done little to stop a dramatic expansion of Soviet power that the Kremlin itself extolled with considerable pride. For a growing number of these skeptics, MAD looked more like an unholy bargain than a guarantee of global peace.

The Countervailing Strategy and the Collapse of MAD

The 1970s were not kind to the United States. From the defeat in Vietnam to the economic shock of an oil embargo, the Americans and their NATO allies were reeling from a loss of confidence at a time when the USSR was surging in power and influence. America was retreating from its alliances and partnerships, while the Soviet presence around the world was growing rapidly. Worse, the Soviets made no pretense of caring what the United States or the hapless Europeans thought about anything. As former Soviet ambassador Anatoly Dobrynin described in his memoirs, the Soviet leadership would discuss their advances and plans in various regions without so much as a passing reference to the United States.[35]

Soviet adventures were difficult enough to handle while the United States enjoyed nuclear superiority, but with the arrival of Soviet-American nuclear parity, nuclear war plans were even less use to U.S. leaders in 1972 than they had been in 1962. The Pentagon, in trying to unite a number of various operational plans for each part of the U.S. nuclear arsenal, by the early 1960s had factored them all into a giant "Single Integrated Operational Plan" (SIOP) for nuclear war with the USSR, but they still envisioned horrendous amounts of destruction. President Nixon and his national security advisor, Henry Kissinger, were as dissatisfied with these war plans as McNamara had been before them, especially because of their inflexibility and their massive human costs. "Nixon," historian William Burr has written, "was plainly troubled by the SIOP, especially the huge number of projected fatalities."[36]

During Nixon's second term in office, Kissinger finally ordered a complete review of strategic nuclear policy. At a meeting in summer 1973, Kissinger noted that Nixon had not been provided with any other nuclear options other than a full briefing on the SIOP "three or four years" earlier, which "did not fill him with enthusiasm."[37] The object, yet again, was to provide Nixon with more flexibility in the new conditions of Soviet parity and Mutual Assured Destruction so that he, or any U.S. president, would be able to deter the Soviets with something less than catastrophe. In a way, the new condition of parity created the old dilemmas of Massive Retaliation all over again.

The targeting process, as always, was still out of civilian control. Kissinger noted that the SIOP given to Nixon did not "distinguish between retaliation and first strike," because it was an inflexible plan that required hitting every target in the USSR. At the outset of the 1973 meeting, Kissinger needled the Joint Chiefs representative, Vice Admiral John Weinel: "We have been discussing this topic for four years and have come to no conclusions. This is probably by JCS design."[38] ("You give us undue credit," Weinel shot back, and Kissinger then pointedly noted that he had expected to see the JCS chairman, not a deputy, at the meeting.)

Kissinger wasn't far wrong. As Burr points out, the Joint Chiefs had resisted coming up with more limited scenarios because they "believed that multiple options would degrade the war plan."[39] Jasper Welch, an Air Force general who was the Defense Department's staff director for the review, protested that the Pentagon was assigning nuclear weapons to objectives according to what it thought the civilian leadership wanted: "The current SIOP calls for [nuclear] attacks on conventional forces. These have not been heavily targeted in the past because we had fewer warheads. As the MIRVs [multiple-warhead missiles] have come on line, and we get more warheads, the targets have grown. In current policy they will grow even further. SIOP is revised every six months and the planners have done what they could within the bounds of legality. I want to dispel any illusions anyone might have that there has been any lack of progress."[40] Kissinger answered, "We are not sitting in judgment here," but there was no way around the political math: the military had been mechanically piling up targets regardless of civilian concerns. In his 1974 final report to Nixon, Kissinger stressed that "until now, there has been no Presidential guidance on how the U.S. should plan for a nuclear conflict."[41] A week later, Nixon issued National Security Decision Memorandum (NSDM) 242, ordering the defense and intelligence communities to generate plans for more limited scenarios.[42]

As Kissinger handled the White House end of things during the review in the summer of 1973, James Schlesinger became the first civilian professional strategist to lead the Defense Department. Unlike his predecessors, he held a doctorate in economics and had spent his career at the RAND Corporation, rather than in business or law. Schlesinger, too, understood the mismatch between the need to control escalation and a nuclear force designed to inflict large and immediate strikes across the Soviet Union at the first sign of trouble.

The search for the more variegated set of nuclear options called for in NSDM-242 led to a menu of scenarios for nuclear use that was briefly called "the Schlesinger Doctrine."[43] This was less a "doctrine" than it was a purely declaratory attempt to squeeze credibility out of the existing strategic arsenal, and it did not produce any serious change in the nuclear force itself.[44] This resistance from the nuclear establishment was not the first time—nor would it be the last—that the Pentagon would smother orders to develop plans for contingencies other than all-out war, even at the regional level.[45] When Henry Kissinger, for example, asked the U.S. military for a "limited" nuclear option to deal with a notional Soviet invasion of Iran in 1974, the Joint Chiefs put forward a plan for nearly 200 nuclear strikes on a wide range of military targets inside the USSR near the Iranian border. "Are you out of your minds?" Kissinger screamed. "This is a *limited* option?"[46] Testifying before Congress in 1975, Schlesinger wondered if nuclear strategy, after years of extensive analysis that always produced the same unacceptable outcomes, had finally reached a "dead end."[47]

President Jimmy Carter came to office in 1977 believing both that the United States had too many nuclear weapons and that Americans themselves had "an inordinate fear" of communism.[48] During his briefing as president-elect, he even suggested that the United States could do with a submarine-deployed nuclear force of some 200 weapons, a proposal that reportedly left the chairman of the Joint Chiefs "speechless."[49] Carter's approach to arms control, however, was flawed from the outset, because he did not understand that he could not blast the Soviets on issues such as human rights while still seeking their partnership in negotiating limits on nuclear weapons. Carter would find in short order that the Soviet leadership, already irritated by the new president's hectoring, was in no mood to cooperate with him on nuclear matters, not least because they saw themselves as an ascending power while the United States had just been through some of its most serious political and economic crises since the American Civil War.[50]

In fairness, Carter inherited rather than created many of Washington's problems with the Soviets. Carter's immediate Republican predecessors had hoped their management of détente and the subsequent slowing of the arms race represented a new understanding between two great powers about maintaining the peace. The Kremlin, by contrast, saw détente as a strategic pause rather than a permanent state of affairs. As Carter came to office, the Soviet military surge of the previous fifteen years was nearing its completion. This included significant Soviet nuclear advances such as the SS-20, an intermediate-range, mobile, multi-warhead weapon that could reach almost all of NATO's European capitals in minutes, and the SS-18 intercontinental ballistic missile, a huge ICBM armed with at least ten highly accurate warheads.

The SS-18 in particular helped to fuel the panicky mathematics of the so-called "window of vulnerability" debate in the United States. The Soviet Union in the 1970s fielded more than 300 SS-18s, and with more than 3,000 warheads on these highly accurate missiles, the argument went, the

Soviets had theoretically acquired the ability to destroy every U.S. land-based ICBM using only a fraction of their strategic forces. Their older and less accurate missiles could thus be held in reserve as a final threat against U.S. cities in order to coerce an American surrender. Whether the Soviets really believed they could do this and escape a full and final retaliation from U.S. submarines and bombers—to say nothing of British and French strategic forces—is unlikely, but to many of Carter's critics the SS-18 and other Soviet nuclear improvements were symbolic of the unchecked growth of Soviet power and required a response.

By late 1978, Carter had been stung enough by Soviet behavior that he became a born-again Cold Warrior. He authorized work on several weapons systems in a vain attempt to catch up with the perceived American lag behind Soviet capabilities, including initiating the B-2 stealth bomber project, the huge ICBM known as the MX (later called "Peacekeeper" by the Reagan administration), and the deployment of improved U.S. nuclear arms in Europe.[51] Politically, these programs came too late to deflect charges from Republicans as well as from conservative Democrats that Carter had pursued a feckless foreign policy, especially with the Soviets. The 1979 Soviet invasion of Afghanistan seemed only to confirm the worst fears of Carter's critics, and raised again the question of whether MAD truly stabilized superpower relations or merely encouraged the Kremlin to act yet more aggressively under the shield of the nuclear standoff.

In the midst of the 1980 U.S. election, Carter issued Presidential Directive 59 (PD-59), which ordered a complete reconceptualization of U.S. thinking about nuclear war. The result was a major declaratory shift in American nuclear doctrine, whether Carter had intended it to be or not. PD-59, sometimes called "the countervailing strategy," upended nearly two decades of stated American policy by moving the United States away from MAD and toward a more confrontational approach that included planning for full-scale nuclear conflict.

PD-59 was based on a key political judgment about the USSR: it assumed that America's enemies in the Kremlin valued the Soviet Communist Party's continued control of Eurasia more than the lives of its own citizens.[52] To this end, PD-59 tried to steer away from the retaliatory killing of millions of Soviet citizens envisioned in MAD by creating a kind of wish-list of political and military targets, including strikes on the Soviet political leadership in its bunkers as well as on a host of other locations ranging from military installations to important economic assets. American leaders had always been reluctant to adopt the same stoic approach taken by the Soviets regarding nuclear war, not least because of the moral horror involved with targeting civilians. Now, however, the United States would attempt to obviate this moral nightmare by sparing innocent Soviet civilians and targeting instead the guilty members of the Party and their police, security, and military forces. Nuclear deterrence would no longer rest on the promise to exterminate the citizens of the Soviet Union, but instead to eradicate the Soviet regime, root and branch, with Soviet leaders henceforth on notice that no matter what happened in a nuclear conflict, the outcome would include their own deaths and the end of the Communist Party of the Soviet Union once and for all.

The actual execution of the strategy envisioned in PD-59 was problematic to the point of absurd.[53] Targeting was bedeviled by the same problems encountered in the "no-cities" concept nearly two decades earlier; specifically, it was impossible to strike so many targets without wiping out most of the USSR in the process. The scope and number of targets slated for destruction rendered the whole idea of a "limited" nuclear war a gross contradiction. In reality, PD-59 was never actually meant to be a functioning strategy. Rather, it was a psychological gamble, an attempt to reestablish a more stable deterrent by convincing Moscow that the United States was not mesmerized by MAD, and planting in Soviet minds the possibility that American leaders were as willing as their Soviet counterparts to consider a protracted nuclear war.

The Soviets were apoplectic. After years of U.S. policies that stressed the impossibility of nuclear war, suddenly an American administration was planning and arming for one. Worse, many senior Soviet policymakers privately realized they were now facing a problem that they had largely brought on themselves through their own aggressiveness and recklessness. In later years, leading Soviet figures such as top Soviet foreign policy advisor Georgii Arbatov would admit that the Kremlin was reaping what it had so carelessly sown:

> The thought of restraint, of moderation in military affairs, was absolutely alien to us. Possibly it was even our deeply rooted inferiority complex that constantly drove us to catch up with the United States in nuclear arms. . . . During those years we were enthusiastically arming ourselves, like binging drunks, without any apparent political need. . . .

We, in essence, became participants in the "dismantling" of détente, actually helping the enemies of détente in the USA and other
NATO countries to start the second "cold war." The negative aspects of our foreign and domestic policies in those years had an
obvious influence on the constellation of political forces and on the
course of political struggles in the USA and other western nations;
we strengthened the position of the right and the far right, even
militaristic, circles.

"It must be acknowledged," Arbatov concluded ruefully, "that Reagan,
along with a whole cohort of the most conservative figures, came to power
[in the 1980 election] not without our help."[54]

But there was much more to PD-59 than electoral politics. In rethinking
nuclear doctrine in 1979 and 1980, the Americans were trying to solve a
puzzle that they would face again in the twenty-first century while trying to
deal with ruthless regimes such as North Korea: what deters a state that
does not seem to value the lives of its own citizens? Since all of the answers
involving nuclear weapons led to the indiscriminate killing of millions of
people, none of them were acceptable. Even the most hardened realists were
uncomfortable with the moral implications of MAD, regardless of how de-
spicable or brutal the character of the enemy regime. In 1979, Henry Kissinger foreshadowed his later call for eliminating nuclear weapons when he
grimly declared that targeting civilians in a general nuclear war would produce more than 100 million casualties, and that "such a degree of devastation is not a strategic doctrine," but "an abdication of moral and political
responsibility."[55]

In a sense, PD-59 foreshadowed Ronald Reagan's early antagonism
toward the Kremlin's leaders. Both Carter and Reagan focused nuclear
strategy on the eradication of the Soviet regime itself, almost personalizing
nuclear war as punishment for the sins of the Politburo and the Soviet high
command while attempting to spare the lives of the Russians and other
Soviet peoples who may not have been willing participants in Moscow's
aggression. Although the term was not used at the time or in the same
context, PD-59 represented nuclear "regime change." PD-59 made clear
that an attack on the United States might not mean the end of the world,
but it would definitely mean the end of Soviet Communism. The Soviet
leadership was so alarmed by this turn in American strategy that by the

time of the 1980 U.S. election they actually preferred Reagan over Carter, thinking that things could not possibly get worse.[56]

They were, of course, wrong. They had terribly misjudged Reagan, who not only accepted the fundamental logic of PD-59, but expanded upon it.

The Second (and Last) Cold War

For most of his presidency, Ronald Reagan was misunderstood by his detractors as being overly enamored of nuclear weapons and too willing to think about using them. The truth was the exact opposite: he viscerally hated them, and wanted their complete elimination. (Journalist John Newhouse was the first to buck this conventional wisdom, when he dubbed Reagan "The Abolitionist" in a 1989 *New Yorker* article.)[57] But Reagan hated Communism almost as much as he hated nuclear arms, and until the nuclear-free utopia arrived, the fortieth president's innate distrust of the Soviet Union led him to stake deterrence on unarguable American nuclear superiority.

In a famous 1982 speech in London, Reagan asked whether civilization was destined to "perish in a hail of fiery atoms." For his part, Reagan intended to forestall that outcome by making it clear to Moscow that the dangerous—and in his view, morally indefensible—days of MAD were over. In the wake of a global Soviet expansion into the Third World dating back to the last days of President Gerald Ford's incomplete presidency and the later Soviet humiliations of President Carter, "détente" had become a term of scorn among conservative Republicans as well as a fair number of defense-minded Democrats, many of whom later served in Reagan's two administrations. Gone was any sense of managing some sort of arms control regime with the Soviet Union; if the Soviets wanted a second, more intense Cold War and a real military competition with the West, Reagan, backed by a new slate of more energetic and anti-Soviet leaders across much of NATO, would give them one.

Reagan and his advisors sought to neutralize the Kremlin's perception that it had gained the psychological upper hand in the arms race, and to that end his officials played a tough game of public diplomacy about nuclear war. Sometimes, these moves were over the top: Undersecretary of Defense Thomas Jones, for example, calmly told the *Los Angeles Times* in 1982 that "with enough shovels" to dig crude shelters before a nuclear attack, "everyone's going to make it."[58] Reagan and his lieutenants sensed, correctly, that after the 1970s the Soviets were increasingly convinced that they were winning the Cold War. What Reagan did not understand, however, was how insecure the Soviet leaders were about the USSR's position in the global competition against the United States, nor the degree to which his policies were inadvertently convincing the Kremlin that the United States was spoiling for a nuclear fight.

In early 1983, Reagan completed what Carter had started, and finally discarded the cornerstone of MAD. Seizing the same arguments made by the Soviets themselves in the 1960s, he embraced the possibility of national missile defenses and argued that constructing them was a moral imperative. Reagan upended the East-West nuclear competition by speaking of a future based not on deterrence but on defense, a world in which "free people could live secure in the knowledge . . . that we could intercept and destroy strategic ballistic missiles before they reached our own soil or that of our allies."[59] At the time, Reagan was both applauded as a hero and dismissed as a dunce. Nonetheless, his vision held a broad appeal for many Americans who were tiring under the intense strain of the decades-long nuclear stand-off with the Soviet Union.

Reagan's Strategic Defense Initiative (SDI) was initially dubbed "Star Wars" by its detractors, but despite this early ridicule, ballistic missile defenses have now survived as a key U.S. strategic goal for more than thirty years. The concept is unlikely ever to be abandoned by either U.S. political party, not least because there is now a bureaucracy dedicated to creating missile defenses, and bureaucracies rarely surrender their own existence willingly. But it is also undeniable that the idea is popular, now as it was then, with an American public that supports the reassuring promise of knocking down incoming nuclear missiles. This public support is understandable, as most people do not understand the costs or technical challenges associated with such defenses; indeed, a plurality of U.S. voters in the late 1990s supported missile defenses because they thought the United States already had them.[60]

Reagan's blistering rhetoric, combined with his administration's adoption of Carter's nuclear strategy and the subsequent additional challenge of SDI, convinced some of the key figures in the Kremlin that the United States was determined to launch a nuclear first strike against the USSR. Even before Reagan came to office, Soviet intelligence stations worldwide were given instructions to note any possible signs of an American nuclear attack; later accounts suggest that this paranoia was heavily centered in the

KGB rather than shared throughout the Soviet government, but within a few years it was a consuming fear among many of the hidebound older leaders in Moscow.[61] In late 1983, a NATO nuclear exercise code-named "Able Archer" triggered a Soviet nuclear alert in Eastern Europe, surprising Reagan and his advisors and serving as one of several incidents that convinced Reagan that he had to ratchet down tensions with the USSR.[62]

U.S.-Soviet talks did not get far, not least because three successive Soviet leaders—Brezhnev, Yuri Andropov, and Konstantin Chernenko—all died in the five years of Reagan's presidency. When the Soviet leadership chose the younger and more forward-looking Mikhail Gorbachev as their new chairman in 1985, both he and Reagan both moved quickly and jointly affirmed that "a nuclear war cannot be won and must never be fought." As Reagan's second term drew to a close, the "abolitionist" was finally able to take steps to realize his dream, one he came to realize he shared with Gorbachev, and together they engaged in a significant step toward denuclearizing Europe. Both the United States and the Soviet Union agreed to remove their most threatening and destabilizing nuclear systems from the Continent in a landmark 1987 treaty, and both sides agreed to pursue further cuts in the future. Gorbachev, however, was soon consumed with trying to hold together the disintegrating USSR, and it would fall to Reagan's successor, President George H. W. Bush, to complete the delicate task of helping to manage the peaceful collapse of a nuclear superpower.

The first President Bush acted with a speed and decisiveness that would rarely be seen again in the American nuclear establishment. Until 1990, nuclear reductions were difficult for the Americans to consider without progress on reductions in conventional forces, but once it was clear that Gorbachev was also going to remove a substantial part of the Soviet Army from Eastern Europe, Bush pressed ahead on nuclear arms and seized the brief window between the Soviet collapse in 1991 and the emergence of the new Russia in 1992 to start shedding Cold War nuclear weapons and practices.[63]

As journalist David Hoffman later described, Bush took dramatic steps during the Soviet interregnum to initiate changes to the U.S. nuclear deterrent.

> [Bush] launched a significant pullback of U.S. nuclear weapons, both land and sea. He did it without drawn-out negotiations, without a treaty, without verification measures and without waiting for Soviet reciprocity.

Bush announced the United States would eliminate all of its ground-launched battlefield or tactical nuclear weapons worldwide, and withdraw all those on ships; stand down the strategic bombers from high-alert status; take off hair-trigger alert 450 intercontinental ballistic missiles; and cancel several nuclear weapon modernization programs. The announcement meant a pullback of 1,300 artillery-fired atomic projectiles, 850 Lance missile nuclear warheads, and 500 naval weapons.

In one stroke, Bush pulled back naval surface weapons that the United States had earlier refused to even discuss as part of strategic weapons negotiations.[64]

Bush also disbanded the institutional guardian of nuclear war planning, the U.S. Air Force's Strategic Air Command, and replaced it in 1992 with the U.S. Strategic Command (STRATCOM), which would thereafter be responsible for all U.S. strategic nuclear weapons. The Air Force and the Navy would continue the day-to-day maintenance and control of their respective nuclear systems, but ultimate authority in time of crisis and war would rest with this new command.

The first Bush administration has since entered the history books as a committee of level-headed realists, including Secretary of State James Baker, National Security Advisor Brent Scowcroft, and others. In many subsequent depictions of the administration (including those of Bush and Scowcroft), these men and women formed a kind of college of foreign affairs cardinals whose policies rested primarily on cold calculations of U.S. national interest. In 1991, however, President Bush himself acted like anything but a realist. Reacting to the changing conditions of international politics, rather than to the distribution of power, he unilaterally discarded weapons and practices that had long ago ceased to serve any purpose.

George H. W. Bush was perhaps the most accomplished of all U.S. presidents in the field of foreign policy. Bush's achievements were undeniable: he helped to reunify Germany, guided the final days of the Cold War to a peaceful conclusion, and organized the most successful United Nations coalition since the Korean War to eject the Iraqi army from Kuwait. But by 1992, his services were no longer required. Voting less than a year after the dissolution of the Soviet Union and in the midst of a recession, Americans turned aside his re-election bid. Fifty years of war were over, the North American heartland was safe once again, and it was time to enjoy the fruits of peace and prosperity. The U.S. electorate was ready to turn its attention away from foreign affairs in general and from the nuclear arms race in particular. It even seemed to many people that the world had reached, in scholar Francis Fukuyama's often-misunderstood phrase, "the end of history."[65]

History, as new U.S. President Bill Clinton would learn, had other plans.

The end of this "second" Cold War and the cessation of political hostilities finally halted the surreal arms race between the United States and the Soviet Union, but it resolved almost nothing among American defense intellectuals, military planners, and policymakers about nuclear deterrence. The legacy of these intellectual divisions lives on in current arguments about nuclear weapons and deterrence. Is deterrence a condition that can be created independently, or is there a way it can be sized or tailored to fit each opponent? Is there a minimum level of nuclear force that guarantees safety? Do nuclear weapons really deter other states at all, and if deterrence fails, can they be used?

These questions, as will be seen, have remained central to a series of dedicated but ultimately frustrating attempts in Washington to make sense of the U.S. nuclear arsenal and its purpose into the twenty-first century.

Chapter 2

Nuclear Weapons After the Cold War:
Promise and Failure

> Over time, as arsenals multiplied on both sides and the rhetoric of mutual annihilation grew more heated, we were forced to think about the unthinkable, justify the unjustifiable, rationalize the irrational. Ultimately, we contrived a new and desperate theology to ease our moral anguish, and we called it deterrence.
>
> —General George Butler, U.S. Air Force, 1997

> We have been unable so far to do better than just sort of go on intellectual autopilot.
>
> —General Butler, a year later

The Power of Inertia

The end of the Cold War was supposed to mean many things: the spread of democracy, the reunification of Europe, an economic "peace dividend," and maybe, with the competition between individual freedom and collectivist repression resolved, even the end of intellectual history. Most important, it was supposed to represent a final release from the nuclear nightmare. Today, some of that promise has been realized. Europe is whole, and the world goes about its business largely free from the fear of global nuclear war. And yet, the weapons and strategies of the Cold War remain: Americans who were young children when the Berlin Wall fell still crew the silos, submarines, and bombers that were all built for service in a previous century. The Soviet Union is gone, but like a ceremonial guard the U.S. nuclear deterrent continues to stand at attention over its remains.

Some of this "nuclear inertia" can be traced to the unexpected speed with which the Cold War ended.[1] Although in retrospect that conflict and the nuclear arms race it spawned might seem to be a long historical process, the Cold War was shorter than the life span of a single human being. The relationship between the United States and the Union of Soviet Socialist Republics went first from suspicion and hostility after World War I into an alliance of necessity during World War II, and then to existential confrontation and the final Soviet collapse of the late 1980s, all in the space of some seventy years.

And then it was all over in a matter of days. Many Western experts, until the very end, clung to the belief that a Soviet collapse was literally impossible—that what was happening could not be happening—and it was remarkable that U.S. and NATO policymakers were not caught more flat-footed than they were. (The advice they were getting didn't help: the late Stephen Meyer of MIT even went so far as to tell the Senate Foreign Relations committee that "hints of military coups [in the USSR] are pure flights of fancy" in testimony he gave on June 6, 1991, just nine weeks before Soviet leader Mikhail Gorbachev's ouster in the Soviet coup.)[2] Even had Washington and its allies been better prepared for the Soviet implosion, however, there was no way for either side to plan for so sudden a peace, and the entire Soviet and American order of nuclear battle remained frozen in place despite the end of the political hostilities between East and West.

The Americans in the early 1990s were reticent about packing away their nuclear weapons. Their caution was understandable: a moment of "peace" does not mean an eternity of "stability," and precipitous moves toward rapid nuclear disarmament immediately after the fall of the USSR would have been irresponsible. Russia's leaders, for their part, had more pressing matters on their minds; in the first years after the Soviet collapse, Russian President Boris Yeltsin and his advisors could not immediately tackle the immense job of securing and consolidating the old Soviet nuclear arsenal in the new Russian Federation mostly because they had their hands full trying to consolidate the new Russian Federation itself. In any case, political leaders cannot sweep away institutions, beliefs, buildings, and bombs overnight, no matter how revolutionary the circumstances. Dismantling the machinery of nuclear war is not a matter of simply turning off the lights and handing in the codes and keys. The disintegration of the Soviet

Union opened a world of possibilities—and created more than a few head-aches—for disarmament, but any serious reconsideration of the purpose and structure of the U.S. deterrent in the wake of the Cold War's end necessarily demanded patience, creativity, and time.

Major reforms of the U.S. nuclear deterrent might have been too much to expect in the immediate aftermath of the Soviet collapse, but in the ensuing two decades since the Cold War's end, Western governments have consistently shown a genuine desire to reduce both their nuclear and con-ventional arsenals. Prominent defense and foreign policy intellectuals, in-cluding former Cold Warriors in the United States and Europe (and even some in Russia), have called not only for reductions, but for the complete abolition of nuclear arms. Other thinkers and leaders, if less sure about reaching "zero," have nonetheless likewise argued for deemphasizing the importance of nuclear arms.

The way forward, then, would seem to be a straightforward matter of simplifying U.S. nuclear doctrine and reconfiguring the strategic nuclear force to correspond to a more limited post–Cold War mission. Unfortu-nately, nothing is ever that simple, but since 1994 each of three successive U.S. presidential administrations of both parties has embarked on a major review of American nuclear policy.

Each of these reviews produced limited and disappointing results. In the end, they all reflected an unwillingness to part with the weapons and strategies of the Cold War. Some of this resistance to changing the U.S. nuclear deterrent reflected the sincere belief on the part of many people in the government, the military, and the American electorate that nuclear weapons kept the peace, and perhaps even saved the world, for more than a half century. Ultimately, however, the reviews of nuclear strategy con-ducted by successive U.S. administrations have been monuments less to the Western victory in the Cold War and more to the sheer power of political and bureaucratic inertia.

Reviewing the Nuclear Reviews

Few nations study their own defense policies as often and as openly as the United States. In the wake of major reforms in U.S. defense policy enacted by the Congress in the mid-1980s, both the executive and legislative branches of the United States government have commissioned repeated studies and reports meant to examine and to explain the various facets of U.S. national security. These documents have included the National Security Strategy of the United States, the National Military Strategy, the National Defense Strategy, the Quadrennial Defense Review, the various reviews conducted by each armed service, and the overarching study of the U.S. nuclear arsenal and its purpose, the Nuclear Posture Review.[3]

In a world free of bureaucratic friction, all of these documents would agree with each other. Taken together, they should provide a relatively complete picture of U.S. national defense: they should explain how the United States views the international security environment, identify areas of particular concern or emphasis, and describe how the United States plans to arm itself in the future. In the real world, however, these reports often miss their required date of submission, end up out of phase with each other, and represent a spectrum of diverse and occasionally conflicting inputs from throughout the government. To be fair, the staffs that create them actually overlap in many cases, and the apparent lack of coordination is sometimes less than it seems, but it is nonetheless difficult to piece together an overall picture of U.S. security policy from these many documents.

The National Military Strategy, for example, is a classified report from the chairman of the Joint Chiefs to the secretary of defense. In theory, it should follow the guidelines of the National Security Strategy, which has been required as an annual submission from the president to Congress since 1986. But the 2011 National Military Strategy was the first in *seven years*, and coordinating anything with the National Security Strategy would be impossible in any case since presidents almost never submit them on time. In more than twenty-five years, only Bill Clinton met the requirement for an annual submission, although it is arguable whether the National Security Strategies of the 1990s actually said anything or whether anyone read them.[4] George W. Bush submitted two reports during the entire eight years of his presidency, and Barack Obama likewise submitted only one during his first term. While quantity is not quality, "annual" does not mean "every four years," either.

These studies and statements more often serve as codification of decisions already taken rather than as guides to choices yet to be made. This is not in itself a sign of any essential political or bureaucratic dysfunction: policy reviews in large organizations are always difficult undertakings, and national security reviews more so due to the nature of the subject and the potentially cosmic costs of getting anything wrong. The formulation of national security policy requires the services of some of the most serious (and expensive) talent the government can muster, including senior military officers, top echelons of the civil service, academic experts, fleets of consultants, and the resources of the best think tanks.

In turn, however, this aggregation of expertise means that official reviews of national security are inevitably riven by both bureaucratic and intellectual conflict. Even when they are finally issued, they may not be "final." As national security analyst Richard Weitz has pointed out, all of these documents "can be updated by speeches by senior officials or superseded by congressional action or other events" and that they "generally lack mechanisms to enforce their guidance at lower levels" because they reflect, at best, "the lowest common denominator of what their multiple authors can agree upon."[5] The resulting studies end up with language approved by everyone but in reality satisfying (or enlightening) no one.

In 1994, 2002, and 2010 the U.S. government produced three official Nuclear Posture Reviews as part of a series of post-Cold War examinations of American defense policy. (The first was undertaken on the initiative of then–Secretary of Defense Les Aspin, while the next two were mandated by Congress.) Each of these reviews bore the marks of collisions between innovation and bureaucracy, change and tradition, and hope and fear. None of them advocated fundamental changes in the U.S. nuclear arsenal mission or its mission of general nuclear deterrence. Ironically, they were all greeted with more fanfare by supporters, and more derision by critics, than their limited impact warranted, reactions which themselves explain much about the continued failure to reform the U.S. nuclear deterrent after the Cold War.

The 1994 Nuclear Posture Review

Bill Clinton came to office in 1993 after a U.S. presidential election that turned primarily on domestic and economic issues rather than foreign policy. Like all presidents, however, Clinton learned how quickly the demands of international leadership and the national defense can muscle aside promises made in the small towns of Pennsylvania or Ohio. Indeed, events threatened to overcome Clinton's priorities even before he was elected: the USSR came to an end less than sixty days after the then–Arkansas governor declared his intention to seek the presidency. After the election, Clinton was able to accept the congratulations of a democratic Russian government in Moscow, but Soviet and American nuclear weapons and their crews remained where they had been for decades, unaffected by a change of administration in one nation and a complete change of regime in the other.

The first Nuclear Posture Review (NPR) was undertaken within a year of Clinton's inauguration. This review was not in response to any kind of public demand or catalyzing international event; the threat of nuclear war, or more accurately, of an *intentional* nuclear war, had receded, and the United States was undeniably safer as a country. But Clinton and his advisors feared that American citizens now faced perhaps even greater threats from the more plausible threats of nuclear terrorism, nuclear proliferation, or accidental nuclear use. Nor were administration officials alone in these worries. After a visit to Moscow in the wake of the failed 1991 Soviet coup, for example, U.S. Senator Sam Nunn later recalled thinking: "I was convinced of two things. One, that there would be no more Soviet empire. And two, that they and we had a huge, huge [nuclear] security problem."[6] The price of the new East-West peace was an environment in which the single major threat from the USSR was replaced by threats from directions, and in forms, Washington had not yet even considered.

The state of the Russian nuclear arsenal was a source of serious concern as much for Moscow as for Washington. In the early 1990s, the loyalties of the former Soviet officer corps were still uncertain, and thousands of nuclear weapons were strewn throughout the former Soviet republics, including ICBM installations in Russia as well as the new and nominally independent republics of Ukraine, Kazakhstan, and Belarus. The Russian high command warned—not entirely disingenuously—that further rifts in the new nations of the post-Soviet "Commonwealth of Independent States," to say nothing of Russia itself, could create a "nuclear Yugoslavia" in which unsecured weapons and fissile material could be targeted for capture and blackmail by warring factions, or sabotaged with ecologically disastrous consequences.[7]

Policymakers in the new Clinton administration did not believe that Boris Yeltsin's Russia was a threat, nor did they try to portray it as one. In later years, critics of both George W. Bush and Barack Obama would argue that the regime of the irascible Vladimir Putin represented a renewed threat to the United States, but for the most part, the 1990s were a time of remarkable Russian-American amity. Still, whatever the warm relations between the United States and the new Russian Federation, the dissipation of the

Soviet threat was a political, not a physical, phenomenon. Communist-built nuclear weapons did not require actual Communists to fire them, and the nuclear force left after the Soviet collapse remained active and targeted at the United States. Moreover, Russian politics in the early 1990s were still in violent flux. Soviet ideology, for the moment, was gone, but matters were far from settled in the remnants of the former USSR.

A friendlier relationship between Washington and Moscow also carried some paradoxical risks. The Soviet implosion led to a Russian retrenchment, in which the new Kremlin leadership washed their hands of troublesome former Soviet clients such as North Korea. As a result, these countries were freed of their Cold War constraints: while they could no longer rely on Moscow's support, they no longer had to follow Moscow's rules, either. And sure enough, within a year of taking office, President Clinton would find himself in a tense confrontation with North Korea over its nuclear program, a situation only temporarily defused by the interference (much to the Clinton administration's anger) of former president Jimmy Carter.[8] The North Korean bomb project, delayed but not defeated, finally came to fruition in 2009.

The first NPR was an effort to reorient America's nuclear bearings in this changed world. It would have been an ambitious project even under better circumstances, but it was bound to be an especially difficult undertaking in the uncertain first years after the Cold War. It was also being undertaken by a Democratic president after twelve unbroken years of control of the executive branch by Republicans, which would unavoidably create internal tensions between the White House and the national security establishment.

The scope of this first proposed review was immense. It was supposed to be, in Secretary Aspin's words, "the first study of its kind to incorporate reviews of [nuclear] policy, doctrine, force structure, operations, safety and security, and arms control in one look."[9] All of the bureaucratic players in the executive branch were expected to pull together on such a comprehensive reconsideration of nuclear policy, but the 1994 NPR had a special priority as Aspin's personal project. As a participant in the review anonymously recalled later, the first NPR was "the Aspin-Clinton show," to be conducted "in the free-wheeling way Aspin was accustomed to and reinforced by the full delegation of authority to him by the president."[10] Given the broad remit of the review and the large cast of characters involved, it should have been no surprise that the process ran into trouble immediately.

No matter how many different players are involved in the nuclear enterprise, the Defense Department is logically the first among equals when it comes to nuclear weapons, especially since it was the secretary of defense himself who had launched the idea of a review in the first place. The result was an unwieldy mass of organizations and actors vying for input and influence from which the Pentagon emerged by default as the most powerful player. All bureaucratic organizations protect their privileges, but few can match the claim of any nation's military institutions that their turf is a higher calling. (As a Soviet general once snorted derisively, the national defense is a "sacred cause," and "not simply a matter for the Ministry of the Timber Industry.")[11]

And so it was with the first NPR, which was dominated at the outset by the defense establishment. "Pentagon officials," according to a 1999 Brookings Institution study, "apparently never considered outside involvement [from other U.S. government departments] seriously."[12] Defense analysts Janne Nolan and James Holmes agree, recalling that military officers and senior Defense Department bureaucrats "stymied the involvement of other agencies, 'amateur' political appointees, and outside experts."[13] The main participants in the 1994 NPR did not agree even on first principles, as Nolan wrote in a later study of the process: "The Pentagon was thus about to launch a review of nuclear policy that involved fundamental theological differences about nuclear weapons between appointees and career officials, and even in some cases among appointees. The basic character of deterrence was in dispute, a metaphor for broader disagreements over the utility of nuclear weapons after the Cold War and even over the extent to which the Russian threat had actually changed."[14] The lack of shared assumptions exacerbated the already tense relations between political appointees and military experts in the Clinton administration. One military officer, for example, was "infuriated by what he perceived to be excessive intrusion by recently appointed and inexperienced Clinton officials," and he resented the trespass on his professional turf. "We know how to produce nuclear war plans," he said. "We have the methodology, we can analyze damage expectancies."[15]

Thinking through the purpose of nuclear weapons, however, is a more complicated matter than producing a plan for nuclear combat. "Damage expectancies" are not the same thing as a "strategy." Nonetheless, the military viewed the civilians as antinuclear dilettantes. In some cases, this judgment was right on the mark, as was the parallel civilian observation that many of the military officials involved were atavistic and obstructionist. What mattered more than the sniping, however, was that different groups in the process were on different tracks right from the start of the NPR process.

The predictable result was that any hopes of a new nuclear doctrine were quickly lost in the shuffle. Instead, "career Pentagon officials changed the subject," as Nolan and Holmes later described:

> Resentful of the intrusive approach of the Clinton appointees and indifferent to the political dimensions of nuclear deterrence, [Pentagon officials] (perhaps unwittingly) shifted the terms of debate. What had been billed as an analytical process joining policy to strategy morphed into a struggle over arcane technical details surrounding the nuclear force structure. Military officers churned out stacks of viewgraphs supporting traditional notions of deterrence based on long-standing targeting and war-fighting plans.
>
> The metric for judging nuclear requirements remained the same as during the Cold War years: the ability to hold at risk and destroy the Russian target base with a triad of forces, including assigning multiple weapons to the assets the enemy valued most.[16]

Whatever Aspin's initial intent might have been, the NPR process quickly mutated into an obstinate defense both of established beliefs and the existing force structure.

Was the 1994 NPR a failure? The answer depends on whether the NPR was really supposed to produce actual revisions of U.S. nuclear policy. In later years, some of the participants argued that the 1994 NPR was only a first cut at an overview of the nuclear arsenal in the absence of a Soviet threat, and that any other expectation was unrealistic. Overviews, however, do not accomplish much. Once any serious changes were off the table, according to one participant in the Brookings study of the 1994 NPR, the final product was nothing more than "slapping a happy face" on what was left of a "disastrous initiative."[17] Another senior official in the same study, however, "disclaimed that there was ever any serious intent to change the U.S. force posture or overall policy," and asserted that significant changes in the nuclear force posture had been ruled out as early as 1993, that further unilateral reductions would have been "idiotic," and that only "self-absorbed arms controllers and unilateral disarmers" ever argued for anything more.

To be sure, some of these recollections reflect the inevitable score-settling that always takes place after a major policy struggle in Washington. Still, it is nonetheless true that the 1994 NPR ended up at the Pentagon and thus was heavily influenced by the traditionalism of the nuclear bureaucracy. At the outset, for example, one of the first NPR working group briefings given to Deputy Secretary of Defense John Deutch in 1994 produced a "twenty-first century nuclear force that looked a lot like the Cold War-era force, only smaller," which led Ashton Carter, the assistant secretary chosen by Aspin to organize the review (and later the deputy secretary of defense under President Obama) to call the presentation a "disaster."[18]

Outside critics agreed. Nuclear scientist Hans Kristensen would later write that the Clinton administration did not "seem particularly interested in revising U.S. deterrence policy, which [still] demanded a grandiose guaranteed destruction of Russia's nuclear forces, command and control, industry, and conventional forces."[19] Scholar Tom Sauer was more succinct, charging that the 1994 NPR "failed miserably" due to "domestic politics, rigid thinking, huge parochial interests, inter-service competition, and a lack of political leadership."[20]

The final 1994 NPR amounted to thirty-seven pages of charts and briefs for public release, and a longer classified version, none of which represented any significant changes in policy.[21] Like the inevitable PowerPoint slides issued in its wake, the result was a muddle. Nuclear weapons still occupied the same role as they did during the Cold War; indeed, their importance seemed magnified, rather than reduced. This was in keeping with the 1994 NPR's cautious conclusion that America must "lead but hedge."[22] This nuclear "hedging" and its demand for high readiness across a spectrum of forces practically ensured that the 1994 review could not serve as a guide for any policy other than maintaining a somewhat smaller version of the status quo.

Aspin left the Pentagon in 1994 and passed away a year later. There was little movement on nuclear issues again until 1997, when President Clinton signed Presidential Decision Directive 60 (PDD-60) on nuclear planning. PDD-60 did not fundamentally alter Cold War nuclear strategy, although it did order the military to stop planning for *protracted* nuclear war with Russia and to refine the targeting of China.[23] It also sought to beef up contingencies for dealing with weapons of mass destruction in rogue states, and allotted more intelligence gathering to Iran, Iraq, and North Korea, with updates to be continuously passed to planners at the newly created

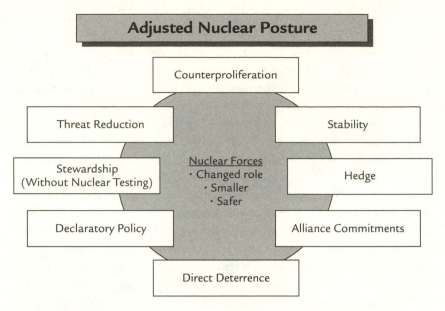

Figure 1. Adjusted Nuclear Posture. Source: 1994 Nuclear Posture Review, U.S. Department of Defense

command in charge of all U.S. strategic nuclear forces, STRATCOM. "There were no immediate plans on the shelf for target packages to give to bombers or missile crews," a Pentagon official told the *Washington Post* at the time, "but we could produce targeting information for those countries within hours."[24]

PDD-60, in fact, did not change the fundamental missions of nuclear weapons, but rather added to them. Clinton White House advisor Robert Bell emphasized in 1997 that the United States even continued to reserve the right to use nuclear weapons first, as it had during the Cold War: "If a state that we are engaged in conflict with is a nuclear capable state, we do not necessarily intend to wait until that state uses nuclear weapons first—we reserve the right to use nuclear weapons first in a conflict whether it's [chemical], [biological,] or for that matter conventional." Bell did allow that a state's "standing under the Non-Proliferation Treaty or an equivalent international convention" could have an impact on the nature of U.S. retaliation, but left unstated what that impact might be.[25]

In any case, presidents make policies, but military officers make target lists, and after the 1994 review the U.S. nuclear force remained largely in its Cold War configuration. As Nolan and Holmes observed:

> For decades, the Strategic Air Command (now the U.S. Strategic Command) has refined elaborate targeting plans and operational criteria to guide the use of nuclear forces in a crisis. But this apparatus, charged with implementing the substance of deterrence, remained largely immune from systemic political oversight or participation for decades . . . there has been no effort to abandon the imperative for large-scale, instantaneous attack against any conceivable enemy. Despite countless changes in nuclear doctrine devised by political leaders over successive administrations, there has been a negligible impact on the configuration and operational objectives of U.S. nuclear forces.[26]

John Deutch likewise wrote in 2005 that the 1994 NPR and later studies led only to "minor alterations" that still left the United States without "a convincing rationale for its current nuclear force structure and for the policies that guide the management of its nuclear weapons enterprise."[27]

The 1994 Nuclear Posture Review posed a series of important questions, but failed to break new ground. The blame can only partially be laid at the feet of the bureaucracy and the military; in 1994, the insecurities of the Cold War were still too close, and the situation in Russia still too unstable, to allow for revolutionary changes in U.S. nuclear doctrine. For the time being, the Americans would adopt a policy that tried to reap the benefits of nuclear deterrence without running the risks of having to make overt nuclear threats.

"Ambiguity" . . . for Them and for Us

After the Cold War, U.S. nuclear doctrine with regard to Russia and China defaulted to a kind of diluted version of Mutual Assured Destruction. This is because Russia and China, as strange as it may be to think of them this way, were the *easy* cases. Wars with either of them were highly unlikely, but such conflicts offered the clearest scenarios for using the U.S. deterrent in all its fury should war come to pass. Far less clear, however, was what role U.S. nuclear forces could play in deterring threats, nuclear or otherwise, from far smaller nations.

History provided no guidance for thinking about possible threats from new nuclear powers. Obviously, the Cold War experience offered few analogies; a promise to retaliate against a small opponent fielding one or two nuclear weapons as if such an attack were functionally equivalent to a full onslaught from the old Soviet Union made no sense. Threats of nuclear retaliation were especially problematic if the point was to deter the use of chemical or biological weapons, the "poor man's bombs" that smaller nations could construct more easily than long-range nuclear missiles. The most vexing issue in the early 1990s, then, was not whether a U.S. president would strike Russia or China in a major exchange, but rather whether any American leader would now have the cold-bloodedness to obliterate thousands, tens of thousands, or perhaps millions of people in a far more limited and regionally contained conflict.

The American solution was not to answer this kind of question at all. U.S. policymakers in the 1990s crafted a position intentionally designed to be vague about whether Washington would resort to nuclear retaliation as punishment for attacks against the United States, its military forces, or its allies with weapons of mass destruction. This refusal to speculate on retaliatory options remains U.S. policy today, and has since come to be known colloquially as "calculated ambiguity."

This position was meant to sidestep the thorny issue of nuclear credibility altogether. Instead, U.S. policymakers tried to shift the psychological burden of deterrence to the target by avoiding specific threats. "We think that the ambiguity involved in the issue of the use of [U.S.] nuclear weapons contributes to our own security," Defense Secretary William Cohen said in 1998, "keeping any potential adversary who might use either chemical or biological [weapons] unsure of what our response would be." Instead, Cohen promised only that the U.S. response would be "absolutely overwhelming" and "devastating."[28] Initially, this policy seemed only to apply to how the U.S. might react to chemical or biological attacks, but by its very definition, "calculated ambiguity" was a minimalist construction that did not rule out, or rule in, any options.

There is an undeniable logic to relying on ambiguity. Why say anything too specific to the enemy ahead of time, other than that bad behavior will bring about bad consequences? Uncertainty—the "threat that leaves something to chance," in Thomas Schelling's often-quoted expression—is the cornerstone of classical deterrence theory.[29] Speculating in too much detail about hypothetical situations is always hazardous, and it makes no sense to lay out to an opponent the matrix of possible responses to an array of unrealized situations.

As a practical matter, adopting a policy of ambiguity solved the ongoing political problem of having to discuss the increasing number of possibilities that did not neatly fit into previous Cold War scenarios. Perhaps most important is that by refusing to specify the nature of U.S. retaliation, American leaders could avoid what scholar and policy expert Scott Sagan has wisely called "the commitment trap," a situation in which too many repeated and explicit deterrent threats potentially create such high public expectations of retaliation that a U.S. president may feel politically forced to use nuclear weapons even when he or she might have wished to avoid them.[30]

The central weakness of this reliance on ambiguity, however, is that it can undermine deterrence in one aspect even if strengthens it in another. It is true that saying less on an issue can sometimes be more unnerving than saying too much. It is also true, however, that characterizing a U.S. response to a chemical or biological attack, or even to a single nuclear event, as some unspecified shade of "bad" could be interpreted as indicating reluctance rather than resolve. Intentional ambiguity leaves a lot of options open for policymakers, but it also leaves considerable latitude for an aggressive opponent, especially one prone to gamble. No American leader should ever be boxed in by a promise to execute any specific kind of military action, but ambiguous warnings of "devastating" retaliation may not mean much to an enemy who may already doubt Western resolve.

Despite these drawbacks, the policy of ambiguity temporarily alleviated the political pressure in the 1990s to say something new about the U.S. nuclear deterrent. Unfortunately, it did little to clarify the strategic situation or provide guidance for the reshaping of the U.S. nuclear deterrent. Notionally, refusing to discuss retaliatory options gave Washington a bit more room to maneuver on lesser, nonnuclear dangers. But it also allowed President Clinton and his successors to avoid clarifying important and specific questions about the use of nuclear force. The point might have been to inflict "ambiguity" on potential opponents, but it served as well to keep U.S. nuclear thinking mired in a twilight zone between nuclear deterrence and nuclear attack. It was, and remains, a position of ambiguity as much for the United States as it is for other nations.

From Clinton to Bush: Unilateralism and the Triumph of Missile Defense

Despite the obvious differences between them, George W. Bush and Bill Clinton were alike in one important respect: neither leader saw any particular usefulness in strategic nuclear arms. Nonetheless, Bush began his first term as president by making two important and mutually reinforcing changes in the way the United States approached nuclear issues. First, he abandoned arms control as a process in itself. Second, he pressed for a renewed commitment to the defense of the United States against ballistic missiles—that is, the *strategic* or *national* missile defenses meant to protect an entire nation, rather than the more limited and more feasible *theater* defenses that are meant to operate over relatively shorter distances.

Insofar as Bush had campaigned on foreign policy, national missile defense was one of his clear promises to a core constituency. Bush, however, was as keen to cull the U.S. nuclear arsenal as his predecessors had been, including his father. In 2001, the new president asked former Reagan administration official Richard Perle to return to the Pentagon to help reverse the same buildup Perle himself had advocated decades earlier, a time when he had been dubbed by his critics as "the Prince of Darkness" for his Cold War hawkishness. "The truth is, we are never going to use [U.S. strategic nuclear weapons]," Perle told *Newsweek* at the time. "The Russians aren't going to use theirs either."[31] A year later, Bush signed the Russian-American Strategic Offensive Reductions Treaty (SORT, or the "Moscow Treaty"), and the United States fulfilled the treaty's mandated nuclear reductions ahead of schedule.[32]

Despite the success of the Moscow Treaty, Bush 43 (the forty-third president, as distinct from his father, Bush 41) and his team had little patience for the plodding and lawyerly nature of arms control negotiations. Such talks may have been a helpful lubricant to East-West diplomatic relations during the Cold War, but in keeping with the general tenor of his foreign policies, Bush wanted to adopt a unilateral approach in which *both* the Americans and the Russians would be free to reduce their own forces to levels they believed commensurate with their own security, rather than haggle with each other. Bypassing formal arms control processes did not mean that Washington abandoned the core reliance on nuclear deterrence, but only that the Americans could now discard what Bush 43 and his advisors saw as the needlessly complicated and restrictive red tape of treaties.

Moreover, Bush did not believe that strategic nuclear reductions could be treated in isolation from other programs, especially missile defense. Nuclear reductions and the pursuit of missile defenses were strongly linked in the Bush 43 administration's approach to nuclear issues. Bush and advisors believed that each policy naturally complemented the other: a move to fewer offensive weapons logically demanded greater investment in defensive systems. Bush in particular apparently assumed that the seamless connection he saw between nuclear reductions and missile defenses would likewise be clear to the Russians, especially given his good relationship at the time with Russian President Vladimir Putin.[33]

It was in this context that Bush made the decision to forego the traditions of East-West arms control and specifically to withdraw from the Anti-Ballistic Missile (ABM) Treaty, originally signed in 1972 by the United States and the former Soviet Union. Bush and his advisors saw the ABM Treaty as a relic from another time that was only impeding American progress in dealing with future threats that had nothing to do with Russia—and they believed that Russians surely knew it as well. Dragging the whole matter into endless rounds of negotiation would thus serve no one's interests.

The Russians, for their part, showed little outward anxiety about the demise of the ABM Treaty. In its own way, Moscow shared Bush's attraction to unilateralism. The Russians are among the most self-absorbed and hard-nosed unilateralists in the world, and they were already readying deployment of the next generation of their own strategic nuclear weapons regardless of any progress (or lack of it) in arms negotiations. Russian decisions on nuclear weapons had little to do with the Americans and more to do with Russian domestic politics, the management of the Russian Federation's fragile military forces, and the fears of Russian leaders that only nuclear weapons guaranteed their freedom of action in the former Soviet region.[34]

Whatever the merits or drawbacks of the ABM Treaty, it is important to note the role that missile defenses played, and continue to play, in the strategic thinking of both its opponents and its advocates in the United States. National missile defenses are a natural source of disagreement, a wedge issue, between American liberals and foreign policy conservatives. The way each group approaches the concept reveals much about the difficulty of reforming nuclear doctrine and U.S. national security policy in general. The debate explains a great deal about the direction of U.S. nuclear strategy in the early twenty-first century, and in particular helps illuminate the reasons behind the eventual failure of the 2002 Nuclear Posture Review to have a strong effect on policy.

The missile defense debate cuts across party lines and ideologies. But as a general observation, American liberals tend to value international institutions, see the processes of international negotiation with opponents as valuable in itself, and are sympathetic—sometimes overly so—to the concerns of other nations about the magnitude of U.S. power. Conservatives, by contrast, focus on the anarchical nature of the international system, and are more attracted to the classical imperative of self-help. They think in terms of outcomes, rather than processes: international institutions and negotiations are important only insofar as they tangibly assist U.S. security, a belief that itself reveals an often corrosive—and often self-fulfilling—cynicism about those institutions and their purposes. American conservatism became somewhat more internationalist in the late twentieth century, particularly during Ronald Reagan's two terms as president, but there is a persistent streak of unilateralism and American exceptionalism that runs through conservative thinking about foreign affairs.

These descriptions are not a judgment on either school of thought, both of which have great virtues and deep flaws. Rather, it is to point out that a notion such as missile defense naturally animates these differences in a highly divisive way. For many liberals, national missile defense is provocative and destabilizing, especially if it involves the extension of American power into space. Defenses are not only a threat to strategic stability but also a needless and self-inflicted wound to American diplomacy. Conservatives see missile defense as an attempt to use America's remarkable capacity for technological innovation to add one more layer of insurance that will save lives and limit damage to the United States should all else fail. (And conservatives, who tend to be pessimistic students of history, assume that sooner or later all else *will* fail.)[35]

Although the appeal of defenses is strongest among U.S. conservatives, President Reagan forced national missile defense onto the agenda of American national security analysts of all stripes when he announced the Strategic Defense Initiative in March 1983. Reagan's early vision was a kind of "peace shield" that would neutralize ICBMs, and thus obviate the need to rely on such dangerously unstable offensive weapons. This made for good political theater, but it was not a technologically feasible concept then or now. Later versions were much less ambitious, with variations that included limited defenses of the U.S. missile fields meant to complicate Soviet first-strike planning, mobile or smaller defenses to catch accidental launches—the GPALS, or "Global Protection Against Limited Strikes," plan advocated by Bush 41—and others.

After Reagan, missile defense never again had such a stalwart advocate in the White House. By the time the fortieth president left office in 1989, however, the institutional and bureaucratic foundations—and especially the budgets—for national missile defense had been rooted deeply enough to sustain the concept through succeeding administrations. George H. W. Bush, Reagan's vice president, did not share Reagan's dream of a world safe beneath a web of space-based defenses, but he supported an active, if more limited, program of missile defense research in his own administration. Under Clinton, the Strategic Defense Initiative Organization was renamed the Ballistic Missile Defense Organization, with an increased emphasis on theater, rather than national, missile defense. Since the Reagan era, neither Congress nor the defense establishment has ever shown the will to disman- tle the expensive and wide-ranging infrastructure put in place during the Cold War.

As a political matter, American politicians are wary of abandoning mis- sile defenses, because the notion has long enjoyed wide support among the American public. This attraction to missile defense is understandable at an emotional level: after all, who could be against protection from nuclear missiles? These high levels of public support, however, are usually a result of the question being asked without reference to cost or trade-offs, and in terms that can only produce agreement.[36] Americans say the same thing, in the *abstract*, about how they support a balanced budget, national health care, immigration reform, and any number of social goods if they are pre- sented with obvious benefits but no reckoning of costs.

Still, the idea of self-defense is powerfully rooted in the human survival instinct, and arguments in favor of defenses have always had the advantage of corresponding to a basic intuition that defenses are legitimate and neces- sary. Indeed, when polled in 1998 by a pro-missile defense group, a major- ity of Americans thought national missile defenses already existed and were positively angered to find out they did not.[37] Presidential administrations come and go, but the concept of missile defenses remains, especially as more nations seek to develop both nuclear arms and the ballistic means to deliver them. (We will return to these issues in later chapters.)

While Bush 43 and his critics may have disagreed about the importance of missile defense programs, Bush shared the feelings of his predecessors in office about the size of the U.S. nuclear arsenal. A few months after taking office, Bush 43 was briefed on the status of the U.S. nuclear deterrent. The presentation, according to journalists John Barry and Evan Thomas, was "dry and crammed with statistics and acronyms, but it got the president's attention." Bush was "stunned at the amount of destructive power" at the president's disposal. "I had no idea we had so many weapons," he said. "What do we need them for?"[38]

Bush's reaction was much like that of every other new president in the nuclear era. Eisenhower once confided that he would head for Argentina if nuclear weapons were used in any numbers; Richard Nixon likewise found the casualty projections embedded in U.S. nuclear war plans nothing less than appalling. Ronald Reagan was so convinced that he would never need the procedures for releasing U.S. nuclear forces that he reportedly fell asleep during his own post-inaugural briefing, and finally had to be convinced by his advisors of the need to take the military's instructions for conducting nuclear war more seriously after avoiding them for nearly two years.[39] President Kennedy's reaction in 1961 was more visceral. After seeing the Strategic Air Command's plans for nuclear war, he muttered to Secretary of State Dean Rusk: "And we call ourselves the human race."[40]

Bush's initial briefing on the U.S. arsenal, however, was four months before the 9/11 attacks, after which nothing in U.S. defense planning, not even nuclear policy, would be the same.

The 2002 Nuclear Posture Review

As in so many other areas of American life, it is impossible to know how U.S. defense policy might have looked had the terror attacks of September 2001 somehow been averted. This is one of many questions about the 2002 NPR that must remain a matter of speculation, since the study was classified and remains so. When it was unveiled, the Defense Department released only an unclassified executive summary, a set of slides highlighting its major points, and a transcript of the press conference that announced its completion.[41]

Still, 9/11 had a clear impact on the Bush administration's thinking about foreign policy in general and about nuclear weapons in particular. The scale and audacity of the terror attacks on New York and Washington, and the stealth with which they were executed, accelerated a growing skepticism among U.S. policymakers about the value of traditional notions of deterrence. Journalist William Arkin claimed that a leaked copy of the 2002 NPR was "striking for its single-minded reaction to those tragedies," and even if that is overstatement, the U.S. defense establishment was obviously shaken by the attacks. The Bush 43 administration's "faith in old-fashioned deterrence is gone," Arkin wrote, and senior Bush officials seemed to confirm this interpretation. "The terrorists who struck us on September 11th," Defense Secretary Donald Rumsfeld said a few months after the attacks, "were clearly not deterred by doing so from the massive U.S. nuclear arsenal." Undersecretary of State (later, Bush 43's Ambassador to the UN) John Bolton added that the "idea that fine theories of deterrence work against everybody . . . has just been disproven by September 11th."[42] President Bush, Vice President Dick Cheney, and other senior officials expressed the same view, leading the veteran scholar of deterrence Richard Betts to note with alarm in 2003 that "leaders in Washington have become curiously pessimistic about deterrence and containment, which sustained U.S. strategy through 40 years of Cold War. . . . Why has Washington lost its faith?"[43]

America was not the only great power anxious about the stability of deterrence in the early twenty-first century. Tony Blair in Britain, Jacques Chirac in France, as well as leaders in Russia, Japan, Australia, and elsewhere were expressing similar fears as they struggled with the meaning of war in the post-9/11 world.[44] But with a full nuclear review already legislated by Congress and under way before the 2001 terror attacks, America's doubts would now be codified into policy.

The 2002 NPR (insofar as can be extrapolated from unclassified sources) tried to attain two contradictory goals at once. Specifically, it sought to preserve the traditional deterrent relationship with other nuclear powers while simultaneously rejecting those same traditional beliefs with regard to rogues and terrorists. The 2002 review flatly reaffirmed the right to use nuclear arms, but also defended Cold War doctrines of deterrence and restraint, at least where Russia was concerned. Elsewhere, however, the NPR called for aggressive planning against specific targets in other nations, including Libya, Iran, Iraq, North Korea, Syria, and even China.[45] Like Clinton before him, Bush was trying to gain some sort of tangible leverage against smaller nations from a huge nuclear deterrent originally built to destroy the Soviet Union. The difference after 9/11, however, was that the threat of a serious enemy attack on American soil was no longer hypothetical.

The drafters of the Bush NPR were trying to reevaluate the classical notion that nuclear weapons deter all opponents in essentially the same way. The pretense of a one-size-fits-all nuclear deterrent was already being reconsidered in the 1990s; it was not hard to conclude that deterring North Korea might not be the same thing as deterring the USSR, or at the least would not require the same kind of forces. A massive retaliatory force on high alert does not make sense against terrorists or rogues who might have only one or two small-yield devices of limited range, and accordingly, defense analysts began to explore the notion of "tailored deterrence," or restraining smaller regimes by matching the size and nature of the deterrent to the threat.[46] The actual content of a "tailored" deterrent was never clearly defined by the Bush administration; nevertheless, the concept and the language of tailored deterrence were later adopted by the Obama administration.

In any case, the shock of 9/11 and the imperatives of unilateralism only go so far in explaining the jumble of ideas and projects in the 2002 NPR. The report's conclusions (or at least the parts released to the public) are difficult to explain, which says something in itself about the nature of the final product. The centerpiece of the 2002 NPR was a "New Triad" that connected three concepts: strike, defense, and research. Here, the old triad of three distinct means of delivering nuclear bombs became enmeshed in a bundle of strategic-range forces, nuclear and otherwise. Subsequently, all of these strategic forces were themselves embedded in a larger trinity, a "New Triad," that included missile defense and "response infrastructure."

This was a "triad" only in the sense that it had three parts. While it managed to keep all three means of strategic nuclear delivery, however, it effectively discarded the original reason they were built. During the Cold War, the existence of a "triad," in both the United States and the USSR, was primarily to protect the strategic deterrent from complete elimination in a single surprise attack. There was virtually no chance that an enemy could wipe out all three legs of the triad at once, at least not without launching an assault so large that the enemy would be left with no choice to be return fire with every weapon left. The 2002 NPR, however, did not even bother to rationalize this New Triad in terms of survivability. Indeed, rather than dwell on this nonexistent danger, the Bush NPR maintained the old triad—which was, and remains, an inviolable concept among foreign policy conservatives—and instead concentrated on the virtue of flexibility. The triad was no longer designed to survive a first strike, but instead

A Capabilities-Based Concept: The New Triad

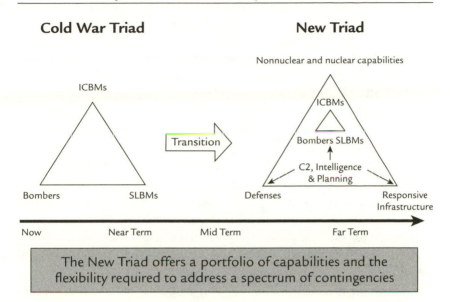

Figure 2. The Cold War Triad and "New Triad." Source: 2002 Nuclear Posture Review, U.S. Department of Defense

remained as just one set of instruments among others against an entire range of threats and targets.[47]

Perhaps anticipating objections that this New Triad did little more than conglomerate all nuclear strike forces without changing their missions, the 2002 NPR added a new wrinkle by arguing for the reconfiguring of some strategic nuclear delivery systems for conventional strikes. The whole basket of strategic offensive weapons would henceforth become "nuclear and non-nuclear strike capabilities," a potentially dangerous blurring of the line between nuclear and conventional force. There were many problems with this proposed change, chief among them the question of how other nations were supposed to be able to tell a nuclear missile launch from one armed only with a conventional warhead. The Pentagon subsequently waffled on the whole idea, until in early 2011 it rejected the concept of conventional ICBMs in favor of an as-yet-undeveloped hypersonic glider for rapid conventional strikes.[48] (This system failed its first several trials, but made at least one successful test flight in May 2013.)[49]

A commitment to missile defense was crucial to the entire concept of the New Triad. With fewer weapons aimed at smaller and more unpredictable countries, planners argued for missile defenses both to enhance deterrence and to limit damage to the United States or an ally if deterrence failed. This commitment was the most speculative aspect of the report, since effective national missile defenses did not exist at the time and even by the NPR's own admission were unlikely to be operational in the near future. They would instead appear in that magical span of time known as "the far term," which in Washington usually means "long after this administration has left office."

The other aspects of the New Triad, however, were attainable. In fact, grouping all American *nuclear* strategic forces together had already been accomplished by Bush's father and consolidated under Bill Clinton with the creation of the U.S. Strategic Command in 1992. As for a "responsive infrastructure," the organizations that would engage in advanced military research already existed and would only need money (or, *more* money) and detailed direction to be "responsive."

If the Bush 43 administration intended to use the 2002 NPR as a means of changing nuclear policy, however, then the document reflected the key bureaucratic error of trying to pursue too many directions at once. Much like Bill Clinton's 1994 policy of "hedging" against unforeseeable future threats, the 2002 review sought to mitigate nuclear tensions with Russia and China, to improve the credibility of U.S. nuclear threats to small proliferators, and to invest in a damage-limiting insurance policy for worst-case scenarios. Since simultaneously fulfilling all of these missions required the continuation of current forces and programs, the review process had once again only produced an elaborate rationalization for the nuclear status quo.

The 2002 NPR did recognize one important issue and its strategic implications: the gap between the kind of strategic nuclear deterrence embodied in the traditions of Mutual Assured Destruction and the new problem of deterring terrorist or rogue-state threats. A new deterrent strategy would require a new deterrent capability; accordingly, the Bush administration sought to create a new capability to deal with future threats, particularly dangers that might appear by surprise or in remote locations far from the United States or Europe. The response was a concept initially called "Prompt Global Strike," or PGS. The eventual objective of the program was to create a set of capabilities that would allow a U.S. president to strike any target, anywhere in the world, in a short time—perhaps even less than an hour—with great precision and destructiveness. In its early conception, PGS was meant to reduce the importance of nuclear weapons and to increase the credibility of the "devastating" conventional retaliation promised by the U.S. policy of ambiguity.

If the intent of Prompt Global Strike, however, was to move away from nuclear options, this goal was obscured by the way in which the "New Triad" in the 2002 NPR mixed nuclear and nonnuclear systems into a single offensive strike force. As Hans Kristensen wrote in a 2006 review of the program: "What makes the nuclear option [in PGS] . . . particularly surprising is that Global Strike is one of the pillars of the Bush administration's vision of a 'New Triad' where advanced conventional weapons were supposed to permit a *reduction* of the number and role of nuclear weapons. Instead, one of the first acts of the Pentagon appears to have been to include nuclear weapons in the very plan that was supposed to reduce the nuclear role" (emphasis original).[50] This, as scholar T. V. Paul noted in 2005, not only failed to restrict the role of nuclear arms, but rather represented "widening the conditions under which they can be used . . . as well as by adding new missions for nuclear weapons," even against nonnuclear opponents.[51] Brookings Institution analyst (and later ambassador to NATO) Ivo Daalder likewise noted that "the distinction between nuclear and nonnuclear weapons fades away" if military planners can "consider the nuclear option any time they confront a surprising military development."[52]

The nature of Global Strike's mission, however, made nuclear weapons an obvious choice. If the question was how to remove any possible dangers to the U.S. or its allies as quickly and as definitively as possible, then it should have been no surprise that the answer included nuclear arms. Conventional firepower can level entire nations, but it takes time and constant reassessment. PGS, by contrast, demanded unprecedented speed and reliability. A year after the Bush NPR was released, STRATCOM commander Admiral James O. Ellis Jr. framed the problem in its most immediate terms: "If you can find that time-critical, key terrorist target or that weapons of mass destruction stockpile, and you have minutes rather than hours or days to deal with it, how do you reach out and negate that threat to our nation half a world away?"[53]

Likewise, Ellis's successor, USMC General James Cartwright, told Congress in 2005: "Nuclear weapons . . . continue to be important, particularly for assuring allies and friends of U.S. security commitments, dissuading arms competition, deterring hostile leaders who are willing to accept great risk and cost, *and for holding at risk those targets that cannot be addressed by other means*" (emphasis added).[54] Cartwright was himself no enthusiast of nuclear force, and eventually emerged as a vocal critic of America's reliance on nuclear force.[55] But it would have taken significant (and unwarranted) confidence for any military officer to assure the American people that non-nuclear systems could accomplish the level of zero-defect certainty that U.S. civilian leaders demanded in Global Strike.

Following the release of the 2002 NPR, the Joint Chiefs in 2003 created a Draft Doctrine for Joint Nuclear Operations, which envisioned a range of nuclear options against regional foes. (This document was a "doctrine" in the military sense, as a specific guide to the employment of nuclear arms, rather than a larger conceptual framework.) In keeping with the goals of the NPR, it envisioned nuclear responses against nonnuclear actors. It also planned for nuclear use against threats that might be difficult to reach with nonnuclear weapons. Some of these plans required using so-called "bunker-busters," small nuclear bombs that could drill into the earth and explode underground. These weapons had been on the drawing board for some years during the Cold War, but had not been funded or built, and the Bush NPR ignited renewed controversy over whether to produce them. Those who supported building bunker-busters claimed that they repre-sented a less destructive option for dealing with threats in small countries; opponents saw them as just another pointless attempt to salvage a role for nuclear weapons in U.S. strategy after the Cold War. Congress quickly set-tled the matter by refusing to fund any further work on bunker-busters, thus eliminating at least one weapon that would have been a factor in turn-ing the concepts in the 2002 NPR into reality.

Critics of the JCS draft charged that it amounted to an affirmation that the 2002 NPR really intended to lower rather than to raise the nuclear threshold. The JCS eventually withdrew the draft, but skeptics continued to assert that the policy remained the same even if the document had been pulled from public dissemination.[56] When National Nuclear Security Ad-ministration Director Linton Brooks, for example, assured an audience in 2004 that "I've never met anyone in the [Bush 43] Administration who would even consider nuclear preemption in connection with countering rogue state WMD threats," arms control advocate Kristensen wryly com-mented that "[this assurance] must have excluded the White House, STRATCOM, the Air Force, and the Navy, for during the past decade they have been busy planning for precisely such a scenario."[57]

The 2002 review did have its defenders, particularly among strategists who accepted its basic premises of maintaining classical deterrence while extending nuclear threats to smaller and putatively more risk-prone opponents. Keith Payne, for one, argued that the 2002 NPR was misunderstood.

What was the [2002] NPR's methodology for calculating force requirements? Although senior officials have publicly presented the basic elements of the calculations, the details of that answer are not fully available for public discussion. In general, the NPR's recommended force structure and number of deployed nuclear warheads was calculated to support not only the immediate requirements for deterrence, but also to contribute to the additional goals of assuring allies and friends, dissuading potential opponents from choosing the route of arms competition or military challenge, and providing a hedge against the possible emergence of more severe, future military threats or severe technical problems in the arsenal.[58]

Here, Payne used the formulation of "assure allies, dissuade and deter enemies, and if need be defeat them" that ran through the major national security documents of the 1990s and early 2000s.

Unfortunately, these public aphorisms were widely used but rarely defined. Terms such as "assure and dissuade" were put forward as though they were new ideas or as if they had inherent meaning. (Was "deter and defeat" meant to displace some previous alternative strategy of "abandon and surrender"?) When applied to nuclear weapons, the intention was apparently to indicate that careful metrics of some sort were applied by the relevant experts—indices they could not share with the American public, of course—and the resulting figures met the specifications for "deterrence."

This notion of deterrence as a function of some kind of objective mathematical or technical determination is especially pronounced in the United States. Americans, as citizens of a scientifically advanced nation, traditionally believe not only that technology solves most problems, but also that most problems have a technological solution. As former STRATCOM chief General Eugene Habinger put it in the late 1990s, deterrence is nothing more than "a package of capabilities, encompassing not just numbers or weapons, but an assured retaliatory capability provided by a diversified, dispersed, and survivable force with positive command and control and effective intelligence and warning systems."[59] This kind of mechanistic thinking is a tradition that goes back to McNamara's Pentagon, when deterrence was defined by the U.S. ability to inflict numerically precise levels of casualties and damage on the Soviet Union.

Of course, objective measurements of brute nuclear force do not have much to do with actual deterrence. Technocratic Americans, and especially policymakers, are nonetheless attracted to such numbers because they are predictable, understandable, and obey the basic rules of logic.[60] It is easier to posit cleanly reasoned models rooted in numbers and systems than to try to figure out the intentions of a regime committed to an extremist ideology, or even just to out-think an enemy leader who, like his American counterparts, may be trying to make decisions in the midst of a crisis after days without sleep.[61]

Deterrence by its nature is imprecise, but every administration claims it is doing only what is necessary to defend the country, and no more or less. In trying to explain Bush's nuclear policies, for example, White House press secretary Dana Perino in 2007 affirmed that the Bush administration was committed to "reducing our nuclear weapons stockpile to the lowest level consistent with America's national security and our commitments to friends and allies," and that "nuclear forces remain key to meeting emerging security challenges."[62] But again, what could that mean? What is the "level consistent with national security," and how will we know it when we see it? For that matter, what administration would say it is keeping a stockpile *larger* than what is consistent with U.S. national security? How do nuclear weapons "meet" emerging challenges? Bush's 2002 NPR, like Clinton's report before it and Obama's after it, did not answer these questions.

The reaction outside the Bush administration to the 2002 review, with its aggressive language and emphasis on new missions, was predictably harsh. Some observers saw worrisome change, others not enough (although again, no one ever saw the actual documents). As one analyst wrote at the time, the 2002 NPR "generally stimulated two contradictory reactions: Fear that the Bush administration would develop new nuclear weapons and move closer to conducting pre-emptive nuclear strikes against a significant number of targets, [and a] view that the new NPR does not represent a significant departure from the 1994 Nuclear Posture Review and other nuclear policy studies performed by the Clinton administration."[63] There were grounds for both of these worries. Bush was explicit in his desire to reduce the nuclear stockpile, and yet his approach to security, especially after 9/11, placed nuclear weapons at the center of a strategy based on traditional deterrence of the major nuclear powers, threats against the smaller and newer proliferators, and unilateral defenses against every enemy, large or small.

The 2002 NPR, like all national security documents, was directed at several different audiences, but because it was mostly classified, the messages it sent were muddled. The Bush administration clearly intended to show the American public its commitment to continue the reductions in nuclear arms begun under Ronald Reagan and continued by Bush 43's father and by Bill Clinton. The Russians and the Chinese were supposed to realize that the NPR only confirmed the administration's earlier assurance that the United States did not consider war with them even remotely likely, and that Moscow, Beijing, and Washington should continue with business as usual. ("One Cold War was quite enough," Bush's Defense Secretary Robert Gates later quipped.)[64] NATO's new allies in East-Central Europe, still jittery over decades of Soviet oppression, were supposed to understand that U.S. military forces would protect them against both the notional Russian threat as well as against any emerging Middle Eastern missile danger.

In the wake of 9/11, however, all of these messages were drowned out by Bush's determination to communicate a stern commitment to defending the United States by any means necessary, even nuclear force. Rogue proliferators were warned that America would not be self-deterred from the use of nuclear arms should the world's madmen slip their leashes. Terrorists and their sponsors were put on notice that the United States would not hesitate to use nuclear force against nonnuclear states.

Bush was not alone in trying to send such messages. French president Jacques Chirac made similar claims in 2001, and a French "white paper" on defense subsequently also suggested preemptive nuclear action against rogues and terrorists. By 2003, the French Defense Ministry found itself forced to clarify the French Republic's position, and to reaffirm the purely deterrence-oriented mission of France's nuclear arsenal.[65] Nonetheless, other countries are rarely held to the same standard, or treated with the same gravity, as the United States, considered the most powerful nuclear-armed nation on the planet, and the prominence of nuclear arms in U.S. national security generated deep concern both within the United States and overseas.

In the end, the 2002 NPR made no serious choices among alternatives, selecting "all of the above" rather than discriminating among nuclear options. Bush's review amounted to a reaffirmation of Bill Clinton's policy of hedging, but this time on a grand scale, and with additional rhetoric fueled by the anger and fear that came in the wake of the sudden sense of vulnerability that gripped the United States after 9/11. Rather than present a coherent view of the mission of the U.S. nuclear deterrent, U.S. security rested on three pillars in the 2002 NPR: the continuation of the Russian-Chinese-American nuclear status quo, an aggressive deterrent threat against smaller nations, and the creation in a far-off future of a missile shield based on unrealized and untested capabilities. As in 1994, the 2002 NPR resolved nothing regarding the larger doctrinal questions of the meaning or purpose of nuclear weapons; if anything, Bush 43's commitment to strategic reductions in one area while expanding more nuclear options in others served only to obscure more than it explained.

None of this mattered very much after Operations Enduring Freedom and Iraqi Freedom were launched in Afghanistan and Iraq, respectively, in 2001 and 2003. Once the United States was embroiled in two wars in Central Asia and the Middle East, the main emphasis of U.S. national security policy shifted to counterterrorism and insurgency operations. The 2002 NPR, like the issue of strategic nuclear weapons itself, receded into the background of the U.S. defense agenda.

Perhaps the most damning indictment of the 2002 NPR is that a significant portion of the U.S. defense establishment, to say nothing of the public, did not understand it. To some extent, the public's inability to comprehend the Bush administration's nuclear policies was a predictable result of the national security hyperactivity that followed 9/11. For the remainder of Bush's time in office, however, his administration did not make any serious effort to put forward any further or clearer explanations of the 2002 NPR. Six years after the Bush review was released, a joint working group of scholars and policymakers at the American Academy for the Advancement of Science still found that "U.S. nuclear policy and strategy . . . have not been well articulated and as a consequence are poorly understood both within and outside American borders."[66]

National security professionals, in the main, agreed with that assessment. Former Secretary of Defense James Schlesinger, for example, reached a similar conclusion after he was asked to look into the U.S. Air Force's handling of its nuclear mandate. This request came from the Pentagon after an alarming 2007 incident in which a U.S. strategic bomber crew flew across the United States without realizing they had six live nuclear weapons on board. His commission issued a report that was unequivocal in its concern:

"The New Triad concept articulated in National and Defense policy documents [i.e., in the Nuclear Posture Review] is not generally understood by many of those involved in the Air Force nuclear mission. This lack of clarity is sensed all the way down to the crew level. In addition, the Air Force has not updated its doctrine on nuclear deterrence since 1998."[67] Another group of external advisors to the Pentagon from the national security community went further in a report issued at the same time, warning that the United States was losing its basic "nuclear deterrence skills," both on the operational and intellectual levels.[68]

These were remarkable admissions, especially so long after the release of the second Nuclear Posture Review. Nor was a solution in sight, since the government was no longer developing experts on nuclear matters. Once the Cold War was over, military officers ceased receiving any graduate education in either the general subject of nuclear strategy or about U.S. nuclear doctrine in particular. Schlesinger's commission found that "the concept of nuclear deterrence and the role of nuclear weapons in international security policy have fallen out of the core military doctrine taught in the Air Force," a finding that was no less true at the other service war colleges.[69] For many reasons, including a poor public relations effort by the Bush administration and the collapse of education about nuclear matters in the U.S. military, in the end the 2002 NPR was largely misunderstood or ignored, even by the few nuclear practitioners left in the United States.[70]

Returning to Zero

A year before the 2008 U.S. presidential election, Henry Kissinger, Sam Nunn, William Perry, and George Shultz published their vision for a "world without nuclear weapons." They challenged all nations to abolish all nuclear arms, and enumerated practical measures toward achieving that goal. This declaration was soon followed by the same call from a similar association of former defense officials in the United Kingdom, and again shortly thereafter by a group of retired Russian and American military officers.[71] Thirty years earlier, Ronald Reagan and Mikhail Gorbachev had put forward similar proposals, but in the tense circumstances of the Cold War, such calls were roundly dismissed on both sides as propaganda.

This time, the atmosphere surrounding "Global Zero" was different. No longer were such entreaties limited to the usual antinuclear groups whose strident demands were largely ignored by policymakers during the Cold War.[72] Now, people who had designed U.S. nuclear strategies, and who had been in the chain of command for their use, were calling for changes that no protester marching on the White House decades earlier would have dreamed possible. Cold War hawks and their former Russian adversaries began advocating for ideas that they themselves had once openly dismissed as radical or silly. In a strange reversal of roles, these proposals were put forward so fast and with such energy that even arms control advocates counseled greater caution. Scholar Robert Jervis, for example—no friend of nuclear weapons himself—noted that the complete elimination of nuclear weapons was impossible, and referred to Global Zero as "an unserious idea espoused by serious people."[73] And of course, nuclear traditionalists in the United States, Russia, and elsewhere continued their steadfast insistence on the utility of nuclear weapons.

What all agreed on, however, was that nuclear arsenals did not need to be so large. Nor did those forces need to be configured for World War III, with multiple systems for their delivery and multiple scenarios for their use. These changes in the nuclear debate represented the last phase in a prolonged tectonic shift from questions about *how many* weapons deter, and toward serious thought about *how few* might deter. At its core, the advocates of "zero" were engaging in a fundamental rejection of the central tenets of fifty years of nuclear deterrence by arguing that nuclear weapons had no real purpose, and that their existence itself was the main source of their danger. "No use" was no longer a "taboo" or "tradition," but a conclusion reached by some of the most prominent men and women of the nuclear age.

This was the state of play in the nuclear debate when Barack Obama was inaugurated in January 2009. The 2002 NPR and its aggressive language may have been consigned to the same bureaucratic limbo that smothered its 1994 predecessor, but with Cold Warriors across the political spectrum in the United States and Europe aligning behind Global Zero, Obama had much wider latitude to reform American nuclear doctrine than any of his predecessors in the nuclear age. Shortly after assuming office, the new president gave a speech in Prague affirming that it would be the policy of the United States to commit to this concept of "Global Zero." Rejecting what he called the "deadly adversary of fatalism," Obama claimed that the United States, as the only nation to have used nuclear weapons, had a "moral responsibility" to act: "So today, I state clearly and with conviction

America's commitment to seek the peace and security of a world without nuclear weapons. I'm not naive. This goal will not be reached quickly—perhaps not in my lifetime. It will take patience and persistence. But now we, too, must ignore the voices who tell us that the world cannot change."[74]

As the president spoke in the Czech capital, preparation of a new U.S. Nuclear Posture Review was already underway back in Washington, set for release in late 2009. For a time, it looked as though the United States might take the lead in reducing its nuclear inventories and altering its national security strategy in accord with a new nuclear doctrine. Despite Obama's rhetoric in Prague, however, it was not to be.

Splitting Differences: The 2010 NPR

The third Nuclear Posture Review was controversial even before it was written. For one thing, previous assumptions about Russian-American amity were harder to defend by 2009. Relations between Moscow and Washington had begun cordially enough under Bush 43, and were especially warm in the days immediately after 9/11, but by the time Obama took office, they were in a shambles. There was plenty of blame to go around for the deterioration of Russian-American relations, including Russia's continued stumble back into authoritarianism, the U.S. determination to create missile defenses and to place them close to former Soviet borders on NATO's eastern flank, open Russian bullying of her neighbors (including a war with tiny Georgia), and other issues both symbolic and substantive. Consequently, any attempt to reform U.S. nuclear policies would unavoidably be tied to Obama's intention to "reset" relations with Russia.

Worse, time had become an issue. The clock was ticking down on START (the Strategic Arms Reduction Treaty). Signed by Mikhail Gorbachev and George H. W. Bush in what seemed like a different world in 1991, The treaty was set to expire in December 2009. The actual reductions envisioned in the proposed next START, or "New START," were not all that significant. Bush 43 and Putin had already agreed in the interim 2002 Moscow Treaty to cap active U.S. and Russian strategic weapons at between 1,700 to 2,200 warheads, and New START would only decrease that level further to 1,550 warheads. But the 1991 treaty's lapse would leave both the United States and the Russian Federation without weapons inspectors in each other's country for the first time since the Cold War, an important change that could only decrease transparency and corrode trust between the former rivals.

Other factors complicated the release of this third Nuclear Posture Review. Leaving aside the political reality that nuclear reductions were not as important to Obama's campaign and his constituency as missile defense had been to Bush and his supporters, a new review of nuclear issues would nonetheless be subject to the same political pressures that existed in 1994 and 2002. Unlike the Bush White House, Obama's national security team did not show any evident uniformity of views, at least on nuclear matters.

This reflected the environment in Washington itself. Arms control expert Jeffrey Lewis observed during the drafting of the NPR in 2009 that "there is no consensus today among Republicans and Democrats on nuclear weapons policy," and that Washington was already "awash" in bipartisan study groups and commissions such as the "Strategic Posture Commission" and others. Lewis's advice to the new administration's strategists was simple: "If the [new] Nuclear Posture Review is truly going, as [President Obama] has promised, 'to put an end to Cold War thinking' on nuclear weapons, *throw out the reports.* . . . Give the President three or four *real* options. Not three flavors of vanilla" (emphasis original).[75] Instead, according to sources inside the White House itself, the nuclear review process was almost immediately bogged down by infighting among the senior officials involved. The final product was the result of 150 meetings, including 30 convened by the National Security Council, and repeated interventions by Obama himself, all of which constituted a bureaucratic round-robin that revealed the inability to reach consensus.[76]

The Obama administration released the third Nuclear Posture Review in April 2010, several months late. Unlike the clumsy politics around the Bush 2002 effort, the Obama review arrived in an accessibly written and unclassified public report.[77] Although a glossier product than its predecessors, it broke no new ground. Clinton's nuclear review process was marked by bureaucratic inertia and internal disorganization that resulted in a diluted report that was of little use; Bush's NPR process was characterized by secrecy and tight control, which produced a vision that was practically indecipherable to those who did not share its basic premises. Obama's NPR, like the group that created it, ended up being characterized by its inability to resolve the broad divisions between the conflicting views of nuclear weapons that have uncomfortably coexisted in U.S. policy since the 1950s.

The 2010 NPR changed some of the tone, but not the substance, of preexisting policies. There were, however, two important rhetorical departures from previous Posture Reviews. First, obviously, was President Obama's declaration that the main goal of Global Zero, the complete elimination of nuclear weapons, would henceforth be official U.S. policy. The second was a "negative security assurance," a promise to nonnuclear states that the United States would *not* use nuclear weapons against them so long as they remained free of nuclear weapons and observed the terms of the Nuclear Non-Proliferation Treaty.

There was much less to these proclamations than their sweeping promises suggested. Without doubt, committing the United States to the eventual elimination of nuclear weapons was an important step, at least as a declaratory benchmark against which to measure future policies. Every American president since Ronald Reagan has left the White House with fewer nuclear weapons in the world than when he took office. Indeed, Obama, reviled by many of his opponents as one of the most liberal of presidents, adopted essentially the same position on nuclear weapons as Ronald Reagan—who was reviled at the time by *his* opponents as one of the most unacceptably conservative presidents. If nothing else, the commitment to zero could be seen as an attempt to ease the contradiction between Washington's attempts to forestall nuclear proliferation while itself maintaining a large American nuclear arsenal.

In practical terms, however, "zero" was a promise that was easy to make and just as easy to ignore. Obama himself said that he did not expect to see the abolition of nuclear arms in his lifetime, and much like Bush's vision of the "far term" arrival of missile defenses, it was a vow for the current administration to make but for future administrations to fulfill. Nor did it require any immediate or concrete steps; in fact, it was a promise that was physically impossible to achieve in anything like the near future, as the U.S. Department of Energy reported in 2009 it was facing a fifteen-year backlog to dismantle weapons already slated for disposal.[78] Obama had campaigned during the 2008 election against constructing new nuclear arms, but in the end Obama had to accept plowing some $80 billion into the nuclear infrastructure anyway as the price of Republican support for New START.[79]

Likewise, the 2010 review's "negative assurance" may have sounded forward-thinking, but it amounted to little more than a restatement of previous U.S. policy and plain common sense. Promising never to use nuclear weapons against a treaty-abiding, non-nuclear state is something akin to the police promising never to shoot at anyone *not* involved in a violent felony. Nor was it new: in a gambit meant to divide the USSR from its allies, the United States offered "negative security assurances" as far back as the 1970s to nonnuclear states and exempted them from nuclear attack so long as they were *also* not allied to any nuclear-armed powers (read: the Soviet Union).[80] The policy was also briefly resurrected again in the 1990s by the Clinton administration.

It is hard to imagine what value such a legalistic policy might have today, or how it could actually be put into practice. The idea, presumably, is that even states that use chemical or biological weapons might be exempt from nuclear attack, thus abandoning at least part of the "ambiguity" strategy, so long as they do not cross the nuclear line. This legal hair-splitting led former Clinton administration CIA Director James Woolsey to ask rather caustically after the 2010 NPR's release whether this meant that if "an ally is attacked by biological weapons, the United States is going to have to do a study to first see if whoever attacked is observing the [Non-Proliferation Treaty] or not."[81]

Moreover, Obama's policy pointedly excluded North Korea and Iran from any such protections. Defense Secretary Gates later emphasized that "all options are on the table" for dealing with those regimes, thus obviating any substance to negative guarantees in all but the most inoffensive cases.[82] Perhaps countries such as Uruguay and Kenya might have been able to breathe a sigh of relief, but for any state opposing the United States, this clarification left a massive loophole for U.S. policymakers to use nuclear arms as they saw fit.

Note that this was not a *positive* warning that the United States *would* use nuclear weapons against troublesome regimes. The 2010 NPR makes reference to some sort of highly damaging, even "devastating," conventional response should weapons of mass destruction be used against the United States or its allies.[83] What form that response might take and whether it would be coupled to eventual nuclear attack was unstated, thus defaulting back to the established policy of ambiguity. The actual names of the countries assembled in Bush 43's gallery of possible nuclear targets were scrubbed from the 2010 Posture Review, but nowhere did the new NPR disavow that they were still targets. In the end, with all of the clarifications and emendations, policy remained almost exactly where it was in 2002 and 1994, with U.S. nuclear weapons fulfilling the roles of a general deterrent, a potential battlefield response, and the final trump card, the ultimate punishment, to be inflicted on unrecalcitrant or undeterrable opponents.

More surprising, and no doubt more disappointing to Obama's supporters, was that the 2010 NPR retained a strong commitment to missile defense. To be sure, Obama scaled back the Bush administration emphasis on a national defense, at least in the near term, in favor of theater-level defenses in specific areas. He cancelled Bush 43's plan to place missile defense batteries in Poland and the Czech Republic, but this was a diplomatic rather than strategic decision. The European basing plans were little more than a parting poke in the Kremlin's eye as George W. Bush left office, an American gesture valued by the newer members of NATO but of no immediate strategic consequence and of no value against Russian missiles. Maintaining Bush's last-minute promise outweighed any political gains in the foreseeable future, and in the end there was little cost to Obama for canceling them so long as the fundamental commitment to missile defense remained.

The fact remained that Obama, like Bush, did not interpret any single formulation about missile defense as excluding any others. The 2010 NPR seemed to accept—again, echoing the logic of the 2002 review, and even harking back to Reagan's original vision—that fewer nuclear weapons should mean more reliance on defenses. "Contributions by non-nuclear systems to U.S. regional deterrence and reassurance goals," the 2010 NPR states, "will be preserved by avoiding limitations on missile defenses and preserving options for using heavy bombers and long-range missile systems in conventional roles."[84] Conservative criticism of a Democratic president's foreign policy was to be expected, but in the wake of the 2010 NPR, there was bitter disbelief among even some self-described progressives who were aghast at this renewed commitment to missile defense and traditional deterrence.[85]

Obama in later years showed no inclination to touch this particular third rail of defense policy. Even under the extreme budgetary pressures of the early twenty-first century, the United States continued to funnel billions of dollars into the search for national missile defenses, testimony to the enduring allure of the concept. In 2011, an analyst at the International Institute for Strategic Studies in London said flatly, and probably correctly, that "no U.S. president can say they're going to stop missile defense. They need to be seen as moving forward. There is this perception in the U.S. that you have to be protected, whether there is a real threat or not."[86]

As a matter of public diplomacy, Obama's NPR was an improvement over the previous two reviews, but that is faint praise. The 2002 NPR suffered a death by a thousand leaks, with skeptics around the world more than willing to fill in the top secret blanks in Bush's strategy. Obama's NPR, by comparison, arrived in a single, coherent package. The main reason the 2010 NPR did not generate controversy, however, is that it did not say very much. Even the few cautious limitations implied in the new NPR posed no real restrictions on U.S. action in the future. Scholar Stephen Walt pointed out almost immediately after the NPR's release that great powers are always free to change their minds, and that "from a purely strategic perspective" the new NPR and its carefully hedged promises were "largely meaningless."[87] Arms control analyst Bruce Blair put it more plainly, calling the 2010 NPR a "status-quo document in every respect."[88]

Still, the 2010 NPR at least acknowledged the existence of the long-standing debate over whether nuclear weapons have actual military utility, or serve only to deter the use of similar weapons. Unfortunately, the 2010 review then tried to split the difference on this critical question. In a division reminiscent of Bill Clinton's 1994 nuclear review, the document tried to have it both ways, wishing at one moment that the world were different, but accepting in the next moment that it was not. In almost wistful terms, the 2010 NPR instead reiterated a goal, rather than a policy.

> The United States is . . . not prepared at the present time to adopt a universal policy that the "sole purpose" of U.S. nuclear weapons is to deter nuclear attack on the United States and our allies and partners, but will work to establish conditions under which such a policy could be safely adopted. Yet this does not mean that our willingness to use nuclear weapons against countries not covered by the new assurance has in any way increased. Indeed, the United States wishes to stress that it would only consider the use of nuclear weapons in extreme circumstances to defend the vital interests of the United States or its allies and partners.[89]

There is, of course, no description of what "conditions" would "safely" allow the adoption of a deterrence-only doctrine in this undefined future. It is also revealing (or perhaps just indicative of poor writing) that the NPR's authors felt the need to affirm that the United States would only use nuclear weapons in "extreme" circumstances. Since it has never been the position of the United States to use nuclear weapons in "routine" or "ordinary" circumstances, this kind of language merely reasserts the traditional right to use nuclear arms claimed in previous NPRs—albeit in gentler and more reluctant language.

In the end, the 2010 NPR backed away from making any categorical determinations about the role of nuclear weapons. Many other important questions remained unresolved as well, since previous nuclear policies remained in place by default, including the needlessly high alert status of U.S. strategic forces, the structure of the land/sea/air nuclear "triad" (or why anyone needs one anymore), or the role of tactical nuclear arms in extended deterrence. Scott Sagan, among others, hoped that the NPR would include a thorough cost-benefit assessment of movement toward a "no-first-use" declaratory policy; such an assessment, he wrote in 2009, "should broaden the traditional focus of such policy reviews on deterrence 'requirements' and also include an analysis of how U.S. nuclear declaratory policy influences the likelihood of nuclear proliferation, the consequences of proliferation, and perceptions of the illegitimacy of nuclear terrorism."[90]

There was no such assessment of this or any similar proposals in the 2010 NPR. The report nodded to such issues, but then retained previous policies with a reluctant tone, noting that steps such as reducing the alert status of nuclear forces were still dangerous because they "could reduce crisis stability by giving an adversary the incentive to attack before 're-alerting' was complete," a passage that reads as though the year was 1980 and a crippling Soviet surprise attack was still possible.[91] A number of other questions that could have been at least approached in an unclassified version were left unexplored.

The 2010 NPR validated traditional concepts, reaffirmed the rationale for the existing force structure and posture, grimly accepted the ongoing need for missile defense, and expressed wishes for a better future. It kept faith with its 1994 and 2002 predecessors, so much so that the impact of all three reports is still difficult to discern in the actual structure and operations of the U.S. nuclear deterrent two decades after the end of the Cold War.

The Devil We Know

Despite the millions of dollars and the many thousands of hours poured into the nuclear reviews, in each case the United States ended up maintaining the same nuclear doctrine and infrastructure developed during the Cold

War. In this, the Americans chose the devil they know rather than risking a new course. The period between the Soviet collapse in 1991 and the signing of New START in 2010 represented two decades of inertia and neglect in U.S. nuclear policies, and as a result, the American strategic nuclear force remains disconnected not only from international realities but also from the hopeful declarations of successive U.S. presidential administrations.

No reform of nuclear doctrine or U.S. security strategy can move forward as long as the Cold War machinery of Mutual Assured Destruction is in place. MAD, and the forces required to make it credible, belong to a different time. To end the pointless bickering over nuclear weapons and missile defenses between Washington and Moscow, to reduce the danger of a possible nuclear crisis, and to move forward against rogue proliferators, it will be necessary to move past both the conceptual and military foundations of MAD. Dismantling MAD will require reducing the U.S. nuclear arsenal further than envisioned in current Russian-American treaties, which themselves are still predicated on the assumptions of MAD. Deeper reductions in strategic arms will provide a better foundation for stabilizing relations among the great powers, and more important, should be the first step in shoring up the ability of the United States and its allies to demand—by force, if necessary—that other nations halt further proliferation.

Three nuclear posture reviews could have begun this process, but each of them left MAD and its infrastructure in place. There is no point in waiting for the next review—assuming another one is ever written. Instead, the Americans should decide sooner rather than later to move toward "minimum deterrence," a doctrine that relies on deterring opponents with very few nuclear weapons rather than thousands.

We turn to this concept, and how it might be implemented, in the next chapter.

Chapter 3

The Return of Minimum Deterrence

> *Dr. Weinberg.* Yes, the bear may come back. And wouldn't it be nice if, when the bear came back, the bear had a few hundred nuclear weapons, and we had a few hundred nuclear weapons, rather than a few thousand on each side. Wouldn't that be a better world if the bear came back?
>
> *Dr. Thompson.* Maybe.
>
> *Dr. Weinberg.* Oh, maybe? Well, I find it hard to imagine any circumstance in which that wouldn't be better.
>
> —Testimony of Professors Loren Thompson
> and Steven Weinberg before the U.S. Congress, 2002

A Deterrent of One?

We know that the Cold War was a "war," not least because its participants thought it was. But we may never know why it stayed "cold." The inescapable logic of Mutual Assured Destruction remains the most obvious explanation for the "long peace" of the Cold War, as both sides buttressed their vows to retaliate under any circumstances with large and intentionally redundant nuclear inventories, robust (or so they hoped) systems of command and control, and intricate scenarios for numerous contingencies.[1] Each side also feigned a kind of cold-bloodedness about nuclear war meant as much to scare the other side as it was to hide their own deep anxieties about the unknowable implications of the use of strategic nuclear weapons.

Regardless of what Soviet and American leaders or their surrogates said in public about a willingness to use nuclear weapons, or even to risk nuclear war, their actions suggested otherwise. In a passage written in 1969 and quoted often since, former White House advisor McGeorge Bundy lamented that only theorists and war-gamers, trapped in the aridity of their own thinking, could contemplate the use of nuclear weapons with anything like detachment or dispassion:

> Think-tank analysts can set "acceptable" levels of damage well up in the tens of millions. They can assume that the loss of dozens of great cities is somehow a real choice for sane men. They are in an unreal world. In the real world of real political leaders—whether here or in the Soviet Union—a decision that would bring even one hydrogen bomb on one city of one's own country would be recognized in advance as a catastrophic blunder; ten bombs on ten cities would be a disaster beyond history; and a hundred bombs on a hundred cities are unthinkable.[2]

This is perhaps why President Richard Nixon vowed in private to the Soviet leaders after a 1973 U.S. nuclear alert that he would never allow a crisis to escalate to war between them, or why Soviet president Leonid Brezhnev had to have his shaking hands steadied as he pushed a button to release Soviet nuclear weapons during a mock drill.[3]

It may also explain Paul Nitze's insistence in 1999 that he could think of "no circumstances under which it would be wise for the United States to use nuclear weapons, even in retaliation for their prior use against us."[4] This might seem easy to say ten years after the Cold War, but Nitze admitted shortly before his death that this was exactly the position he had advocated to President Ronald Reagan during the 1980s: "You know, I advised Reagan that we should never use nuclear weapons. In fact, I told him that they should not be used even, and *especially*, in retaliation" (emphasis original).[5] The history of the Cold War is replete with such moments, many of which only now are coming to light.[6]

Then, as now, critics enamored of classical deterrence theory have derided this kind of thinking—or at the least, this kind of thinking *out loud*—as little more than unproductive emotionalism. Only madmen do not fear nuclear war, but the concern on both sides was that to admit such a fear might only embolden the enemy or weaken one's own resolve. In the mid-1980s, for example, Henry Kissinger pointedly responded to the spate of movies made at the time about the horrors of nuclear war by asking if it was wise to make policy by "scaring ourselves to death."[7]

Over time, however, both logic and the accumulation of evidence have confirmed that Bundy was correct. The number of nuclear weapons required to deter policymakers in "the real world" has long been far fewer than several thousand or even several hundred. It may in fact be much closer to the simplest number of all: one.

This is the condition of "minimum" deterrence, in which leaders refrain from using nuclear weapons not because they fear complete national destruction, but because they instinctively fear the risks and consequences of any nuclear use at all. If this fear is at the heart of nuclear peace, then numbers and plans did not matter, and still do not matter, to ordinary human beings untutored in the arcane arts of nuclear planning. A study by a group of faculty at the U.S. Air War College summed it up concisely by noting that "all states strive to survive," and that "all statesmen want a state to rule."[8] Additionally, as analyst Jeffrey Lewis has argued, a policymaker "sane enough to be deterred in the first place is unlikely to consult force exchange ratios or find comfort in strategic superiority when contemplating a nuclear war," and that "despite the fine calculations of strategic planners," political leaders will "recoil at the terrible destructiveness of nuclear war" at practically any level.[9]

Recreating the U.S. nuclear force as a minimum deterrent would have several advantages over the current attachment to the tenets of Mutual Assured Destruction. Fewer nuclear weapons in the world means fewer dangerous assets to maintain and protect, and a lower probability either of an accident during routine operations (of which there have been many), or worse, a malfunction of some kind during a crisis that is misread by the other side.[10] The strategic effects of a minimum deterrent, of course, are far more important: a small force postured only for retaliation need not be tied to high alerts, complicated war plans, "signals," or other risks.

All of this assumes, however, that any probable enemy is deterred by the prospect of being struck with relatively few weapons rather than thousands at a time. During the Cold War, the specialists who populated the intellectual infrastructure of U.S. nuclear strategy generally rejected such assumptions, and with them the whole concept of minimum deterrence. Herman Kahn lamented in the early 1960s that minimum deterrence was based on "unreliable mechanisms," such as "taboos." He condescendingly noted that he would not call minimum deterrence the "layman's view" because he did not want to be "gratuitously insulting" to any of his

colleagues who gave it credence.[11] Oskar Morgenstern—an "escalation opti-
mist of the first order," as scholar Andrew Ross has described him—
asserted in 1959 that it was "unmitigated nonsense" to assume that "*any*
atomic weapon, *any* atomic explosion, is a disaster of a magnitude that the
world cannot stand, that it spells the beginning of the end of the earth, that
it poisons the atmosphere for future generations" (emphasis original).[12] As
Lewis points out, Kahn and other thinkers saw this dread of nuclear weapons, the so-called "Armageddon syndrome," as a peculiarly American af-
fliction that "undermined rational defense planning."[13]

Another impediment to thinking about minimum deterrence was that
both experts and ordinary citizens during the Cold War became accustomed to dealing with large numbers of weapons and the innumerable casualties they could inflict. Once the human imagination could no longer
generate a comprehensible picture of war, it mattered little whether the end
of civilization would come after a rain of ten, twenty, or thirty thousand
warheads. And if building weapons seemed to keep the peace, then there
was little reason to stop. The point of complete saturation had already been
reached, and if arms racing could substitute for war, then arms racing was
better.[14]

Today, without the smothering pressures of the Cold War, political
leaders and defense thinkers in many nations have begun to admit (or to
admit once again) that they may be just as deterred by small arsenals as by
massive ones. "American policymakers," scholar Stephen Walt wrote in
2010,

> clearly understand the compelling logic of minimum deterrence, or
> else they wouldn't be so worried when states like North Korea or
> (maybe) Iran seek to join the nuclear club. U.S. leaders recognize
> that even a handful of nuclear weapons in the hands of a hostile
> country constrains what we can do to that country (which is of
> course why some states want to get them in the first place). But if a
> very small number of weapons can induce such sobriety on our part,
> why exactly do we need *thousands*, especially when our conventional
> forces are already far stronger than any other country on the planet?
> [emphasis original][15]

This time there is no Herman Kahn (and no glowering Soviet marshals) to
make short work of the argument, and the debate has already shifted to

how few, rather than how many, nuclear weapons are required to keep the nuclear peace.

Still, there is significant resistance to declaring a commitment to minimum deterrence in both the United States and the Russian Federation, despite the fact that Washington and Moscow have repeatedly affirmed that they no longer have any dire ideological issues between them. Neither side regards the other as an enemy: the Russians, for their part, regularly refer to the Americans as "our partners" even when castigating them. And yet, when explaining their nuclear postures, both governments resort to Cold War tropes that do not correspond to their day-to-day diplomacy with each other.

This disconnect between policy and postures occurs because defense planning is based on concerns about capabilities rather than intentions. In the Western technocratic tradition, capabilities are measured and quantified, while intentions are left necessarily as a matter of interpretation. Pure military logic dictates planning for what other states theoretically *can* do, rather than what they *might* do.

Relying on indices such as hardware and numbers, however, can also result in muddled strategic thinking. In March 2011, for example, U.S. Director of National Intelligence James Clapper was asked by the U.S. Senate Armed Services Committee for his view of the major threats to U.S. security. Clapper answered: "Certainly, the Russians still have a very formidable nuclear arsenal, which does pose potentially a mortal threat to us. I don't think they have the intent to do that. . . . China is growing in its military capabilities . . . So they too do pose, potentially from a capabilities standpoint, a threat to us as a mortal threat."[16] The legislators at the hearing were understandably confused, and when Senator Carl Levin (D-MI) asked Clapper to clarify his answer, the general responded that the issue for the intelligence community was "gauging intent versus capability." This wasn't much of an answer, and so the committee again pressed Clapper about which state could be the greatest single menace to the U.S. heartland. "Probably China," he said, despite the fact that the American deterrent is still configured for the rapid destruction of *Russian* strategic nuclear forces.

The Russian position is no less contradictory and in some ways significantly more dangerous. Twenty years after the Cold War, Russian military guidance still officially defines the United States and NATO as the primary threats to Russia's security.[17] Meanwhile, Russian civilian leaders, including the foreign minister, continue to reaffirm that "NATO poses no threat to us."[18] A commentator in one of the major Russian dailies captured this contradiction perfectly when he observed that "in contrast to the era of Stalin and Harry Truman" there is "a complete lack of incentives for us to destroy one another," while warning that "as early as 2015–2020, Western-ers will in theory be able to rain nuclear missiles down on us, while we will not be able to respond in kind."[19] Why the "Westerners" would do such a thing was not discussed.

None of this detracts from the remarkable progress Russia and the United States have made in cutting their strategic inventories. Both nations also cooperate in other areas, such as nonproliferation efforts. The same week in late 2011 that Russia threatened to pull out of New START, for example, the Russians and Americans signed a ten-year contract for ura-nium enrichment services.[20] These cuts, however, have generated no obvi-ous change in strategy. Although the arsenals are smaller, they remain configured in much the same way as they have been for decades, like minia-ture models of their Cold War ancestors.

The irony in all this is that the United States is already poised to move to a minimum deterrent. In January 2012, two years after the Obama ad-ministration's Nuclear Posture Review had quietly faded from view, Presi-dent Obama again opened the door to thinking about further nuclear reductions: "We will field nuclear forces that can under any circumstances confront an adversary with the prospect of unacceptable damage, both to deter potential adversaries and to assure U.S. allies and other security part-ners that they can count on America's security commitments. *It is possible that our deterrence goals can be achieved with a smaller nuclear force*, which would reduce the number of nuclear weapons in our inventory as well as their role in U.S. national security strategy" (emphasis original).[21]

To say that further reductions are "possible" does not exactly constitute a ringing endorsement of minimum deterrence, but it is at least a step away from Cold War nuclear orthodoxy. Meanwhile, the surest sign that neither nation values large nuclear stocks in the way they once did is the speed with which they both reduced their nuclear arsenals after 1991. From a high of roughly 10,000 warheads on each side in 1989, Washington and Moscow agreed on a total of 6,000 strategic arms in 1991. A decade later, they low-ered that cap to 2,200 active weapons. In New START, both sides signed off on reaching a new limit of 1,550 warheads each by 2018. In all of these negotiations, both Russian and American hard-liners argued at each stage that the absolute floor had already been reached and that deeper reductions could only endanger national security—that is, until the next limits were proposed. These lower numbers in turn would become the *new* minimum that could not be breached. In practice, this means that opponents of reductions tend to define whatever amount of nuclear weapons exists at the moment as the absolute lowest level of force required to meet the notional bar of "deterrence."[22]

This is not a "strategy" so much as a dogma, a reflexive belief that nuclear deterrence demands the maintenance of a rough equivalence, at any level, to the forces of the potential enemy. This fixation on numerical equality is due as much to the inertia of the nuclear bureaucracies as it is to a force of habit in which Moscow and Washington each continue to treat the other as its only real peer. And because the basic tenets of MAD remain in place, the triad-based strategies of rapid and heavy retaliation remain in place as well, regardless of how many weapons are involved.

Unfortunately, these reductions are still disconnected from the question of how many nuclear weapons are really needed to protect the United States from a nuclear attack. Russian and U.S. planners, for example, came up with the numbers in New START by agreeing that deterrence was stable so long as each side could retaliate against a staggering 150 to 300 urban targets.[23] This kind of thinking is the ultimate result of a circular logic in which "deterrence," as a 2009 report from the Federation of American Scientists charged, is always "*defined* as whatever it is that nuclear weapons do" (emphasis original).[24]

Optimists might argue that New START represents a retreat from MAD, but if the annihilation of a total of 300 to 600 cities does not constitute "mutual destruction," nothing does. This many strikes would more than cover every major urban center in both nations, since there are fewer than 100 metropolitan areas with more than a half million people in the United States. (There are only about 350 places with a population of a million or more in the entire *world*.) As a group of American and Russian authors— including former U.S. Air Force officer Bruce Blair and Viktor Esin, the retired chief of staff of the Russian Strategic Rocket Forces—lamented in 2010, nuclear planners on both sides are still operating on the assumption that deterrence "requires the ability to retaliate against an opponent's leadership bunkers and nuclear installations, even empty missile silos. But this Cold War doctrine is out of date." Deterrence, they argue, "today would remain stable even if retaliation against only ten cities were assured," an estimate that might even be too high.[25]

While previous Russian and U.S. nuclear reductions are a positive step, they are only reductions to amounts that are still high enough to sustain MAD-like strategic concepts. The former head of the U.S. Strategic Command, U.S. Air Force General George Butler, spoke scathingly about these number games in a 1999 speech. "It is imperative," he argued, "to recognize that all numbers of nuclear weapons above zero are completely arbitrary; that against an urban target one weapon represents an unacceptable horror; that twenty weapons would suffice to destroy the twelve largest Russian cities with a total population of twenty-five million people—one-sixth of the entire Russian population; and therefore that arsenals in the hundreds, much less in the thousands, can serve no meaningful strategic objective. From this perspective, the START process is completely bankrupt."[26] Nuclear reductions do not have much meaning if they merely replicate the nuclear dead-end of mutual destruction at lower levels, but that is how the United States and the Russia Federation have proceeded since the end of the Cold War. MAD remains not only a "one size fits all" deterrent, but also one where "all sizes fit."

This was not always the case. The first forays into thinking about minimum deterrence actually took place at the very outset of the Cold War itself, when both Soviet and American arsenals were small and military and civilian leaders were just beginning to comprehend the immense capability of nuclear arms. These debates held great promise, but were quickly overwhelmed by the grim and complicated arguments of the nuclear strategists, as well as by the virtually uncontrolled expansion of the military-industrial complex and its nuclear cottage industries in the 1950s and after. In the end, it was unavoidable that the pressure of "assured destruction" would trump the common sense of "minimum deterrence"—at least as long as the Cold War dominated the security agenda. To understand why the nuclear establishment in the United States, in particular, still resists embracing minimum deterrence, it is important to understand how the whole concept was so soundly defeated at the outset of the nuclear age.

The Assured Destruction of Minimum Deterrence

The idea of minimum deterrence is not new. Sometimes called "finite" deterrence in earlier years, minimum deterrence was, like MAD, a result of the efforts of early Cold War strategists to make sense of the destructive power of the new nuclear instrument of military power. American leaders hoped for a strategy that would deter the Soviet Union, but that would also, if all else failed, terminate a nuclear conflict before the complete destruction of the United States. It was impossible to reconcile these competing goals; U.S. leaders, then as now, could not resolve the tension between nuclear warfighting and nuclear deterrence. And since no one could answer the question of what nuclear weapons were supposed to do, the default solution was to prepare for everything.[27]

Regardless of what Soviet leaders may have thought, early American war planning was centered on the ability to retaliate rather than to conduct a surprise attack. President Dwight Eisenhower was hardly a nuclear hawk, and he resisted calls both for a larger arsenal and for a crash program of civil defense. "You just can't have this kind of war," he said in 1957. "There aren't enough bulldozers to scrape the bodies off the streets."[28] Still, deterring World War III through pure retaliation ran against the grain of the men who had fought World War II. If war came, Washington would take the battle to the Soviets as quickly as possible, wiping out whatever was left of the enemy's nuclear arsenal once the incoming nuclear Pearl Harbor was discovered.

These notions of protracted battle were thwarted by the destructive capacity of nuclear weapons themselves. The sheer power of nuclear forces in small numbers implied short and catastrophic exchanges rather than a long war, and this in turn drove the logic of a minimum deterrent. A top-secret 1957 memo from Rear Admiral Roy Johnson, then in the office of the Chief of Naval Operations, explained why deterrence would work at very low levels of nuclear arms: "Assured delivery of rather few weapons is sufficient to inflict terrible punishment. . . . The first 10 delivered weapons would produce a major disaster with fully a quarter as many casualties as the first hundred. For this reason the 'assurance of at least some' capability is vastly more important than the achievement of any arbitrarily derived 'adequate' deterrent level."[29]

The Navy determined that a force of 232 weapons would be enough to destroy the entire Soviet Union, and that more strikes would not translate into significant military consequences.[30] Accordingly, adding more weapons to the inventory, even to survive a first strike, made little sense. As U.S. Admiral Arleigh Burke quipped in the late 1950s: "You never see a cowboy wearing three guns. Two is enough."[31] Of course, the U.S. Navy was especially quick to advocate the minimum deterrence position not least because a strategy built on a small, sea-based retaliatory force would make the Navy the sole guarantor of American nuclear security. But the fact that the idea carried a parochial benefit for the Navy does not mean the reasoning behind it was wrong. Nor was the Navy alone in its thinking: Army General Andrew Goodpaster recommended a force of only 100 weapons to Eisenhower in the late 1950s, a number he continued to advocate into the 1990s.[32]

Still, while there was strategic virtue in the Navy's proposal, it wasn't exactly the product of rigorous analysis. The Navy, convinced of the reality of minimum deterrence, was content simply to argue for basing the entire American deterrent on U.S. Navy submarines carrying the new POLARIS missile, which was set to enter service in the early 1960s. When Maurice Stans, an advisor to President Eisenhower, was briefed on POLARIS, he asked why the United States needed to accumulate more nuclear force in addition to the underwater deterrent. The Navy briefer had no substantive answer, and instead responded that the other weapons were "someone else's problem."[33]

Three years after Admiral Johnson's memo, a major U.S. study authored by a team of experts called the Weapons Systems Evaluation Group (WSEG) also reached much the same conclusion. "Once an effective basic force level consisting of the more promising weapons systems is deployed," WSEG wrote in 1960, "it does not make much difference whether increments of one system or another are added in the retaliatory force."[34] The initial limited strike would achieve the same practical effect as a protracted nuclear bombardment, a reality of which the enemy was no doubt aware as well. Later strikes would only fall on areas that had already been eradicated, a concept captured in the term "overkill," meaning the redundant ability to destroy the enemy serially and repeatedly.[35] In a simpler expression first popularized by Winston Churchill, subsequent bombings would achieve little more than "bouncing the rubble."

By the late 1950s, however, it was already too late to consider anything like a minimum deterrent. The Navy and the Air Force, in preparing for nuclear war with the USSR, had already gone to war with each other, and the conceptual issues were soon lost in the institutional scuffle over the guardianship of the U.S. strategic nuclear arsenal. The Navy would get POLARIS, but it lost the larger argument over minimum deterrence. In 1960, Burke complained bitterly in a private memo that U.S. Air Force officials were as ruthless as the Soviets and had used the same methods as Communists to win the bureaucratic fight over nuclear arms.[36] In short order, the production of nuclear weapons on both sides overtook any ability to think in limited terms about a nuclear exchange.

President John F. Kennedy's defense secretary, Robert McNamara, was attracted to the logic of a minimum deterrent. Like other American leaders, however, he could not fully accept it for both political and conceptual reasons. Caught between the arguments of thinkers such as Bernard Brodie for a minimum deterrent on one hand and the Air Force's argument for a preemptive, "full first strike capability" on the other, McNamara in 1961 advised JFK to reject them both.[37] Instead, McNamara settled on a strategy in which counterforce strikes would be followed by attempts to end the conflict before escalation to cities could take place, thus inserting an interval of nuclear warfighting as the bridge that would make the transition from peace to all-out nuclear war more credible and therefore—hopefully—less likely. This was something of a straddle between a minimum deterrent and a force designed for all-out attack, based on the gamble that Soviet aggression against the United States or Western Europe needed to be held at bay by more than the threat of a minimum nuclear strike, but not necessarily by incredible promises of complete annihilation.

How much, then, was enough? No one really knew, and so McNamara and his team chose imaginary numbers based on assumptions rather than evidence. "What amounts and kinds of destruction we would have to be able to deliver" to deter the Soviets, McNamara explained to President Lyndon Johnson, "cannot be answered precisely." The Defense Department provided a precise answer anyway. "It seems reasonable," McNamara told LBJ in 1964, "to assure that the destruction of, say, 25 percent of its population (55 million people) and more than two-thirds of its industrial capacity would mean the destruction of the Soviet Union as a national society. Such a level of destruction would certainly represent intolerable punishment to any industrialized nation and should serve as an effective deterrent."[38] Why McNamara or anyone else assumed that the Kremlin was working off the same charts and calculations as the Pentagon's analysts was irrelevant. McNamara's point was that after a certain level of destruction, *anyone* would be deterred—which was little more than an unhelpful truism.

McNamara's numbers represented purely mechanistic thinking. But they were comforting, because such calculations took nuclear strategy out of the realm of human emotions, the mysteries of a foreign culture, or the dictates of an alien Soviet ideology, and instead placed them safely in the universal language of mathematics and engineering. The 1964 motion picture *Fail-Safe* illustrated this kind of thinking with stark simplicity when Professor Groteschele (a stand-in for Herman Kahn played by Walter Matthau) explains to the head of the Strategic Air Command why the Soviets will surrender in the face of an accidental U.S. nuclear attack on Moscow: "They do not reason the way you reason, General Black. They're not motivated by human emotions such as rage and pity. They are calculating machines. They will look at the balance sheet, and they will see they cannot win."

The problem for McNamara and others in this period was that U.S. nuclear analysts kept raising the level of weapons at which this notional deterrence was triggered as both sides relentlessly produced yet more nuclear arms. In the early 1950s, the Joint Chiefs of Staff told Eisenhower that the Soviet Union could be defeated with 70 nuclear strikes. In 1959, the Navy came up with its figure of 232. In 1960, a special committee led by Army General Thomas Hickey produced a list consisting of 2,021 Soviet bloc targets, including every military asset of any appreciable value and more than a hundred targets in urban areas.[39]

As new weapons were built, the military identified more targets, which in turn created a circular pressure for more weapons to serve the expanded target sets. The Air Force was pressing the new Kennedy administration for nearly two thousand land-based Minuteman missiles in addition to the nuclear forces already based on bombers and submarines. In the end, McNamara would support building half that number of ICBMs. By 1965, the total U.S. nuclear inventory numbered more than 30,000 weapons.

Any notion of "minimum deterrence" was for the rest of the Cold War out of the question. As a 2009 study by nuclear expert Hans Kristensen and his coauthors describe, what constituted "deterrence" soon reached "grotesque proportions," with a U.S. "deterrent" force configured "to destroy a heavily protected Soviet leadership, to effectively target Soviet nuclear forces, and retain command and control of U.S. nuclear forces during a 'protracted' nuclear war. While the new war goals seemed to focus on military targets instead of population, in fact, the war plans included attack on political leadership, command centers, transportation hubs, defense industry, and other targets that were in the heart of all major cities." The resulting millions of casualties meant that "counterforce" and "countervalue" became "a distinction without a practical difference as far as the civilian populations were concerned."[40]

The Soviets, for their part, never seriously considered a minimum deterrent. They were obsessed with their near-death experience in World War II, and so they immediately misapplied its lessons to the nuclear world, including a fixation on large quantities of force.[41] Most important, Soviet leaders were determined never to be surprised again as they were by the Nazi attack that nearly destroyed the USSR in 1941. The Soviets prepared their society in all respects for nuclear war, from civil defense to propaganda, while in foreign affairs Moscow took the art of bluster to remarkable lengths with an icy insistence that a nuclear war, however terrible it might be, was survivable. Some Soviet leaders, particularly in the Soviet high command, may have even believed it. More to the point, however, the Soviets put their money where their mouths were: in 1960 the USSR created an entire military service dedicated to nothing but land-based strategic nuclear missiles. The Strategic Rocket Forces were the jewel in the Soviet military crown, and they remain today as the most privileged branch of the Russian Federation's armed forces.

In the tense and hypercompetitive environment of the Cold War, minimum deterrence stood no chance. The idea itself nonetheless persisted in U.S. national security debates for several more years, but the intensity and speed of the arms race insulated both Soviet and American nuclear strategies from any serious danger of reconsideration. It would take the collapse of the ideological struggle between East and West before there could be any hope that minimum deterrence might displace MAD as the centerpiece of deterrence.

The Dangers of Minimum Deterrence

Is it possible, with the Cold War behind us, to adopt a doctrine of minimum deterrence? Although the United States and the other major powers are already headed in that direction, there are some reasonable, if not insurmountable, arguments against explicitly adopting a minimum deterrent in the twenty-first century.

First, very small nuclear arsenals could have unsettling implications for crisis stability. How low can any nuclear-armed power go before it is inviting a disarming strike on itself, either as a preventive move by a dedicated enemy, or as a preemptive reflex during a crisis? The most dangerous time in the life of a new nuclear power is not when it has many nuclear weapons, but when it has only a few. As Stephen Younger, the former director of nuclear weapons research and development at Los Alamos National Laboratory, has argued, "a small nuclear stockpile could actually *increase* the probability of nuclear war, tempting an attacker to think it could destroy all or most of our weapons in a first strike, effectively eliminating our ability to respond" (emphasis original).[42]

This argument has led some prominent scholars to argue that "more is better," in the sense that secure nuclear arsenals, at least among the larger powers, would actually help to stabilize international peace.[43] Academic theorist John Mearsheimer, for example, even wrote in 1990 that it might not be a bad idea for Germany to develop nuclear weapons.[44] Mearsheimer's thought experiment obviously found no takers in the real world, but there is a certain logic to it: why not assume that nuclear weapons in other countries will have the same effect they supposedly had on the superpowers? But if states really do follow the iron dictates of realism and seek to remedy imbalances of power if the opportunity arises, why court the risk that only a small cache of nuclear bombs could actually be more dangerous than an imposing arsenal of many more?

Consider the standoff between India and Pakistan. If both nations reduced their arsenals to a mere handful of easily destroyed weapons, and Pakistan were gripped by a political crisis or even a civil war that caused the Indians to move to high alert, low numbers might have a destabilizing effect. The Indians might decide "better safe than sorry" with regard to the enemy's arsenal, while the Pakistanis might feel the crushing pressure of a "use them or lose them" moment. A similar dynamic might play out between the United States and China at the height of a terrible crisis. Would Washington gamble that it could wipe out the Chinese deterrent in one strike? Or would Beijing launch its small ICBM force and hope that an imminent Chinese loss could be turned to a nuclear cease-fire and a subsequent draw?

These are only a few of far too many hypothetical situations to consider. The fact of the matter is that we have no evidence about whether small nuclear arsenals increase the risk of preventive war or preemptive strike; obviously, we cannot generalize from previous attacks on small nuclear arsenals. There is evidence, however, that small arsenals increase the temptation to *think* about preventive strikes. This was, after all, an option that was seriously considered by U.S. policymakers both in the early 1950s, when the Soviets were building their first nuclear arsenal, and again a decade later when the Chinese approached the nuclear threshold.[45]

We also know that proliferators can make even the most powerful states jittery. The idea of legitimizing preventive strikes against nuclear proliferators has been gathering steam in the international community since the late twentieth century. Attacking a nuclear program before it can bear fruit was pioneered—unsurprisingly—by the Israelis more than thirty years ago, and the concept itself is approaching the status of something like a new norm with alarming speed in the twenty-first century.[46] It would be extremely dangerous if the great powers were to reverse-engineer that norm to apply it among themselves if their own arsenals ever shrink to the point where their weapons became vulnerable to complete elimination in a first strike.

A minimum deterrent is also inflexible. A nuclear arsenal that is configured only for retaliation—that is, solely for deterrence through punishment—cannot be employed in a more limited war-fighting capacity. A strategy of minimum deterrence not only implies, but in fact requires, a force that is not capable of any kind of graduated or prolonged military engagements. Hypothetically, a nation fielding a small arsenal might spare a handful of weapons for a demonstration attack, or for a single strike on a massed enemy force, or for a desperate attack against a small set of nonmilitary targets, but a minimum force cannot engage in waves of attacks against an array of military objectives. By definition, a minimum deterrent forecloses the ability to engage in iterated rounds of strikes that might offer the hope of "intrawar" deterrence, in which gradual escalation to greater destruction helps to put a stop to the conflict before it reaches all-out nuclear war.

Critics of minimum deterrence are understandably concerned that this kind of inflexibility might result in a strategy that is little more than the second coming of Massive Retaliation. Stuck with plans that rely solely on the launch of strategic nuclear weapons, an American president could face a situation of something less than mortal danger, such as a tactical nuclear attack on U.S. forces overseas or against a U.S. ally, with no options but the simple binary choice of either destroying the enemy with strategic nuclear strikes or accepting the damage and retaliating by other means. As in the 1950s, the choice might come down to a humiliating peace or a devastating nuclear war.

In addition to these purely strategic objections, there is a strong moral argument that a minimum deterrent violates the fundamental Judeo-Christian precepts at the foundation of Western thinking about the conduct of "just war."[47] This is because a small deterrent can, in the end, really only have a single target: the enemy regime. Destroying the regime with nuclear weapons consequently involves attacking targets ranging from infrastructure to the civilian population, especially since most nations—including all the current members of the nuclear club—locate their means of political and military control in or near their major cities. Nuclear targeting under a doctrine of minimum deterrence, then, rests not on calibrated attacks against purely military objects, but instead on threats to destroy population centers, or "city-busting."

This, more than any other objection, is the ostensible Achilles' heel of minimum deterrence. "City-busting" is morally abhorrent even by the almost nonexistent moral standards of nuclear war. Targeting cities is hostage-taking on a grand scale, a violation beyond all reckoning of any civilized notions of self-defense or just war, especially if the United States has already been struck first and all is lost. The Allies engaged in these kinds of city attacks during their strategic bombing raids against the Axis in World War II; the ethicist Michael Walzer has argued that the "supreme emergency" of national survival justified at least some of these raids, including the initial British bombing of Germany. But none of the campaigns of World War II, not even the later Allied fire-bombings of German and Japanese cities or the final nuclear attacks on Hiroshima and Nagasaki, inflicted damage comparable to the kind of slaughter that would result from even a single attack with modern nuclear weapons.[48]

Concerns about targeting cities have in fact stopped U.S. policymakers from moving closer to a minimum deterrence approach in the past. After the Cold War, Bill Clinton kept a large and flexible nuclear force intact as a hedge against Russian instability as well as against unknown threats from future proliferators. Neither Clinton nor George W. Bush faced a serious possibility of nuclear war, but the dissipation of the nuclear threat did nothing to alleviate the dilemma that would be created by significant nuclear reductions. As a pre-9/11 *Newsweek* report about Bush 43's new national security team noted, "to bring down nuclear forces to, say, 1,000 weapons or less, Bush is going to have to give precise marching orders. That may mean confronting a painful reality: targeting Russian cities in order to maintain deterrence. . . . [and] no president, including Bush, is going to feel comfortable explicitly aiming at the Russian population."[49] Bush never gave those orders, and it is unlikely that Barack Obama or his successors will issue them either. Bill Clinton, both Bushes, and Obama all showed a clear interest in creating a slimmer post–Cold War nuclear deterrent of some kind, but the implications of a minimum deterrent are daunting, and would require far more political capital and credibility in foreign affairs than most U.S. presidents can command.

All of these limitations add up to the greatest objection of all: that a minimum deterrent is not a deterrent at all. While it might be a credible means of preventing a genocidal attack on an entire nation, it makes no provision for deterring anything else. U.S. leaders caught in a crisis would have no choice but to escalate to grand nuclear threats in order to make the use of their arsenal credible, and thus find themselves in exactly the trap Eisenhower and Kennedy were trying to get *out* of in the 1950s and early 1960s when they abandoned the surreal threats of Massive Retaliation. If a deterrent must be usable to be credible, then it stands to reason that when nuclear options are limited, so are the possibilities for peace.

Minimum Deterrence in the Twenty-First Century

Can these objections to minimum deterrence be overcome? It is important to grant at the outset that concerns about minimum deterrence are persuasive because they are logical—but only if the premises on which they are based are accepted. These premises, however, are deeply flawed. They are rooted in a traditionally American paradigm, developed and perfected during the Cold War, which sees deterrence as an objective phenomenon that can be summoned into existence with technological expertise and mathematical calculations that always seem to arrive at the need for large numbers of nuclear arms.

"Deterrence," however, is not a physical condition. Weapons systems do not by their existence generate it like a magnetic field. Deterrence is a subjective experience, a political relationship between states. More precisely, it is a psychological dynamic between national leaders.[50] Neither nuclear deterrence nor nuclear war can be discussed in the abstract, nor can they be calculated as the predictable outcome of competent political or mechanical engineering.

War with Russia or China is not impossible. They are both frustrated powers, seeking to gain (or regain) what they see as their rightful place in the international community. Like petulant teenagers, they are alert to every slight and insult, and willing to raise the specter of war even when to do so seems more comical than threatening. In late 2011, General Nikolai Makarov, chief of the General Staff of the Russian armed forces, cautioned NATO over further eastward expansion (as though that were still on

NATO's agenda), and warned that the risks of Russia being pulled into local conflicts have "risen sharply." In fact, Makarov added, "under certain conditions local and regional conflicts may develop into a full-scale war involving nuclear weapons."[51] Makarov declined to explain how this could happen, but with a conventional army on the skids, he probably assumed that the only remaining way to reassert Russian influence was to invoke vague nuclear threats.[52] (Moscow can barely project power across its own borders into the former Soviet space, much less overseas.)

The Chinese, for their part, are not reticent about bellicose language. A Chinese general in 1995, for example, raised the possibility of the nuclear destruction of Los Angeles if the United States were to come to the aid of Taiwan during a Pacific war.[53] Worse, the Chinese regime continually sees U.S. nuclear conspiracies no matter what Washington does or who is in the White House. They were deeply worried about George W. Bush's intentions after parts of the 2002 Nuclear Posture Review was leaked, but they were no less reassured by Barack Obama's NPR eight years later. As China scholar (and later U.S. Deputy Director of National Intelligence) Thomas Fingar wrote in 2011, the Chinese manage to regard both increases *and* decreases in U.S. nuclear forces as a threat:

> A number of [Chinese academics and military officers] interpreted decreased US reliance on nuclear weapons as implying greater reliance on conventional arms, an arena in which the United States enjoys unrivaled superiority. Some described this as a "trap" that would require Beijing to engage in an expensive and potentially ruinous conventional arms race with the United States that would harm China's image and prospects for continued rapid economic growth.
>
> Even the reductions in American and Russian nuclear forces agreed to in New START and referenced in the [2010] NPR were interpreted as intended to put pressure on China to reduce its own nuclear arsenal or to embarrass Beijing by pointing out that it was the only permanent member of the United Nations Security Council that was not reducing its reliance on nuclear weapons.[54]

A large U.S. nuclear arsenal, then, threatens the small Chinese deterrent, but a reduction in that arsenal embarrasses Beijing. Like the Russians, the

Chinese also charge that national American missile defenses, if they are ever built, are meant to undermine their strategic deterrent.

Beneath all of this is a Chinese fear, one obviously shared by some Russian leaders, that nuclear weapons are the only instrument that really guarantees their nation's status among the great powers. Russia does not qualify by any standard as an economic superpower, and China, although richer, is still only a regional power whose glittering coastal cities are tied to a woefully underdeveloped interior. The Russians and the Chinese rely on nuclear weapons to compensate for a variety of their own shortcomings including a lack of conventional reach. These attempts at nuclear compensation are especially worrisome because they suggest that Russian and Chinese strategists unwisely think military power is somehow fungible and that nuclear force can therefore substitute for conventional weakness.

The important point in all this is to realize that these insecurities are internal to the Russian and Chinese regimes. They are, literally, their problem, not ours. Of course, these Eastern fears could become an American problem if Beijing and Moscow believe that nuclear threats are their only recourse in the face of the superior power, military and otherwise, of the United States and its allies.

These dangers, however, only make sense if it is assumed that that the Russians and Chinese still believe that there are things other than survival that are worth a nuclear war. It is here, in thinking about an actual war, that the criticisms of minimum deterrence break down. It is a maddening characteristic of most nuclear scenarios that they are built on the assumption that war has already broken out, which might be a convenient device for gamers and modelers but is of little help to policymakers. Sir Michael Howard challenged this kind of detached thinking about nuclear conflict in a 1981 response to the nuclear strategists of the time.

> When I read the flood of scenarios in strategic journals about first-strike capabilities, counterforce or countervailing strategies, flexible response, escalation dominance and the rest of the postulates of nuclear theology, I ask myself in bewilderment: this war they are describing, *what is it about?* The defense of Western Europe? Access to the Gulf? The protection of Japan? If so, why is this goal not mentioned, and why is the strategy not related to the progress of the conflict in these regions? But if it is not related to this kind of specific object, what are we talking about? [emphasis original][55]

More than thirty years later, there is still no answer to Howard's question. Modern strategists merely assume that something, somehow, has driven the United States, Russia, or China into a nuclear confrontation. As Kristensen and his colleagues observed in their 2009 study, when trying to design a nuclear deterrent for even a limited conflict with Russia or China, we can only speculate on why the war went nuclear. "Nothing presents itself," they conclude.[56]

The determined critic of minimum deterrence will still fall back on "what if?" Howard, Kristensen, and others might be correct that we cannot imagine anything *today* worth national destruction, but that might say only that our imaginations are too limited and our horizon too short. What if Georgia had been a member of NATO when it was attacked by Russia in 2008, for example, and the Georgians had in turn invoked NATO's Article V and demanded a common defense against the Russian invasion? What if a new leader in Pyongyang sparks war for the second time in North Korea's miserable history, and China then attempts to shield its troublesome ally from Western retaliation under its own nuclear umbrella? The nightmares continue on and on, until any advocate of minimum deterrence must concede that there is *some* scenario in which a nuclear war with Russia or China is possible, in which case we will ostensibly be left wishing we had kept the doctrine, plans, and systems of the Cold War.

At some point, however, the parlor game of imagining horrible alternatives must end. Not everything that is possible is probable. If the United States were to plan against every nation that *could* do it nuclear harm, the Pentagon would have to develop contingencies for destroying French and British strategic nuclear forces. This is not a flip observation: planning based on capability rather than probability is one of the reasons the United States maintained "War Plan Red" for a conflict with the British Empire, including the invasion and permanent seizure of Canada (or target "Crimson"), right up until the outbreak of World War II.[57]

To be fair, advocates of a large and variegated nuclear force accept that an existentially threatening nuclear conflict with Russia or China is unlikely. As a final backstop against change, however, they will argue that a major war is unlikely precisely *because* all sides have a range of nuclear options short of full-scale war, and the existence of these options induces caution among the nuclear states. In this view, the major powers are like good poker players sitting on a large reservoir of chips. They must be able to raise and bluff, rather than be forced either to fold or to go all in.

This reasoning, however, is rooted in the most dangerous fallacy of all in strategic nuclear planning: that there is a difference between "limited" and "all-out" nuclear war, between "counterforce" strikes aimed at military and war-related targets, and "countervalue" strikes against population centers and civilian infrastructure. These are purely theoretical distinctions, however, that make sense in the peace and quiet of a seminar or conference room, but would have no relevance to a national leader contemplating the first American use of a nuclear weapon in anger since 1945.

Limited War and Minimum Deterrence

As discussed in Chapter 2, the debate over limited nuclear war dates back to beginning of the Cold War. Whether a limited nuclear exchange with the Soviet Union was possible will never be known, since the bold pronouncements of both U.S. and Soviet leaders were never tested. As a concept, limited nuclear war was a political tool in managing the Cold War; even just discussing it was a way of signaling to a stoic Soviet adversary that the United States would not be self-deterred by a fear of nuclear use during a general war with the USSR. Many historians and analysts of the Cold War continue to believe that this kind of nerve-wracking test of nuclear wills helped to keep the peace by convincing Soviet leaders not to take unpredictable risks. Others believe that this addiction to what George Kennan called "the nuclear delusion" prolonged the Cold War and made it more dangerous than it had to be.[58] That debate will continue for many years to come and cannot be resolved here.

Whatever role limited nuclear war scenarios played in Cold War deterrence, however, they are irrelevant today. First, the previous escalatory paths to general nuclear war between Russia and the United States no longer exist. The inter-German border where NATO and the Warsaw Pact poised for war has been erased. The Warsaw Pact itself is gone, and former Soviet satellites are now free participants in the Atlantic alliance. NATO's Cold War–era nuclear targets in east-central Europe are actually now inside NATO itself. A Russian dash to invade Europe is no longer physically possible. And if the Russians, for some unfathomable reason, wanted to invade Poland or Germany once more, they would have to march across 50 million independent Ukrainians to get there, only to find themselves at war with another 26 European nations and two North American powers—most of whom are their trading partners and neighbors on a continent no longer divided physically or ideologically.

Second, without these Cold War nuclear battlefields outside of the superpower heartlands, any exchange today will involve striking targets on Russian or Chinese territory. The Russians no longer have Central Europe as a nuclear buffer. In the Pacific, fanciful descriptions of nuclear war at sea between the United States and China in a conflict over Taiwan do not account for the reality that should the People's Republic kill thousands of American military personnel by wiping out U.S. carriers, there is nothing of value available for a U.S. counterstrike outside of China itself, even assuming that the American public would accept anything less than full retaliation against China.[59]

And third, no matter how much American policymakers might wish to limit a nuclear exchange, there is no way to strike targets in Russia or China without inflicting grievous casualties and lasting damage. During a global Cold War, there was an argument, however tenuous it might have been, for deterrence through a layered and redundant nuclear force. In a globalized post–Cold War world, those arguments are outdated and dangerous.

In the end, there is no way to place meaningful limits on strikes against enemy strategic nuclear forces. Discussing such limitations especially with regard to an attack on the Russian deterrent is pure nonsense; there is no serious analysis that produces any option to neutralize hundreds of Russian silos and submarine pens without creating a Eurasian holocaust. Nor is there anything in Russia's history or current military doctrine to suggest that Moscow would consider anything but all-out retaliation against the United States and NATO in return for any attempt to destroy the Russian deterrent force. Theorists, presumably, might argue that a "limited" strike against Russia might mean the detonation of a nuclear weapon over a military facility in the middle of Siberia as a demonstration meant to make the Kremlin lose its nerve, but there is no militarily significant strike against Russia that would do anything but produce similar devastation against the United States. (And "demonstrations" only make sense to theorists; it is not hard to imagine how an actual U.S. president would react to a Russian "demonstration" over North Dakota or Wyoming.)

China, with its small, concentrated missile fields deep in its own territory and relatively far from population centers, at least superficially seems to be a different case. While an attack on the Chinese deterrent might not produce an instant holocaust, however, the damage would still be immense.

A 2006 study by Federation of American Scientists and the National Resources Defense Council modeled a modest strike against China's ICBM silos, assigning just one warhead to each silo (a dangerously slim margin should any of them fail). They calculated more than 1.5 million Chinese casualties, including nearly a half million fatalities.[60] A larger attack that more responsibly assigns two warheads to each silo, or tries to account for dummy silos, pushes those figures up to between three and four million casualties, with a million dead, mostly through fallout.

These studies probably underestimate damage and casualties from a U.S. strike, because they assume the static placement of enemy weapons in silos. But the trend in China and Russia, as well as smaller powers such as North Korea, is to place nuclear weapons on mobile launchers rather than in fixed, visible, and easily mapped holes in the ground. Mobile launchers make counterforce attacks far more difficult than attacks on silos and thus increase the chance that at least some enemy weapons will survive. Should a gamble against the Chinese nuclear force fail and the Chinese get any of their strategic weapons off the ground, the FAS/NDRC authors estimate that the subsequent attacks on U.S. urban centers (the only sensible targets for China's retaliation in the aftermath of a failed disarming strike) would mean nearly 800,000 American deaths per surviving Chinese warhead.[61]

Some scholars see this post–Cold War nuclear imbalance between the United States and its potential enemies in Russia and China as a source of instability. American scholars Keir Lieber and Daryl Press, for example, opened a major debate over nuclear strategy in 2007 when they claimed that Russian and Chinese vulnerabilities, combined with U.S. superiority, effectively gave the United States complete nuclear "primacy," meaning that the United States could launch a first strike against the Russian or Chinese nuclear arsenals with a high chance of wiping them out instantly. "Russian (and Chinese) leaders can no longer count on having a survivable nuclear deterrent," they wrote, and as a consequence of this insecurity and asymmetry, nuclear weapons "may no longer produce the peace-inducing stalemate that they did during the Cold War" due to the fears other countries may have of U.S. supremacy.[62]

Lieber and Press then advocated for an updated, more accurate counterforce arsenal. Such a force could threaten potential enemies with an effective disarming strike that would be far more precise than the clumsy and ruinous plans attached to the current U.S. arsenal. This smaller, more accurate force would be a more credible deterrent, they contend, because it would be far more precise, much less destructive, and thus more "humane," particularly against a smaller arsenal like China's.[63] Objections to this analysis were quick in coming, not least from an indignant Russian military leadership who sought to reassure their people that the Federation could achieve the destruction of the United States under any conditions.[64]

Less offended critics on both sides of the Atlantic took issue with the idea of "supremacy" itself and whether it matters to anyone. Belgian scholar Tom Sauer noted that U.S. "primacy," insofar as it existed, was more of an accidental outcome than the result of any nefarious intent, and that in any case the United States would never risk the chance of retaliation: "Even in the extremely unlikely event the United States uses nuclear weapons against Russia or China, whether either country can retaliate with one, five, ten, or a hundred nuclear weapons does not really matter for deterrence calculations. . . . Because a minimum deterrent is sufficient, Russia and China need not worry greatly about the exact nature of the United States' nuclear posture."[65] James Wirtz of the U.S. Naval Postgraduate School put it more bluntly: "U.S. officials," he wrote in 2007, "would have to possess nerves of steel or brains of lead to undertake an attack on Russia based on the assumptions that guide Lieber and Press's analysis."[66]

In response, Lieber and Press were flatly dismissive of minimum deterrence-type arguments that the survival of even a single strategic weapon would be enough to deter a U.S. first strike. "The notion that deterrence will hold as long as countries face the mere possibility of losing a single city—or even a few—is comforting," they chided their critics, "but is not well supported by historical evidence. Major wars always begin with at least one country taking a tremendous risk, and these gambles are often bigger than the terrible prospect of losing a city."[67] It is not clear to what "historical evidence" Lieber and Press were referring; while it is true that states take huge, even existential gambles when they go to war, no state has ever gone to war knowing they are likely to suffer the complete, instantaneous, and *permanent* destruction of a city, and all of the consequences that would go with it.[68] The great powers are accustomed to military action, but no Russian, Chinese, or American leader has been under direct attack in the modern age, and no academic debate can prepare them for contemplating anything comparable to the immediate and irretrievable loss of a city.

Lieber and Press also rejected the assumptions in Kristensen's FAS/NDRC study of nuclear war with China, eschewing what they saw as its Cold War assumptions about nuclear targeting and consequent casualties.

They contended that a different attack profile against China's strategic forces using a new generation of far smaller nuclear weapons could keep casualties far lower than the FAS/NDRC calculations, perhaps even as low as 700. (That is not a typo: seven *hundred*.) They pointed out that this was "comparable to the number of civilians reportedly killed [between 2006 and 2009] in Pakistan by U.S. drone strikes."[69] Thus, they argued, by using missiles tipped with very small "mini-nukes" in the low to sub-kiloton range, the United States could hold the Chinese deterrent at risk while sparing China's people, government, and infrastructure. Lieber and Press did not explicitly link low-yield nuclear weapons to regime change, but held out the promise of their further usefulness "if an adversary acts in a truly egregious fashion," although one can only wonder what further depths of "egregiousness" would have to be reached to induce additional U.S. nuclear strikes.[70]

This kind of theoretical elegance discounts the unpredictable and emotional fears that would come to the fore in the world's first nuclear exchange. Relatively tiny nuclear bombs would indeed minimize damage and fallout. Of course, if they are so small, the question arises of why they have to be *nuclear* weapons in the first place, since the U.S. arsenal already has conventional weapons in the low-kiloton range. More puzzling still is the inclusion of a requirement for high precision, perhaps even guided by the Global Positioning System (GPS), since any U.S. strategist contemplating a retaliatory strike against China (or Russia) would have to assume that the enemy's first target would be America's sensors and the GPS itself.[71] Thus, only the dimmest enemy strategist would regard a U.S. nuclear weapon guided by GPS as anything but a destabilizing first-strike weapon—which defeats the purpose of constructing a usable deterrent in the first place.

It is also unrealistic to assume that the Chinese will be able to discern, in the wake of several nuclear explosions on their territory, how many casualties have been sustained or how widely they have been attacked at that moment. It is hard to envision a Chinese leadership embroiled in a hot war with the most powerful nation on earth waiting to see if a few dozen nuclear explosions killed "only" a thousand Chinese, just as it is hard to imagine that any U.S. president contemplating a nuclear strike on China—as usual, for unstated reasons in the midst of a war-gamer's generic conflict—would really accept such optimistic presuppositions during a crisis-drenched briefing in the Oval Office.

None of this, by the way, is meant to dismiss the importance of certain kinds of war games, which play important roles in designing and testing operational concepts. (I am particularly well aware of the importance of games because my home institution, the Naval War College, remains a leader in this field.) Nonetheless, *nuclear* war-gaming is an intellectual exercise of, at best, questionable utility or relevance to policymakers. Operational war-gamers worry about variables such as the weather over the "target set," but a U.S. president contemplating the destruction of a swath of North Korea is unlikely to ask whether it is raining at the moment in Pyongyang. More important, the secondary effects of a nuclear conflict, including the emotional and psychological effects on leaders and the public alike, are likely to be far more traumatic and complicated than dispassionate modelers assume.[72] Brave talk of limited nuclear exchanges far overestimates what people and their governments are capable of handling as national disasters.

Consider how poorly the United States, Russia, and Japan have all dealt with large-scale disasters under far better circumstances than a nuclear war: the 1986 nuclear accident at Chernobyl in the former USSR, the 2005 wreckage of Hurricane Katrina in the United States, and the 2011 one-two punch of an earthquake and a tsunami that destroyed the Fukushima nuclear plant in Japan. None of these disasters resulted in a huge loss of life, nor did they disrupt the larger U.S., Soviet, or Japanese infrastructure, yet each of them strained the resources of these three technologically capable nations, with enormous costs and lasting effects. (Chernobyl, in particular, was a far greater shock to the Soviet political system than it was to the Soviet economy.) If the Soviet Union and Japan feel permanently scarred by one nuclear disaster each, and the United States is still engaged in political recriminations for the inability to respond to one killer hurricane several years ago, how likely would any advanced nation be able to cope with five, ten, or twenty actual nuclear explosions?[73] And how likely would they be to restrain their desire for full retaliation?

In the end, there is no difference between "counterforce" and "countervalue" strikes, or at least not any difference that an actual political leader will be able to discern in the heat of battle. As veteran White House and Defense Department official Jan Lodal has called it, this is "the counterforce fantasy," in which concepts for nuclear warfighting all collapse "under even the most superficial examination."[74] The many nuclear "options" that opponents of minimum deterrence wish to preserve in the name of flexibility and credibility are, in fact, not real options at all. They exist only in the complicated models of nuclear warfare that policymakers, when faced with a real crisis, will neither understand nor consider.

At present, without a clear line between counterforce and countervalue targeting, if a conflict somehow reaches the nuclear threshold—at least between Russia, China, and America—the decision will be only whether to cross the line into nuclear war to defend the national existence of the United States. This is effectively the same and only choice that would be available under a doctrine of minimum deterrence. The United States should lead the major powers by accepting this reality, declaring such a doctrine, and reforming its nuclear arsenal to support it.

A New U.S. Strategic Deterrent

Despite American apprehension about minimum deterrence, other nations have been less reticent about accepting the concept. Since the end of the Cold War, the United Kingdom has openly referred to its strategic nuclear arsenal as a "minimum" deterrent, meant only to deter "the most destructive forms of aggression."[75] When France arrived as a nuclear power in the 1960s, Paris maintained a minimum deterrent on the assumption that the USSR would fear the great damage that could be leveled by a relatively modest arsenal. The French have since dismantled their small ICBM force, and a French scholar noted in 2007 that it is "unlikely that France would embark on a military nuclear weapons program today if it did not already have one."[76]

The Chinese, although more aggressive in their public statements, have constructed a minimum nuclear force.[77] India, Pakistan, and Israel together maintain arsenals that are a fraction of the American or Russian inventories, and the Indians, for their part, have made definitive statements about the meaning of their arsenal. "Let's be quite clear on it," General V. K. Singh, the chief of the Indian Army, said in early 2012. "Nuclear weapons are not for warfighting. They have got a strategic significance and that is where it should end."[78] This leaves only the United States and Russia maintaining strategic triads capable of protracted nuclear exchanges.

A new U.S. nuclear deterrent would require several major changes. Some of these changes are already within reach, while others would require a significant reform of American foreign and defense policies. Material changes would include a unilateral reduction in the size of the U.S. nuclear arsenal and a restructuring of U.S. strategic nuclear forces to support a retaliation-only doctrine. Even more important, American leaders will have to undertake several politically challenging decisions, including declaring a public commitment to minimum deterrence, embracing a "no first use" pledge, revising the policy of extended deterrence for our allies, and the cancellation of national missile defenses.

Critics will charge that these proposals amount to unilateral nuclear disarmament. Such a description would be correct. There is no point in trying to create a euphemism for disarmament, nor is there any need for one. Disarmament gained a bad name from the end of World War I to the end of the Cold War, not only because any practical application of the notion was limited by genuinely dire international circumstances, but also because of the way some of its adherents advocated it. Too often, nuclear disarmament efforts during the Cold War were the product of a synergy between sanctimony and hysteria, and showed no understanding of the real danger presented by the Soviet empire.[79]

In the twenty-first century, however, there is an opportunity to reclaim the concept of disarmament as a legitimate part of statecraft. Ridding the world of nuclear weapons is the stated goal of the U.S. government, and of a broad and bipartisan coalition that includes some of the most conservative and stoic figures in the nuclear history of the Cold War, including Americans, Europeans, and Russians who would never have countenanced such thinking even a decade ago.[80] While some of them might be criticized for coming to their changed beliefs late in life, this is hardly a crusade of smug activists or terrified gaggles of college students.

Each of the following changes would produce a more stable nuclear deterrent, and support larger American goals in the post–Cold War world.

Changing Declaratory Policy

The first and most achievable step would be for the President of the United States to declare a doctrine of minimum deterrence. The United States would vow never to use nuclear weapons first, neither for strategic attack nor as a battlefield weapon. Henceforth, the only use for American nuclear weapons would be to deter the use of other nuclear weapons against the United States, and failing that, they would be used purely for retaliation in the event of a nuclear attack that could threaten the national existence of the United States.

This "new" doctrine is effectively U.S. policy already with regard to Russia and China. Both of these American competitors understand the rules of a nuclear game into which they were socialized over the course of the Cold War. They have no illusions that a nuclear launch from Russian or Chinese territory against the United States, NATO (or other close U.S. allies such as Japan or Australia) will be regarded as anything but a direct attack on America's continued existence as a democratic superpower at the head of a global alliance system. Their governments will not survive the exchange intact, no matter what happens. Destruction might not be complete, but it will be assured, and more than enough to render pointless whatever was initially at stake.

A "no first use" pledge is central to a minimum deterrent. Reserving the right of first use undermines any claim that a strategic arsenal is meant only for deterrence and retaliation, because, as many defense analysts have pointed out, there is no logical *military* need for a first-strike force absent a first-strike strategy.[81] Such a declaration would be an important first step, if only a symbolic one, because a large triad based on nuclear "hedging" (which has been the American practice since the Cold War) raises doubts about intent: such a force structure will always contain more weapons than is needed for a minimum deterrent and is therefore always going to look suspiciously like it is designed for a first-strike. At the least, the question deserves more serious consideration; in 2009, scholar Scott Sagan forcefully argued that Cold War objections to such a pledge no longer make sense, especially now that the United States commands such overwhelming conventional capabilities, and he called for the 2010 Nuclear Posture Review to include a thorough review of the concept.[82] (It didn't.)

Critics of the "no first use" pledge do not believe it is worth making, and argue that no one would believe it anyway. French scholar Bruno Tertrais notes that "during the Cold War, we did not take Soviet no-first-use statements seriously. I doubt that governments that see the United States and its allies as adversaries would believe our own."[83] Tertrais is correct about the way the West viewed Soviet pledges (and not just about "no first use"). The United States, however, is not the Soviet Union, and saying that Soviet promises were not credible does not then logically lead to the conclusion that no such promises should ever be made by anybody.

Other analysts, such as Keith Payne, object that a pledge not to use nuclear weapons will convince potential enemies that it really reflects an unwillingness to use nuclear weapons at all. This, he fears, would open the door to unconstrained proliferation. This claim is too extreme, especially since the American refusal to commit to "no first use" so far seems to have achieved exactly nothing in preventing nuclear proliferation. (And is projecting a severe reluctance to use nuclear weapons a *bad* thing?)

A pledge not to be the first to use nuclear weapons can be given form and substance by changing the size, composition, and targeting of the American deterrent. This would help to affirm that the pledge of "no first use" really means *no first use* rather than "no use unless we think it is necessary." During the Cold War, NATO had to rely on the threat of the rapid use of battlefield nuclear weapons against a Soviet war machine whose forces heavily outnumbered the Atlantic alliance and threatened the freedom of Europe and eventually of North America itself. No such threat exists today, nor is one likely to emerge, and there is no reason for the United States to continue to reserve the right to resort to the first use of nuclear arms.

Changing Nuclear Targeting

Once Washington adopts a doctrine of minimum deterrence, the United States can publicly revise its nuclear strategy. There is no need, for example, to maintain an alert status based on the imminent threat of a disabling Russian first strike. U.S. strategic forces have gone to lower states of alert since the Cold War, although a significant portion of the American deterrent still remains ready for war in a matter of minutes. Taking the nuclear arsenal off this relatively quick trigger would not only reduce the chance of an accident, but it would communicate more clearly a new policy in which U.S. strategic forces exist not to fight a nuclear war, but instead to guarantee inevitable punishment without the need for a nearly instantaneous decision either to escalate or to surrender.[84]

When it comes to targeting, some analysts, most notably Kristensen and his colleagues, have advocated an alternate strategy of "infrastructure targeting" to support a doctrine of minimum deterrence. In this approach, U.S. retaliatory targeting would do its best to avoid cities and civilians, but would seek to neutralize remaining Russian or Chinese military capability while inflicting grievous damage to industry, energy, transportation, and other key elements of enemy infrastructure.[85] This strategy is not the same as the fictive counterforce strategy, in which military assets are targeted as part of a larger nuclear warfighting effort. As Kristensen observes: "A true minimal deterrence mission has no need for a capability to attack enemy nuclear forces, hardened facilities, or underground structures, and certainly not to do it promptly. The objective is no longer to destroy enemy nuclear forces so as to achieve an advantage in a nuclear exchange or limit damage against the United States or to 'win' a nuclear war."[86] Rather, this strategy attempts to deter attack by promising that a U.S. response is not instant but inevitable, and when it arrives, it will reduce the enemy—or what's left of it—to the status of a less-developed country.

This option is not an attractive one, but at lower numbers of strategic nuclear weapons, it is at least more credible than the complex and fragile warfighting scenarios that require the immediate incineration of millions of Russians or Chinese. Nor is it a particularly merciful alternative: despite the attempt to avoid striking cities, casualties will still be horrendous. Kristensen and his colleagues estimate, for example, that an attack on the Russian energy sector that targets refineries and other assets that are generally far from civilian centers will still kill tens of thousands of Russians, and perhaps well over a million, instantly.[87] Many more will die later from fallout, and unknowable numbers of people will eventually starve or freeze from the collapse of large parts of the Russian infrastructure. Strikes against Chinese infrastructure could be even worse because of China's already lower level of development. There is no imaginable objective worth Moscow or Beijing risking this level of destruction short of Russian or Chinese national survival.

A true minimum deterrence theorist might argue that this much damage is unnecessary and destabilizing, because the possible loss of so many people, or even just one city, is enough to deter a nuclear attack. No serious policy of deterrence, however, can simply state that an unspecified act of nuclear aggression will cost one million lives, or one city, as a soulless reprisal meant to balance some sort of karmic ledger. In the end, city-busting is an empty and amoral threat. A retaliatory strike meant to unravel the enemy's country, however, is something any aggressive regime can grasp. Even a handful of successful strikes against Russia and China will fracture and politically disintegrate those unsteady nations. If that possibility itself is not a deterrent, then the threat of another thousand strikes is unlikely to induce any greater terror.

Unilateral Reductions

A reduction in the absolute number of nuclear weapons is the one area where there has already been tangible progress. Further reductions are well within the power of the United States. The reason these moves should be unilateral rather than mutual has nothing to do with earning Russian good will, which is unnecessary and will be impossible in any case until the current generation of Sovietized autocrats such as Vladimir Putin leave the Russian political stage. Rather, the Americans should rescue one of the few positive legacies from the George W. Bush administration and declare the era of arms control to be over in order to release the United States from the self-imposed and anachronistic need to synchronize the U.S. and Russian arsenals.

Russia and America have different defense needs and different political environments. As in other areas of their society and their economy, the Russians are still dealing with a Soviet legacy in nuclear affairs. Moscow is saddled with an expensive defense sector whose engineers and military officers still must be fed and treated decently by their government, which means allowing them to continue work on nuclear systems until they can be absorbed elsewhere in the still-recovering Russian industrial and scientific infrastructure. The Russians also have a different force structure because of their geography: the United States is a maritime power, while the Russian Federation is a territorial giant, and it has always been a somewhat tricky matter to negotiate reductions between one nation whose megatonnage travels largely at sea and another whose weapons are scattered across Eurasia.

Another reason to discard traditional approaches to symmetrical arms control is that further conversation with the Russians may be pointless, at least in the near future. Current Russian political and military leaders, for many reasons, are unwilling to abandon their beliefs about the importance of Russia's nuclear status. It is instructive to note that when pressed about whether the warhead limits in New START could have been lower, an unnamed Obama administration testily replied: "We wanted to go lower. This was a negotiation with the Russians, not the Arms Control Association."[88]

So be it. Russia's desire to pay for a large and useless nuclear force is a Russian problem. By junking the complicated legalism of formal arms control, the United States could construct a deterrent that suits America's needs and reflects American assumptions about the types and numbers of weapons needed to serve American purposes. Russian objections serve no purpose, and certainly no American interest, other than to slow overall progress in nuclear reductions. The United States could press ahead rather than seek the grudging permission of arms negotiators in Moscow who either do not understand, or who do not care about, U.S. national interests, and who have their own headaches back in Russia that have nothing to do with the United States.

At the least, moving toward unilateral reductions will eliminate the tiring international haggling over the arcane details of weapons systems and peculiar counting rules that make no sense.[89] America's B-52 and B-2 strategic bombers, for example, are counted as one nuclear weapon under New START. This is, of course, ridiculous; bombers can carry a lot of armaments, and no nation is going to launch a fully crewed strategic bomber with only one weapon aboard. The reason for this pointless counting rule is not strategy but convenience: satellites can see bombers on a runway, but they cannot see inside them, and the Russians would rather not have U.S. inspectors wandering around their bomber bases. Rather than dither over the matter, New START counts bombers as "one" and is done with it, a rule that arms expert Kristensen succinctly described in early 2010 as "totally nuts."[90] This itself is a sign of how little Russia and the United States really worry about the nuclear balance or how it would affect an actual nuclear conflict.

Just how many weapons, then, would be needed to serve a new minimum deterrence doctrine? If the goal is to maintain the ability to strike a set of targets in Russia or China that would destroy the existing regimes with as little loss of life as possible, the number could go quite low, and certainly below 1,000. A group of scholars and officers at the U.S. Air War College, for example, has argued that the Americans can maintain a comfortable margin of security with a total of 311 strategic weapons.[91] (Their peculiarly precise number comes from their mix of bombers, ICBMs, and submarine-launched weapons.) As two of the authors, Gary Schaub and James Forsythe, later wrote, 311 warheads "may seem a trifling number" but it is equivalent to "nine-and-a-half times the amount that Secretary of Defense Robert McNamara argued in 1965 could incapacitate the Soviet Union."[92]

Schaub and his colleagues thus returned to the heritage of Bernard Brodie and the early theorists who argued that almost any level of nuclear damage is unbearable. In a 2010 response to their critics, they explained that a state "does not have to demonstrate a capacity to win a nuclear war to deter one, because the devastating consequences of nuclear war are transparent, well understood, and universally recognized. . . . [T]he political effect of nuclear weapons does not stem from countervalue or counterforce targeting but from the destructive power of the weapons themselves."[93] Other analysts have mooted forces numbering in the low hundreds as well. Kristensen, for one, claims that an arsenal of some 500 weapons, based solely on bombers and ICBMs, is achievable by 2025, five years after New START expires.[94]

Unilateral reductions would generate an additional, ongoing political benefit. An energetic program of nuclear reductions would enable the United States to seize higher moral ground in demanding an end to nuclear weapons programs in other nations. Would-be nuclear proliferators, as well as general critics of American foreign policy, constantly point to the large U.S. nuclear arsenal as the prime example of American hypocrisy and selfishness when it comes to nonproliferation efforts. Some of this criticism can never be quelled; there are autocrats and despots who would not be happy were America to disarm completely.

More honest critics, however, have a point. Although the United States has eliminated thousands of weapons from its nuclear arsenal, it retains thousands more, far in excess of any credible claim for self-defense and vastly more than any smaller nation will ever be able to build, despite the requirement in the original 1968 Nuclear Non-Proliferation Treaty that the superpowers reduce their own arsenals. The resulting "two-tier system," as U.S. Ambassador James Goodby has called it, of nuclear and nonnuclear states "was doomed to break down," because saying "that certain nations can have nuclear weapons and others can't is somewhat unnatural."[95] As U.S. Air Force General Charles Horner put it in 1994: "It's kind of hard for us to say to North Korea, 'You are terrible people, you're developing a nuclear weapon,' when the United States has thousands."[96] Over a decade later, Senator Sam Nunn made the same argument: "The general view out there when you get behind the scenes, even with some of our allies, is, 'We don't like Iran and North Korea, but what kind of hypocrites are you?' "[97]

The Americans should dash past the sluggish Russians and begin a serious reduction of the U.S. strategic nuclear arsenal. This move would strengthen U.S. and allied demands on regimes with nuclear pretensions, since an America that is steadily dismantling its own arsenal would have

every right to demand that other countries cease the creation of new nuclear weapons. Enemies of the United States have continually demanded
American disarmament, and so it should be given to them, with reciprocity
as the price—by force if necessary—so that rogue states and their apologists
might yet learn the wisdom of the words of St. Theresa of Avila that more
tears are shed over answered prayers than unanswered ones.

Changes in Force Structure

Does the nuclear triad need to remain intact? Advocates of the triad insist
that American security depends upon a nuclear force that can survive a
surprise attack. As former Bush 43 administration officials Elbridge Colby
and Paul Lettow argued in 2011: "If an opponent figures out how to shoot
down stealthy bombers and cruise missiles, we can respond with ballistic
missiles. If it figures out how to track submarines, we have ICBMs and
bombers. If it tries to take out our land-based forces, we have submarines
at sea. The bottom line is that there is no plausible contingency in which
an opponent could succeed in frustrating our ability to retaliate. This means
there is no reasonable course of action leading to a major attack on the
United States."[98]

This is a curious argument, largely because Russia and China, to say
nothing of smaller countries, have no prospect of developing so many ways
of neutralizing U.S. strategic forces. It is also a position that turns the original reason for having a triad at all on its head: at least initially, the triad
was designed mostly as a means for the overall U.S. nuclear force to survive
an attack and then retaliate, rather than to keep a variety of means for
conducting a range of nuclear strike options. With survivability no longer
a worry, advocates of the triad now rest their arguments on keeping open
options, in some cases against threats that do not yet exist and may never
be realized.

To some extent, questions about the triad are a matter of cost and pref-
erence. So long as the retaliatory force is small but invulnerable to eradication in a first strike, it may not matter very much where or how it is based.
Bombers, for example, may not have much of a future at all in a world
where a triad is no longer needed as an insurance policy against an overwhelming Soviet strike. Nuclear expert Stephen Younger has suggested that
bombers might be "a backup measure should an adversary develop an effective means of defeating ballistic missile warheads, a remote but nonetheless conceivable possibility."[99] Kristensen, for his part, dispenses with the

costly submarine fleet—which now numbers fourteen submarines and car-
ries more than a thousand weapons—while Schaub and Forsythe would
reduce that number to twelve, with eight submarines on station at any
given time. Whether the bomber force is eliminated or the submarine fleet
is reduced are important questions, but they are less pressing so long as the
strategy for their use is predicated on minimum deterrence rather than
counterforce targeting.

Whatever the decisions about submarines and bombers, land-based
ICBMs must remain in the U.S. arsenal. Their location in the continental
United States, rather than their number, is the source of their deterrent
power, because there is no way to destroy them without violating the North
American heartland and killing hundreds of thousands of Americans instantly. For an attacker, this endeavor is far more terrifying than playing a
game of hide and seek on the high seas with U.S. submarines, or investing
in the hope that American bombers can be stopped somewhere along the
many hours of travel to their targets. As long as the U.S. deterrent includes
land-based ICBMs, an enemy who is truly determined to escape nuclear
retaliation will have no choice but to attack those missile fields and thus
risk all-out nuclear war with the United States and its allies.

One other change that would be relatively easy to make would be to
remove the last U.S. tactical nuclear weapons from Europe. Their battlefield
is gone and their former targets are now in Allied territory. The United
States has already removed more than 90 percent of its tactical inventory
on the Continent, leaving less than 200 weapons that today serve no purpose other than as a diplomatic irritant both among NATO nations and
between NATO and Russia.[100] A European observer, commenting on the
Alliance's 2011 deliberations over its security concepts, noted: "The most
acrimonious point in the current [NATO nuclear] review is not whether
the last remaining U.S. nuclear weapons should be withdrawn, but when
and how. Even the U.S. military agrees that the missiles' military utility is
close to zero. The real question is whether or not NATO should link their
withdrawal to reductions in Russia's arsenal of tactical nuclear weapons."[101]

There have been no serious arguments in favor of keeping these weapons other than that the Russians have some two thousand tactical nuclear
arms of their own and will not countenance destroying them. Moscow's
stubbornness, however, has little to do with strategic purpose. Russia is
stuck with a large tactical inventory whose continued existence reflects the
Russian high command's traditional nuclear fixations as well as the squalid

mess inside the Russian defense establishment.[102] There is no reason the United States must emulate this idiosyncratic Russian approach, and a unilateral dismantling of these weapons would remove a thorn from NATO's side while obviating many of the specious Russian complaints about NATO's outdated nuclear forces.[103]

Extended Deterrence

Removing nuclear weapons from Europe and creating a minimum deterrent raises obvious questions about extended deterrence, or the guarantee of a nuclear umbrella over friends and allies to protect them from attack by a nuclear-armed enemy. Extended deterrence was another necessity of the Cold War, a strategy meant to forge a nuclear link between the United States and its allies. The U.S. nuclear guarantee strategy made sense at the time, because Soviet foreign policy was directly aimed at splitting NATO apart by driving a wedge of doubt between the Europeans and the Americans. The attempt to convince the Soviet Union that the Americans valued European freedom as much as they valued their own was a huge gamble, buttressed by the placement of nuclear weapons on the frontlines of Europe. The Soviets may never have believed the theory that the Americans would risk a nuclear war for NATO, but they were unwilling to invade Europe and test it.

Today, there is no plausible future in which the United States must engage in nuclear threats to protect a weak and menaced NATO. The British and the French both command minimum deterrent forces in Europe, and U.S. submarines patrol the waters of the Atlantic and the Pacific armed with nuclear weapons. Perhaps more to the point, if the Russian Federation decides to invade and attack NATO, something has gone wrong far beyond what any "extended" deterrent could have prevented. NATO, in any case, is rapidly taking on many of the characteristics of a collective security organization whose goal is to keep the general peace, rather than a bulwark against a Eurasian superpower. An alliance trying to hold the line against the Soviet Union needed nuclear guarantees. A collective security organization enforcing good behavior on the unruly playgrounds surrounding a core of European democracies does not.

With the Cold War long over, it is time to consider whether extended deterrence of any kind is wise, and whether it really deters anything. Schaub and his colleagues at the Air War College tackled this question directly, noting that even during the Cold War the West's nuclear guarantees were of questionable value: "Critics contend that a small number of nuclear weapons will prevent the United States from extending its nuclear deterrent to allies and friends who might be threatened by other nuclear states. One might think, 'Thank goodness.' "[104] Extended deterrence is a yet more complicated question now that NATO is larger than it was during the Cold War. In those dark days, the Alliance was composed of fifteen countries. When Spain's dictatorship collapsed in 1982, Spain joined and NATO remained at sixteen members for the remainder of the Cold War. Today, NATO has twenty-eight members representing the addition of a dozen nations of varying strength and uneven democratic development.

The enlargement of NATO meant the consequent extension of American nuclear protection to nearly the entire continent of Europe. This expansion of the nuclear guarantee, however, took place without serious public debate or strategic analysis. The original 1999 inclusion of Poland, Hungary, and the Czech Republic made sense, but the next eleven additions, or an average of about one country a year, took place too precipitously.[105] There is nothing to be done about the size of NATO at this point, but Americans must now ask themselves if they are really willing to risk a nuclear crisis over, say, a civil war or a border dispute along NATO's eastern edge. It is one thing to commit to the security of Poland in case of a massive Russian invasion. It is another entirely to keep a nuclear bullet in the holster as a guarantee against threats, whatever they are, to newly formed nations whose politics and foreign policies may still be unstable.

Other extended deterrence policies left over from the Cold War are tenuous today as well. The nuclear commitment to Japan is no longer well understood even by the Japanese, who now see U.S. nuclear promises as a hedge against a North Korean attack with nuclear or chemical weapons rather than as a deterrent against Soviet or Chinese aggression.[106] South Korea, too, has sought assurances that Washington will treat any nuclear attack by the North as equivalent to a nuclear attack on the United States, a dramatic proposition that would represent an unprecedented expansion of the Cold War deterrence model, and so far the United States has quietly declined to return tactical nuclear arms to the Korean peninsula.[107] A 2010 RAND study asked: "The question becomes how the United States would respond to attacks on Seoul or Tokyo. Would it employ massive retaliation, as some think, but in apparent contravention of the Geneva Convention? Would North Korea think that the United States had the will for such an escalation?"[108] These are good questions, and ones no doubt being asked in Pyongyang as well as in other Asian capitals.

The same imponderables about extended deterrence apply to the Middle East. In 2008, U.S. Democratic presidential candidate Hillary Clinton threatened to "obliterate" Iran if it used nuclear weapons against Israel, a statement for which she was roundly criticized. (The *Boston Globe*, for one, referred to her as "Hillary Strangelove.")[109] When she suggested in 2009, this time as the U.S. Secretary of State, that the American nuclear umbrella might shield states in the region from a future Iranian nuclear capability, her comments set off "tremors" throughout the Middle East and the Obama administration backtracked quickly.[110]

Extended deterrence has run its course. It is time to admit it, so that the United States and its allies will no longer lean on a nuclear crutch and instead begin the more difficult (and admittedly more expensive) task of preparing its conventional forces for operations in support of U.S. friends and allies across the globe. The most visible component of U.S. commitment to its various allies is not the vague promise of nuclear use, but the physical presence of U.S. forces. These troops, when based on an ally's territory, are a deterrent because any attack that kills American soldiers thus courts war with the United States. Some of the members of "new NATO" along the eastern frontier have admitted as much, and have pursued cooperation with U.S. missile defense primarily as a way to guarantee the stationing of U.S. troops on their territory.[111] Russia, China, and the rogues are far more likely to fear contending with U.S. and NATO conventional forces—still by far the most advanced and powerful in the world—then they are to quail at half-hearted nuclear threats that the Americans themselves might not know how to execute if the need arose.

Rethinking Missile Defenses

The political third rail of nuclear reform has less to do with nuclear weapons than with defenses against them. Ever since Ronald Reagan committed the United States in 1983 to creating a space-based shield against nuclear attack, missile defense has become a matter more of religion than rational debate among both opponents and advocates of the idea. Both sides complicate the cause of nuclear reform because of their absolutist positions on the subject. For proponents, defenses are a moral imperative, and it is doubtful that missile defense supporters in Congress will ever agree to major cuts in the U.S. nuclear arsenal, by treaty or otherwise, without a solid guarantee of further work on such projects. Many opponents, for their part, tend to hate the idea of missile defense in all its forms, and dismiss objections or counterarguments that eliminating dangerous offensive weapons should be coupled to the creation of defensive systems.[112]

There is not much room to maneuver between these two positions. With the adoption of a minimum deterrent, however, there might be a middle way. The first step is to disentangle *theater* missile defenses from *national* missile defense. The United States and other nations have for decades worked on systems designed to intercept short- and medium-range ballistic missiles, such as the antiquated Scud missiles Saddam Hussein fired at random during the 1991 Gulf War. The Americans are planning to base many of those theater defense systems at sea so that they can be speedily repositioned during a crisis. This is the so-called "Phased Adaptive Approach" approved by the Obama administration in late 2009 and slated for completion sometime around 2020.[113]

Theater defenses are valuable both as military assets and and as political instruments. The movement of defensive systems into troubled waters (literally) not only signals to a regional opponent like Iran or North Korea that the United States is bracing for conflict, but holds out the hope, however slim, of limiting damage to U.S. forces or allies should the situation spiral out of control. They are a warning to the enemy that a missile launch will be only the beginning, not the end, of a major conflict with the United States, and that the damage from such a launch, while awful, will not be fatal to the U.S. and allied war effort—if the enemy weapon makes it to the target at all.

Concentrating on theater defenses would also allow the United States and NATO to dispense with disingenuous Russian and Chinese objections. Theater missile defense systems will never be able to stop any sizable ballistic nuclear attack, and the Chinese and the Russians know it. Bogus arguments about missile defense are essential to rationalizations made in Moscow and Beijing about the need to modernize the Russian and Chinese strategic arsenals, but those programs have progressed, and will continue to do so, regardless of American moves.[114] The Russian decision to replace the aging SS-18 "heavy" ICBM, for example, was made many years ago, even though the Kremlin later carped about the need to counter future NATO missile defenses. On occasion, Russian defense analysts themselves have blurted out the truth that Western plans for theater defense systems pose no real threat to the Russian Federation.[115]

The same characteristics that make theater defenses useful, however, make the pursuit of national missile defenses destabilizing. National defenses, unlike their smaller regional counterparts, could be interpreted by potential opponents as an active attempt to limit damage during central nuclear war, a concept which in turn suggests a nuclear warfighting mentality, especially when combined with a large, MAD-sized offensive nuclear inventory. Indeed, memories in international relations can be short: this kind of thinking was exactly the source of a great deal of American concern about the Soviet obsession with missile defenses in the 1960s.

Another particularly dangerous aspect of national defenses is the chance that a U.S. leader might actually believe they will *work*. There is virtually no possibility, nor will there be in our lifetime, of stopping a strategic launch of any appreciable size against the United States, especially one consisting of several missiles over a long range with scores of warheads arriving at fantastic speeds. It would be reckless in the extreme for an American president to risk the lives of millions of people on a system that has never been tested in combat, and whose effectiveness might only be as high as 80 or 90 percent; when it comes to defending against nuclear strikes, "100" is the only percentage of reliability that matters. Still, under inhuman levels of duress, a commander-in-chief might give in to the fervent hope that a launch against the United States can be intercepted. The U.S. military has already made confident statements about shooting down North Korean missiles, and the only thing that might be worse than making such claims would be if a U.S. president, in a moment of weakness, acted on them.[116]

This hazard is compounded by the outsized claims that some supporters of missile defense make whenever anything fired into the sky manages to strike anything else. Missile defense enthusiasts argued, for example, that the success of Israel's "Iron Dome" theater defenses against rockets fired at Israel from Gaza in late 2012 proved the efficacy and necessity of missile defenses. Conservative journalist Max Boot even took to the pages of *Commentary* magazine to insist that Iron Dome's high rate of interception—Israeli officials put it somewhere near 85 percent—"vindicated" Ronald Reagan's original conception of SDI.[117] (That number has since come under serious challenge by experts in the U.S. and Israel, with critics placing the number of actual intercepts at less than half the original claims, and perhaps lower.)[118]

Any claim that the 2012 successes of Iron Dome somehow proved the wisdom of trying to pursue national missile defenses is ridiculous on its face. Iron Dome is meant to destroy objects in a regional conflict that travel over a much shorter range and are far slower and easier to detect than long-range ballistic missiles. The rockets aimed at Israel had a speed of some 500 meters per second; Saddam's Scuds, by comparison, reached 2,200 meters per second, while ICBMs travel through space at 7,000 meters per second.[119] Moreover, the Gaza rockets did not have the countermeasures and decoys that would accompany a long-range missile strike. It should also be sobering to consider that knocking down four out of five rockets sounds like a great success—so long as that fifth projectile isn't packing a nuclear warhead.

In the end, intercepting nuclear missiles is nothing like intercepting short-range rockets. It would be dangerous folly if U.S. leaders entered a conflict thinking they had a functional SDI-like system if in fact all they had was, to use the Israeli newspaper *Haaretz*'s description of Iron Dome, a "rocket-swatter."[120] Missile defense opponent Joe Cirincione put it best when he acidly responded to the exuberance of missile defense supporters by suggesting that trying to translate the success of Iron Dome's short-range interceptions into an argument for national missile defenses was "like being good at miniature golf and thinking you can win the Masters."[121]

Theater missile defenses can be an important component of a new American national security policy. *National* missile defenses, however, have no value in creating a stable minimum deterrent and in fact will undermine it. Americans must finally outgrow the unrealistic claims that continue to contaminate discussions of missile defense. The goal of SDI during the 1980s, at least in its initial incarnation, made sense: it was meant to complicate Soviet first-strike planning by inducing greater risk and uncertainty into Soviet calculations, and thus to gain time during a crisis by undermining the Kremlin's confidence in nuclear escalation. Absent such a threat, national missile defenses create more problems than they can ever solve.

A mature and unemotional conversation about missile defense systems should engage advocates and opponents of defenses, including those among America's European and Asian allies. Such a discussion, however, need not spend inordinate time trying to placate Moscow or Beijing. Short of completely abandoning any discussion of the concept of defenses at all levels, the Russians and Chinese will never be comfortable with any project that harnesses the energies of the American technological base to military purposes. A reconsideration of national missile defenses coupled to significant cuts in offensive strategic forces would create a more stable and smaller U.S. nuclear deterrent, and the Americans would do well simply to exit their *pas de deux* with the Russians and leave Moscow to tend to its own nuclear problems.

The Political Challenge of Nuclear Reform

Adopting a new deterrent will require a significant change in the way national security policies and nuclear postures are debated in the United States. The President of the United States will have to rely on his or her authority as the Commander-in-Chief and make a persuasive case to the American people, who by and large do not understand nuclear issues but who generally support the current nuclear establishment because of the experience of the Cold War. They have an intuitive sense that nuclear deterrence, as they have seen it, works. And the fact of the matter is that it *did* work: the Soviet Union was defeated in a real sense by holding it at bay with nuclear weapons until its system could finally complete the internal processes of rot and collapse. While some scholars will complain that any talk of a Soviet defeat or a Western victory is merely jingoistic American "triumphalism," ordinary Russians no less than their American counterparts know what happened in 1991, and nuclear deterrence was central to those events.

The Cold War, however, cannot define U.S. defense policy forever. Russia is not the USSR, and stabilizing the nuclear relationship with Russia and China should be the easiest part of reforming American nuclear doctrine. In any case, the harder questions revolve not around deterrence with established competitors such as Russia or China, but with small nuclear powers. These nations are the far more likely threats to U.S. and Western safety, and deterring them is a more agonizing problem because any American use of nuclear weapons will be by choice rather than necessity. How should the United States respond to threats from small states that could inflict huge damage with deaths in the tens of thousands or more, but which do not threaten the very existence of the United States? Even if Washington and its allies resolve to maintain a deterrent that can level Russia or China, how does that help prevent an attack by a nation of starving North Koreans, or by a group of religious fanatics holding millions of their innocent neighbors hostage?

In the classic 1975 motion-picture thriller *Three Days of the Condor*, John Houseman played a senior CIA official who is asked by one of his deputies if, in the twilight world of Cold War intelligence games, he misses the kind of direct action he saw as a young man in World War II. "No," Houseman intones gravely. "I miss that kind of *clarity*." The threat represented by the USSR gave meaning, however confused, to the U.S. nuclear arsenal. No one knew exactly how it should be used if deterrence failed, but all agreed that deterrence of the Soviet Union was why it existed at all. As will be seen in the next chapter, when a nuclear challenge finally arises from a small nuclear rogue, the nuclear dilemmas of the Cold War will seem like clarity itself by comparison.

Chapter 4

Small States and Nuclear War

I just don't think nuclear weapons are usable . . . I'm not saying that we militarily disarm. I'm saying that I have nuclear weapons, and you're North Korea and you have a nuclear weapon. You can use yours. I can't use mine. What am I going to use it on? What are nuclear weapons good for? Busting cities. What President of the United States is going to take out Pyongyang?
—General Charles Horner, U.S. Air Force, 1994

I have no sympathy for the man who demands an eye for an eye in a nuclear attack.

—George Kennan, 1976

"Sacred War"

In October 2006, North Korea successfully tested a nuclear bomb. Nearly four years later, as the United States and South Korea mounted a major joint military exercise in July 2010 that included the massive American aircraft carrier *George Washington*, North Korea thundered that such an "unpardonable" provocation would mean war. The North Korean regime is a bizarre, pseudo-Communist dynasty governed by the fanatically oppressive Kim family since World War II, and it routinely makes such threats against actions it finds offensive or insulting—which is almost everything.

This time, however, Pyongyang brandished a new addition to its military and rhetorical arsenal. "The army and people," the official North Korean news agency declared, "will legitimately counter with their powerful nuclear deterrence the largest ever nuclear war exercises to be staged by the U.S. and the South Korean puppet forces." The North's National Defense Council also promised a "retaliatory sacred war" in response to the maneuvers.[1] Less than two years later, in late 2012, North Korea finally succeeded in launching a crude, three-stage ICBM prototype, placing a small satellite in orbit and proving not only that Pyongyang now had a bomb, but that the regime was on the way to achieving an intercontinental delivery capability as well.[2] "We are not disguising the fact," North Korean defense authorities said in early 2013, "that the various satellites and long-range rockets that we will fire and the high-level nuclear test we will carry out are targeted at the United States."[3]

The post-Cold War problem of rogue state nuclear proliferation is no longer hypothetical. These small powers, whom Clinton administration national security advisor Anthony Lake in 1994 termed "outlaw" or "back-lash" states, not only remain "outside the family of nations," in Lake's words, but also "assault its basic values."[4] North Korea's nuclear tests and rash threats represent more than the entry of a new member into the nuclear club. Nuclear weapons are now in the hands of a small, unpredictable state whose foreign policy remains centered on hostility to the United States, whose arsenal is not dedicated to a specific opponent (as in the cases, for example, of India and Pakistan), whose regime remains in a state of declared hostilities with a U.S. ally, and whose leaders remain outside of any constraining alliance system. The North Korean regime has joined the nuclear game with no pretense to being a status-quo power, and no superpower competition to restrict its ambitions.

The North Korean challenge raises issues that go far beyond Pyongyang and Washington. Other states that are no friend to the liberal international order, particularly the terror-supporting theocracy in Iran, are seeking nuclear arms as well. While a minimum deterrent can keep the peace among the great powers such as Russia, China, and the United States, how can small states, crowded by innocent neighbors and commanding only comparatively tiny arsenals, be deterred? The sheer disparity and imbalance of power between the actors involved, and the location of the possible hostilities, complicates the question of what to do if deterrence fails. What threats can actually be *executed* without unacceptable geopolitical—and moral—consequences? U.S. policymakers have unwisely avoided making difficult choices about these questions for two decades. They have relied instead on intentional ambiguity while pursuing nuclear policies better suited to the Cold War than to the twenty-first century.

Now, however, the threat is no longer notional, and ambiguity will no longer suffice. The United States and its allies need to create a new and radically different deterrent against small nuclear powers. Before constructing that new deterrent, it is important to consider the existing alternatives and their limitations and problems, especially those related to nuclear retaliation.

The Retaliation Imperative

On an immediate and intuitive level, striking an enemy with nuclear weapons after a nuclear attack is the only reaction that makes sense. The logic of retaliation is both linear and seductive: if a nuclear weapon is used against the United States or other Western powers, it will mean that the fear of a nuclear response was somehow insufficient to deter the attack. It will mean, in other words, that deterrence has failed. The imperative will be to respond in kind in order to restore that fear, and to salvage nuclear deterrence by reinforcing the consequences of its failure.

On a more emotional level, nuclear retaliation will fulfill the inevitable urge to balance the karmic scales of revenge. Even a small terrorist nuclear device will create a catastrophe that will make memories of jetliners crashing into skyscrapers seem like a reassuringly manageable crisis in comparison. In the chaos that will follow the detonation of a nuclear weapon amid hundreds of thousands of people, the urge to retaliate will not only be understandable but virtually irresistible.

Nevertheless, threats to engage in a nuclear exchange with a small power have to be examined more closely. Such threats are heavily complicated by the asymmetries between the United States and its potential enemies. The Cold War is no longer a reliable template, if it ever was: the promise to retaliate against the USSR for reducing the United States to ashes cannot be translated into the same threat to destroy a small nation for an attack with a few bombs, or even one. The military and moral enormity of nuclear use, the potentially disproportionate scale of the response, the unavoidable damage to innocent parties near the actual target, the risks of escalation, and the lasting effects of nuclear weapons make retaliation a vastly more complicated equation than the simple logic of assured destruction.

It is not difficult to sympathize with the fears of successive U.S. and allied leaders, and it is understandable how those fears have prolonged a reliance on nuclear threats. Despite their many efforts, Western leaders and their populations have faced, over the years, the inexorable march of proliferation, a steady movement that at best has been occasionally slowed but not stopped. Meanwhile, traditional notions of deterrence no longer seem as predictable or as durable as they once were.[5] Much of the anxiety among status quo powers such as the United States is rooted in confusion about the nature of new nuclear powers in the twenty-first century, as the nuclear ambitions of these small, personalized regimes do not fit well in the Cold War paradigm. Their erratic behavior frustrates traditional thinking about nuclear weapons.

Unlike the superpowers in the early Cold War, the rogue proliferators of today have not stumbled into an arms race in the aftermath of global war. Instead, they seem bent on swimming against the tide of international events. States such as North Korea and Iran are creating nuclear weapons primarily as a means of upsetting the status quo, even as the established nuclear powers are heading in the other direction and trying to reduce their nuclear inventories. These proliferators are not interested in rising into the ranks of the nuclear powers through the steady creation of a relatively institutionalized nuclear infrastructure; instead, they are determined only to bolt across the nuclear threshold by any means possible. North Korea shocked the world with its demonstration of a nuclear capability, while Iran, for its part, for years has claimed to have no aggressive designs for its nuclear program, even as its leaders have made apocalyptic threats against Israel and its military has regularly rattled the international community with various threats to the region.[6]

Elsewhere, other proliferators are accelerating their efforts. The Syrians were apparently engaged in a nuclear program of some kind before 2007; more interesting than the fact that the Israelis destroyed it in an air raid is that the Syrians refused to press charges, so to speak, probably because pursuing the issue would have involved allowing international inspections of the attack zone.[7] (We will no doubt learn more in the wake of the Syrian civil war and the collapse of the Assad regime.) In Asia, a United Nations panel in spring 2010 found that North Korea was sharing nuclear technology with other states, including Iran, Syria, and even Myanmar, a program that does not have much promise but whose existence is bizarre and worrisome in itself.[8] The Americans, and especially the Europeans—who will sooner be in range of Iranian threats than the North Americans—might be

forgiven for feeling that they have reached the limit of their ability to tolerate nuclear or other WMD risks.

Under such tense and unpredictable conditions, it is tempting to believe
that the only recourse is to fall back on the kind of nuclear threats that
seemed to keep the peace during the Cold War. Whatever happened during
the Cold War, it seemed to work, and in its wake the world's most powerful
nations enjoy far more amicable relationships than they once did. While it
is a refrain that has been heard before, it is difficult to disagree with Henry
Kissinger's 2006 observation that "contrary to historical experience . . .
what used to be called the 'great powers' have nothing to gain by military
conflict with each other. They are all more or less dependent on the global
economic system."[9] British general Rupert Smith likewise wrote in 2005
that war, "as a massive deciding event in a dispute in international politics,"
no longer exists.[10]

Like most complicated international phenomena, however, this peace
among the great powers is the outcome of many conditions. The cessation
of the East-West ideological conflict was central to this new stability, but
the benefits of globalization, including improved communication and
trade, have played important roles as well. None of these factors, however,
appears to be at work between the great powers and the would-be nuclear
rogues. History, for these small powers, has not ended; rather, it has only
begun now that they have been freed from the constricting competition
between the superpowers. These regimes are at best ambivalent about
globalization, which provides them access to technology and wealth, but
which they correctly perceive as a threat to their control over their own
people. And they see no reason to adopt the rules of the Cold War game,
built on concepts instituted by the United States and the Soviet Union and
thus congenial to the interests of large, established states rather than small
upstarts.

The most important difference between the great powers and small proliferators lies in a dangerous asymmetry of power and interests. The Cold
War was a contest between two superpowers who represented evenly
matched military coalitions and who were each challenging the core tenets
of the other's political system. Both the United States and the Soviet Union
brought immense amounts of economic power, ideological warfare, and
military force to bear in their defense because each nation thought, ultimately, that its own existence was at stake. Today, however, an issue that is

only of limited value to the United States could be considered a matter of life or death to an opponent. Likewise, the West and its probable enemies are no longer military peers, and damage that a large power could shrug off in a conflict could mean regime collapse to a smaller or less stable state. These asymmetries might thus lead to a catastrophic choice by a nation whose leaders are desperate, delusional, or suicidal—or who become so after an ill-advised game of chicken with the United States or another major power.

At such a moment, the balance of interests will be violently reversed, and the Americans or Europeans will face horrific damage from a regime with nothing to lose. As Richard Betts wisely noted nearly two decades ago, the ability of a small power "to destroy the downtown of one or two American cities would be puny, indeed infinitesimal, by comparison to the old standard of Soviet capabilities. It could, however, more than offset whatever is at stake in a confrontation with some Third World trouble maker or non-state actor."[11]

The current American policy of "ambiguity" hopes to avoid all this by assuming that small powers, and perhaps even terrorist organizations, are subject to the same supposedly iron laws of deterrence that constrain large powers. This assumption had better be right, because Western security is currently built upon it. But what if it's wrong? Deterring budding nuclear programs with threats of nuclear retaliation might seem obvious. In reality, the simple equation that nuclear use will beget nuclear use is easy to assert, but is too difficult to execute, for a host of practical, political, and moral reasons.

Nuclear Retaliation: Targeting and Secondary Effects

Nuclear retaliation is not an abstract notion. If deterrence fails and a nuclear threat has to be carried out, it will have to be carried out against someone or something. Targets in a small nation, however, will not be as obvious as the large nuclear forces and military assets of a country such as Russia or China. Nor will they be hardened against nuclear attack and protected against immediate elimination by the kind of redundancies the superpowers built into their nuclear systems. The United States would have no fear of national destruction in an exchange with a rogue nation, and there would be no question that America would be the eventual victor, at least in a military sense, in such a conflict. None of these advantages, however, would alleviate the dilemmas of targeting and the residual effects of nuclear strikes in regional conflicts, all of which present obstacles to nuclear counterattack against small states that cannot be overcome.

During the Cold War, nuclear targeting followed the mechanical logic of MAD: planners assigned new weapons to every identifiable asset in the Soviet Union. The first attacks would cripple the Soviet military and limit damage to the United States. Escalation would lead to strikes on industrial infrastructure and urban centers. The last act of this tragedy would be the destruction of the entire Union of Soviet Socialist Republics and their allies in a final, spasmodic salvo. Both sides would be destroyed, and if the inevitability of this result did not deter the Soviets from resorting to nuclear war, at least in theory the rest of the world would have a chance to recover without falling prey to the surviving pieces of the Soviet Union. Those who were not dead would at least not be Red.

This kind of targeting reflected a fight to the death, and so U.S. and Soviet strategists did not need to concern themselves with what the world would look like on the day after the war. The remnants of both states, they assumed, would be crawling out of the ruins for years. Bureaucracies, of course, made all kinds of plans about setting up forwarding addresses for the postal service and other such inane details, but thinkers and analysts in both capitals understood that the world as anyone knew it would be gone. The failure of deterrence itself would result, as the grim humor of the time put it, in "dynamic disarmament," after which there would no further pursuit of discrete political objectives beyond survival and recovery.

A nuclear counterattack on a small state would be an entirely different matter. The combatants would not resolve some sort of global ideological confrontation, nor would U.S. forces worldwide be engaged in battle. The retaliatory strike would not be designed to erase the targeted country. Instead, the goal of retaliation would likely be unconditional surrender and regime change. As scholar George Quester has argued, this goal should be "the demand of the civilized world," because a nuclear attack "could be so outrageous, so much beyond the normal standards of governments around the world, that the offending government would have to be replaced from the top down. . . . The constraints on political goals that seemed so self-evident during the Cold War would no longer apply, as an actual renegade's use of [nuclear] WMD might require that the perpetrator's entire political system be overturned and reformed."[12] Quester even goes a step further and argues that nuclear retaliation would be necessary not only for "the simple satisfaction of revenge and justice," but as a means of "'setting an example' for the deterrence of similar acts in the future."[13]

Quester's point about regime change is well taken, but it's unlikely there will be a consequent need to reestablish deterrence after a small nuclear war, not least because the United States or NATO is unlikely to tolerate the existence of any other rogue arsenals once one has been actually used. As scholar Stephen Krasner (for a time the head of policy planning at the State Department in the George W. Bush administration) has argued, it would probably take a lot less than a nuclear war—perhaps only a few incidents of nuclear terrorism would be enough—to overturn the current international order and return global affairs to a kind of nineteenth century arrangement in which peace and disarmament are imposed by force by the great powers.[14] In any event, Quester is correct that no U.S. president or any other Western leader would allow a rogue regime to walk away from a nuclear attack with its political structures intact and its leaders alive. This sensible observation, however, does not answer the questions of which targets to strike and how to strike them without inflicting damage so disproportionately that the United States itself transgresses the very values and laws that it is seeking to uphold.

Assuming that U.S. leaders believe they have no choice but to respond with nuclear arms—or feel driven to it by the public's demands for revenge—they would still have to choose a target or package of targets. Retaliatory strikes would logically fall into two broad categories, depending on whether the Americans were trying to send a political message or if they were seeking to further a larger military campaign. These two groups of targets are not mutually exclusive, but there are significant practical, political, and psychological differences involved in attacking them with nuclear weapons. Attacks on any of these objectives create considerable dilemmas.

One set of targets would consist of military assets. If there is the least amount of doubt about whether the enemy has any unexpended nuclear warheads or delivery systems, these targets would require immediate destruction through prompt means such as submarine-launched missiles or ICBM strikes. There is no moral or military prohibition on such attacks; the onus for the horrors to come would rest with the aggressor, not the defender. If the enemy has held even one more nuclear weapon in reserve, it would be an act of criminal irresponsibility for any Western leader not to destroy that secondary force instantly.

This is the one eventuality that would command broad agreement on the retaliatory use of nuclear weapons. In 2008, nuclear expert Stephen Younger proposed such a scenario:

> Are there *any* conditions in which the United States might use nuclear weapons? Are they really no more than an existential deterrent, threatened but never used? There are several situations where the limited use of nuclear weapons could prevent catastrophic damage to the United States. Suppose that North Korea, in an insane demonstration of its military power, were to launch a nuclear weapon against Los Angeles, with bellicose threats that San Francisco is next. Having suffered one attack, with a credible threat of a second, the United States might respond in kind by a limited nuclear attack against North Korean missile locations and military installations. [emphasis original][15]

In this case, arguments about proportion and overreaction that might have stayed American retaliation will quickly dissipate in the face of the necessity to preempt whatever might be left in the enemy inventory.

The important assumption here is the certainty about the existence of a second-strike capability. The urge to act against a follow-on strike, regardless of further information, will be intense, especially if the enemy attack was conducted with easily hidden mobile missiles. Unless they feel they have virtually perfect intelligence, U.S. leaders will be under immense pressure to make sure they have destroyed any further nuclear threats. History, insofar as it matters, will be no comfort at such a moment: in the Gulf War of 1991, for example, the Allied coalition spent an extraordinary amount of time and effort hunting Saddam Hussein's short-range Scud missiles in the Iraqi desert, but their efforts did not prevent Hussein from launching nearly ninety missiles at Israel, Saudi Arabia, and other nations in the region.[16]

Under these conditions, the strategic and moral equation is simple: a nuclear attack is going to take place, and it will take place either on Allied or enemy territory. There is no third way, and the President will be choosing not *whether* people *should* die, but *which* people *will* die. To accept one, but only one, nuclear disaster after being caught by surprise would show restraint. To accept a second, knowing it was coming, would be a dereliction of duty that would probably result in the President's removal in a crisis that would shake the U.S. constitutional order.

This scenario is attractive to deterrence theorists and planners because the enemy's actions would relieve U.S. leaders of responsibility for retaliation by forcing an almost automatic response. To focus on this eventuality, however, is to plan for what would be convenient, and not necessarily for what the enemy is likely to do. While it might seem logical to assume that a canny opponent will threaten the further use of nuclear weapons, even if they do not exist, in the hopes of seeking a cease-fire or avoiding retaliation, in reality a small attacker, unless bereft of any strategic wisdom, will almost certainly have to use all the weapons available to make good on a threat to attack the United States or its allies for several reasons.

First, there is the issue of technical reliability. To use one or two—or even five or ten—missiles on the assumption that they will operate perfectly while holding more nuclear weapons in reserve would be suicidal. The very worst outcome for rogue attackers would be to watch their "sacred" retaliation blow up on the launch pad, corkscrew into the ocean, or detonate over their own territory, all of which are possible with the kind of primitive systems likely to be fielded by such regimes. A failed attempt to inflict nuclear damage on the Americans while sitting on a vulnerable second-strike capability would not only leave the United States and its people unscathed, but would release them from any prohibition on striking back with nuclear weapons.

A would-be attacker will also have to consider whether the accuracy and destructiveness of U.S. nuclear weapons will complicate attempts to hold a second strike in reserve as a gamble on intrawar deterrence. Even a power with a larger and better arsenal, such as China, may not be able to gain such an advantage due to the increasing quality of U.S. reconnaissance and targeting capabilities. Despite the difficulty the Allied coalition faced in finding Iraq's conventionally armed Scuds in 1991, a rogue nuclear power cannot replicate Saddam's gambit. It will not have hundreds of ballistic nuclear weapons at its disposal, nor will it be willing to disperse those weapons and their crews into the desert—even if it has one—with nothing to defend them but prayers. War will not come from out of the blue, and the entire world will be watching the enemy's nuclear forces; the American ability to peer into other nations from space is far now beyond what was possible a quarter-century ago. As British scientist James Acton has argued, improvements in U.S. capabilities "would simply encourage an adversary to launch more of its weapons initially (leaving fewer behind as targets)."[17]

Finally, if the Americans or another large nuclear power decide that suppressing further nuclear attacks can only be achieved with nuclear force, it will be difficult to limit the damage from the counterattack. In the best but most unlikely eventuality, U.S. leaders will know exactly where the enemy's second-strike force is located and will be able to strike it precisely and immediately with as little damage to populated areas as possible. But if intelligence can provide only the general area where those weapons *might* be located, U.S. leaders might feel they have no choice but to bombard an entire area with nuclear weapons. This would be the surest solution, but it would also create a disaster of astonishing proportions. There is no good solution in such a case: the possibility of an enemy second strike is unacceptable, but levying wide nuclear strikes at suspected enemy installations is a terrible option, especially if Western intelligence about the location of the weapons turns out to be wrong—as has been known to happen in the past.

If the enemy does use its entire stock of nuclear arms in one strike, the argument for nuclear retaliation as a matter of military necessity evaporates. Less pressing military targets would include airfields, troop concentrations, military command centers, and communication nodes. It is far more difficult to argue that these objectives must be eliminated immediately with nuclear weapons, since none of them pose a further nuclear threat and all of them could be struck by a variety of nonnuclear means. While these installations might well be a danger to U.S. forces or allies in the region, they would be neither time-urgent nor immune to conventional attack, and thus could be degraded or destroyed without unnecessary civilian deaths or long-term radiation effects.

A different set of nuclear targets would have a more overtly political character. These targets could include the enemy leadership, their capital, their political institutions, or other assets of great value or meaning to the enemy. This kind of political retaliation would be aimed less at degrading the enemy's military capability and more toward inflicting punishment and generating eventual regime collapse. Such strikes would not only satisfy the need for revenge, but would represent an attempt to reestablish nuclear deterrence, and even the nuclear "taboo," insofar as one exists, by showing that the use of nuclear weapons against the United States will produce all the misery, and more, that people rightly fear from a nuclear exchange.

Presumably, the shock of the American retaliation would be so great that no nation will ever again consider the use of nuclear arms against the

United States. Destroying these targets with nuclear weapons means high civilian casualties, and perhaps intentionally so. The argument for engaging in this kind of nuclear retaliation might be to make the enemy regime's population understand, like the Germans and the Japanese before them, that they cannot escape the consequences of their leadership's actions, and they will share in the suffering that their nation has inflicted on the Americans or their allies.

There are severe practical barriers to these choices, whether the aggressor is in East Asia, the Middle East or any other area where U.S. leaders will want to limit the impact of conducting what they will hope is a "small" nuclear war. Possible nuclear targets might be too close to a range of objects the United States and its allies may not wish to destroy, including natural or historical treasures. They will certainly be too close to millions of innocent human beings both in the targeted country and nearby.

As discussed in previous chapters, this is the problem of "co-location," the nesting of military or nuclear-related assets near civilian areas. Iran's most important nuclear reactor, for example, is less than ten miles from the city of Bushehr and its 160,000 inhabitants; likewise, the Iranians have placed a uranium enrichment facility some 20 miles outside Qom, one of Iran's treasured holy cities. North Korea's Yongbyon nuclear facility is slightly more than 50 miles from Pyongyang, the capital city of more than three million that itself could be a target for retaliation.

Co-location is almost always a problem with strategic attacks, as experiences with the use of aerial bombing from World War II to Vietnam and the Gulf War have repeatedly shown. These problems are magnified many times over when it comes to nuclear targeting against a country of any size, even large nations with bases scattered around the world. (It is impossible, to take but one example, to neutralize the United States Pacific Fleet Command headquarters with nuclear weapons without destroying most of Honolulu, Hawaii.) The dilemmas of targeting in small countries are especially aggravated by co-location issues because of the narrow geography of these states; military, civilian, and infrastructure assets are close to each other because literally everything is close to everything else.

An additional problem is that small nations are situated in crowded neighborhoods, and the effects of a nuclear exchange would be traumatic on nearby states. Not only can rogue regimes hold their own populations as human shields against nuclear attack, but they are also protected by the many innocent people who live near them—or more precisely, by the unwillingness of more civilized nations to kill or injure those innocent populations. North Korea, for example, shares land borders with three other nations, one a U.S. ally and two who are nuclear-armed U.S. competitors. Over water, Japan's shores are less than 700 miles away from North Korea, with Pyongyang less than 800 miles from Tokyo. On the other side of the world, Iran borders the Islamic-majority NATO nation of Turkey as well as nuclear-armed Pakistan. Nor is it far from Iran's borders to a collection of former Soviet republics, including southern Russia itself. Iran's greatest regional enemy, Israel, is only a thousand miles away—not a great distance where nuclear explosions are concerned.

These geographic problems have already frustrated American planners in previous conflicts and crises. As U.S. Air Force General George Butler noted in 1999, "this lesson has been made time and again, in Korea, in Indochina and most recently in the Persian Gulf, [when] successive presidents of both parties have contemplated and then categorically rejected the employment of nuclear weapons even in the face of grave provocation."[18] Before the 1991 Gulf War, for example, the Americans were intentionally vague about what might happen should the Iraqis use chemical weapons against Allied troops, precisely because U.S. leaders did not want to get boxed in by their own threats. President George H. W. Bush's national security advisor, Brent Scowcroft, later recalled a January 1991 White House meeting: "If Iraq resorted to [chemical arms], we would say our reaction would depend on circumstances and that we would hold Iraqi divisional commanders responsible and bring them to justice for war crimes. No one advanced the notion of using nuclear weapons, and the President rejected it even in retaliation for chemical or biological attacks. *We deliberately avoided spoken or unspoken threats to use them on the grounds that it is bad practice to threaten something you have no intention of carrying out*" (emphasis added).[19]

During another briefing, Joint Chiefs Chairman Colin Powell told Secretary of Defense Dick Cheney: "Let's not even think about nukes. You know we're not going to let the genie loose."[20] Butler, for one, later asserted that U.S. officials knew early on from their own analyses that "a nuclear campaign against Iraq was militarily useless and politically preposterous."[21] There have since been assertions that implied nuclear threats played an important role in deterring Saddam from using chemical weapons in 1991, but Scott Sagan and General Butler, among others, dispute this.[22]

The same concerns arose after the Gulf War in the many attempts to constrain Saddam Hussein. When the United States and its allies resolved to launch Operation Desert Fox in 1998 and bomb various targets in Iraq,

U.S. Secretary of Defense William Cohen openly admitted that the goal was to attack the regime while minimizing civilian casualties. "We're not going to take a chance and try to target any facility that would release any kind of horrific damage to innocent people."[23]

Long before Iraq and Iran, however, the United States was already wrestling with the problem of how to strike North Korea, where planning for the use of nuclear weapons repeatedly ran into various dead-ends. Declassified U.S. documents show that in 1969, for example, President Richard Nixon sought plans for dealing with North Korean military provocations, including an April 1969 North Korean attack that resulted in the downing of a U.S. reconnaissance plane.[24] The Pentagon eventually provided Nixon with twenty-five alternatives, including an operation code-named FREE-DOM DROP, the "pre-coordinated options for the selective use of tactical nuclear weapons against North Korea."[25]

There were three overlapping options in FREEDOM DROP.[26] The first was a "punitive attack against up to twelve military targets with nuclear weapons of a yield of .2 to 10 kilotons." (By comparison, the bomb dropped on Hiroshima was about 15 kilotons.) The next plan added an attack to neutralize North Korea's air force (now obsolete, but then a major threat) by striking all sixteen major North Korean military airfields with nuclear weapons in the 70-kiloton range. Finally, the third alternative was a broader attack with nuclear weapons ranging from 10 to 70 kilotons "aimed at diminishing greatly North Korea's offensive capability" and included everything in the first two options plus twenty-two additional military targets.

In the end, Nixon and his advisors realized that nuclear force held no answers for dealing with Korea. The United States would have had to engage in wide strikes to suppress the North Korean military, which would have caused immense destruction and risked escalation to a wider war in the region. In 1969, of course, the Cold War situation in East Asia was far more dangerous and complicated than it is today, with America's Soviet and Chinese adversaries nearby (and already in an undeclared shooting war with each other along their common Asian border), and a much stronger North Korean force facing a weaker U.S. and South Korean defense. Still, U.S. presidents since Nixon have all faced the same problems when thinking about the use of nuclear weapons in North Korea.

One option for retaliating against small states might be to engage in the kind of infrastructure targeting described in the previous chapter. Such a plan would aim to destroy the regime with coordinated nuclear attacks on industry, energy, and other targets besides populations. Again, however, the problem is that small nations do not have significant strategic depth or wide expanses of territory, and there would be almost no way to establish practical differences between bombing only infrastructure and bombing everything else. From the Russian border to the thirty-eighth parallel, North Korea is less than 500 miles long, or about the distance from Boston to Washington, D.C. In places, it is narrower than 200 miles. Iran presents a similar problem, if on a slightly larger scale. The entire length of Iran is some 1,500 miles, and in overall territory it is roughly the size of Alaska. This might seem like a fairly vast space, but fewer than 740,000 people live in Alaska, while Iran has a population of 78 million, with more than a fifth of its people concentrated in its five largest cities and most of its military and nuclear facilities in or near those cities.

In the case of North Korea, there is an added problem: the Democratic People's Republic of Korea is an impoverished country with very little infrastructure worth striking, or at least none that would require the use of nuclear weapons. In a tiny state, with an almost nonexistent economic infrastructure and most of its 22 million people already starving, even a small number of nuclear attacks could end up killing, in one way or another, almost the entire population. American leaders have implied that they know and understand this problem, and that it might even enhance deterrence. The complete destruction of the North may have been what President Bill Clinton was implying in 1993 when, in the spirit of "ambiguity," he warned that if North Korea ever used a nuclear weapon, not only would the United States "quickly and overwhelmingly retaliate," but that for the North Koreans it "would mean the end of their country as they know it."[27] In 1994, Senator John McCain (later the 2008 Republican presidential nominee) was even clearer when he was asked about North Korean motives and whether Pyongyang's usual threats were bluffs. "I don't know," McCain replied. "But I know what they understand and that is the threat of extinction."[28]

Nuclear attacks on North Korea, Iran, or other small states may not result in complete extinction, but they will effectively destroy them as functioning nations, at which point victory will bring its own complications. The United States and its allies have always in previous wars assumed their proper responsibilities to their defeated enemies, including feeding and caring for the occupied population, reconstruction of the conquered territory, and reintegration of the defeated nation into the international system. (As Secretary of State Colin Powell warned before the 2003 invasion of Iraq, this is the rule that says: "If you break it, you own it.")[29] The aftermath of a nuclear attack, however, will overwhelm both the immediate palliative and long-term reconstructive capacities of the winner and the loser alike.

The sheer number of burn victims, to take but one example, will represent a disaster beyond any hope of remedy. The specialized facilities needed to treat burn victims are a rare resource across the world: the United States itself has only 2,000 of these so-called "burn beds" in the entire country. A nuclear attack of almost any size, even in relatively under-populated areas, will produce more burn injuries than any coalition of medical establishments can handle.[30] U.S. hospitals have had problems coping with far smaller emergencies: a 2006 nightclub fire in Rhode Island that killed 100 people in one night absorbed the medical aviation, transport, and burn resources of every New England state and most of eastern New York for days. Rhode Island's single trauma-capable hospital had to resort to disaster procedures, while fewer than a dozen patients from the fire completely overwhelmed the burn unit at Massachusetts General Hospital, some sixty miles away in Boston.[31]

Policymakers, and especially the public, choose to ignore these kinds of consequences when speaking so casually and reflexively of nuclear retaliation. Neither the Americans nor anyone else will really want to care for thousands, perhaps tens of thousands, of horribly injured people in the remains of a state that has already used nuclear weapons against the United States or its friends. But many of the sick, injured, and destitute will be civilians, and the victorious powers will have no choice but to render whatever assistance they can. In reality, where burns and other severe injuries will be beyond medical help, U.S. and allied military forces advancing into the enemy damage zones in the aftermath of a nuclear counterattack will have no humane choice but to euthanize the untreatable casualties on the spot. Such actions could retroactively make America's nuclear retaliation seem violent beyond reason, perhaps even genocidal, to friends and enemies alike.

Radiation will be a longer term problem. Because the amount of nuclear fallout and its subsequent dispersal will depend on factors ranging from wind patterns to the choice of targets, it is impossible to say in advance how far any contamination might spread. Nuclear tests are not much help as a guide, since those carefully controlled explosions took place far from populations and provide models based only on extrapolation. (There is, after all, a reason the great powers used to test their nuclear bombs in deserts and on remote islands.) The 1945 attacks on Japan are also difficult to use as a measure, since they were conducted as isolated airbursts with small weapons over cities built largely of paper and wood.

Some analysts have tried to model small nuclear strikes and exchanges under modern conditions. One study of a regional nuclear war in South Asia involving up to fifty Hiroshima-sized weapons aimed at each side found that it would produce climate change "unprecedented in recorded human history" with "catastrophic and long term" effects lasting a decade or more on a global scale.[32] While this might be a helpful exercise when thinking about an exchange between India and Pakistan, even this kind of limited war is far larger than the handful of strikes that would occur as part of a rogue attack on the United States and the subsequent U.S. retaliation.

As an example of a much smaller nuclear attack on just one city, analysts at the RAND Corporation in 2010 modeled a single ten-kiloton explosion (again, smaller than Hiroshima) at ground level in Seoul. They estimated that some 160,000 people would die or suffer serious injuries for miles downwind from fallout alone. RAND also pointed out that this single nuclear strike in the South would "vastly outstrip medical supply" and "could cause panic," problems that would be far worse should the United States engage in multiple strikes in North Korea, where modern medical care is unavailable.[33]

One or several nuclear explosions in the Middle East will replicate these problems across several nations with common land borders. In the Iranian case, the political impact of long-term radiation will be fractured and multiplied across a matrix of various cultures, political systems, and religious movements. Even a small retaliatory strike will mean at least some radioactive contamination and consequent social and physical disruption throughout the Arab Middle East, and Islamic radicals would no doubt welcome the anger and suffering that would persist long after the war's end. As a practical matter, aside from injury to innocent civilians, the destruction or contamination of crucial sea lanes, ports, and other assets could make the tangible costs of whatever started the war seem tiny by comparison.

The Fukushima Effect

Regardless of the actual long-term health effects from small nuclear strikes, the fear of nuclear fallout itself might place significant inhibitions and limits on U.S. action in a regional war. In addition to emotions that will already be running high in the midst of a crisis or war, U.S. and NATO leaders will have to contend with anxiety and perhaps outright panic among their own populations should they consider the use of nuclear weapons. These concerns about public reactions to the use of nuclear weapons are not hypothetical: in 2011, the worst nuclear accident since the 1986 Chernobyl fire in Soviet Ukraine took place in Japan, and the global reaction to that disaster is an instructive case in nuclear panic.

On March 11, 2011, the combined effects of a huge earthquake and its consequent tsunami crippled the four nuclear reactors at the Daiichi power plant in Japan's Fukushima prefecture. Although all of the facility's safety mechanisms initially worked properly and the reactors were sent into immediate shutdown, the disruption of power to the plant led to a failure of the cooling apparatus, and the reactors overheated. Three of them soon went into meltdown. Subsequent releases of hydrogen gas produced a series of explosions, and radioactive material, including highly dangerous cesium-137—a long-lasting contaminant with a half-life of about thirty years—was released into the atmosphere.

At first, the Japanese government was literally in the dark about the extent of the damage or the danger to public safety, and Japanese leaders secretly considered the drastic option of evacuating Tokyo itself.[34] Emergency crews managed to contain the threat, but the accident still reached the most severe level on the International Atomic Energy Agency's International Nuclear and Radiological Event Scale, although the actual radiation released was about one-tenth as much as that produced by Chernobyl.[35] Japanese authorities established a twelve-mile exclusion zone around the disaster site, displacing some 75,000 residents who were never allowed to return.

Where nuclear retaliation is concerned, the actual event at Fukushima is less interesting than the reaction to its aftereffects. Although the reactor's location on the eastern edge of Japan ensured that most of the debris would be blown out to sea, some contamination from the fire headed for North America. As the radioactive plume from the reactor spread, the U.S. Navy's Seventh Fleet, operating about 100 miles northeast of the reactor complex, was repositioned "as a precautionary measure."[36] The Navy also advised personnel at Japanese bases 200 miles away to take precautions as well, such as limiting outdoor activities.[37] While the reactor was still burning, nuclear expert Joe Cirincione told interviewer Chris Wallace that radiation from the plant could reach the United States. "Really?" Wallace asked. "I mean, thousands of miles across the Pacific?" "Oh, absolutely," Cirincione accurately replied.[38]

Meanwhile, people across the world had already assumed the worst. Despite repeated warnings from health officials not to take iodine supplements without medical advice, panic-buying produced a global run on iodine from California all the way to Finland. (Iodine supplements fill the human thyroid with "clean" iodine and thus prevent the absorption of its radioactive isotope.) Residents of the U.S. West Coast sought iodine tablets—which many of them called "nukepills"—so aggressively that prices of the element shot up to as high as forty times their usual levels. "They did it during Chernobyl. They're doing it again," one California vitamin retailer told the *Los Angeles Times*. "Everybody's out of iodine everywhere. People worry and panic about things."[39] There was also a spike in the sales of gas masks and other surplus military gear in a rush that one supplier said was reminiscent of the reaction to the 9/11 terror attacks.[40]

In the ensuing months, radioactive contamination was found in ordinary Japanese products hundreds of miles from the Fukushima site, including rice, tea, milk, fish, beef, and mushrooms.[41] "Radiation fears," according to a 2012 report, "have become part of daily life in Japan."[42] Reassurances from international monitoring bodies, including the United Nations, that there are no major health risks outside of the exclusion zone have since done little to quell such anxieties, including across the Pacific in the United States.[43] A year after the disaster, the *Los Angeles Times* duly cited reports by scientists who found traces of radioactive iodine in kelp along the California coast, even though the report noted that "the effect of radioactive material in kelp is not well known" and the levels found "were likely not harmful to humans" or to the crustaceans who ingested the kelp after its contamination.[44] Two years later, the United Nations affirmed that the health impact of Fukushima would be "negligible," especially compared to Chernobyl.[45]

None of this is to say that these public fears are rational, but only that they are real. Panic is a powerful force, and policymakers will have to take it into account when weighing the costs of nuclear retaliation. If the world is reeling from the rogue or terrorist use of a nuclear weapon, U.S. or allied leaders may be faced with demands to forego retaliation if there is already significant destruction, casualties, radiation, and electronic damage from the first nuclear detonations. Despite Japan's reliance on U.S. guarantees of extended nuclear deterrence, for example, if North Korea were to use a nuclear weapon in a conflict in East Asia, which would be the greater pressure: to retaliate in kind, or to cease further escalation and forego more nuclear explosions? An attack on North Korea will have a traumatic impact not only on the Japanese, but potentially on millions of South Koreans, Chinese, Russians, Americans, and Canadians, among others. These same pressures will be just as intense, if not more so, in the Persian Gulf, where the effects of nuclear strikes will cross crowded borders more easily and quickly.

In the wake of Fukushima, it is difficult to make the argument that the United States or its allies can continue to make nuclear threats with the same steadiness that characterized the reliance on deterrence during the Cold War. While the heat of battle may create the immediate urge to retaliate with nuclear weapons, public fears about the long-term consequences of nuclear use could quickly undermine any such plans. Western governments may soon find that deterrent threats do little good if they are more frightening to their own people than to their potential enemies.

Mini-Nukes: Small Is Beautiful?

Nuclear strikes cannot be executed without the hazard of fallout. These concerns have led some analysts to call for reviving research into extremely small nuclear weapons, or better yet, small weapons combined with earth-penetrating capabilities, sometimes called bunker-busters, EPWs (earth penetrating weapons), or RNEPs (robust nuclear earth penetrators). Whatever their nomenclature, the objective is the same: the weapons carry a rocket motor that ignites after reaching their target, and this motor helps the warhead to drill deeply into the ground so that the nuclear payload detonates beneath the earth and explodes nearer to buried or reinforced facilities. Developed (like so many nuclear systems) during the Cold War, their original purpose was to penetrate the frozen tundra above Soviet nuclear installations. Like an underground nuclear test, this kind of attack minimizes the amount of blast, heat, and fallout damage to the surrounding area.[46]

Mini-nukes and EPWs represent attempts to deal with the challenges of using nuclear weapons to deter the use of nuclear arms or other WMD by small nations. In 1991, two U.S. analysts expressed their "doubt that any

President would authorize the use of the nuclear weapons in our present arsenal against Third World nations," and "it is precisely this doubt that leads us to argue for the development of nuclear weapons with very low yields."[47] Twenty years later, strategist Elbridge Colby argued:

> Bluntly, we need to be able to say credibly that "wherever you go, we can get at you." If enemies can make themselves immune to retaliation, deterrence is seriously compromised. Yet the trend among our potential adversaries towards hiding underground, beyond the reach of our weaponry, poses precisely this challenge. . . . The capability to destroy [deeply buried targets] would give the United States a more sensible option that would enable us to get at what our adversaries most value while avoiding the most serious pitfalls posed by occupation or attacks upon cities as such.[48]

Colby and others also accept that EPWs need not be nuclear weapons, but they argue that only nuclear arms can assure either the preemption of enemy nuclear forces or the certain destruction of enemy leadership bunkers in a retaliatory strike.

The problem is that bunker-busters don't really solve the problems of nuclear retaliation: they just temporarily make them smaller. Small EPWs can alleviate some of the immediate effects of a nuclear explosion, such as the flash blinding of innocent civilians nearby. They are still nuclear weapons, however, and they still carry many of the same political and practical ramifications of their larger brethren. More to the point, the United States does not actually *have* any weapons capable of producing only minimal effects. According to defense analyst Michael Gerson's calculations, a weapon of any reasonable size (his assumption is 300 kilotons) would have to be detonated 800 meters below ground both to avoid fallout and to destroy its intended targets, and this is more than 200 times deeper than current U.S. warheads are capable of penetrating.[49] In the end, as scholar Derek Smith has written, strategies for the use of small nuclear weapons still "fall prey to the same flaws that have foiled plans for tactical nuclear weapons before, from nuclear artillery to neutron bombs: no matter how tiny, they simply cannot be used without causing intolerable radioactive fallout."[50]

Debates about effects such as burns and fallout too often and too quickly devolve into mathematical duels that do not interest policymakers, even if they had the technical expertise to understand them.[51] But there is a larger conceptual problem in all this: advocates of low-yield weapons and EPWs discuss these arms as though they are little more than conventional super-bombs that will make only a bit more of a mess than a nuclear device. They also argue that the very existence of such weapons communicates a willingness to attack a small enemy, even if in reality we have no intention to engage in such an attack; merely having such a capability, they would argue, shores up increasingly weak deterrent threats against rogues.

The danger here, as thinkers from Bernard Brodie to Robert Jervis have warned, is that this kind of approach represents a "conventionalization" of nuclear weapons, in which strategists and policymakers become too accustomed to thinking of nuclear attacks as similar to any other kind of military operation.[52] Joseph Nye warned more than a quarter-century ago of the severe strategic and moral consequences that could result if national leaders somehow ceased to think of nuclear weapons as unique:

> One can construct and aim a nuclear weapon that is so small and accurate that it will do about the same damage as conventional "iron bombs" full of high explosives. But even those miniature nuclear weapons must never be treated as normal usable weapons, because politically and technically they are too closely related to their big brothers of mass destruction. . . . Declaratory policy affects perceptions and procedures, and, given the potential immoral consequences, it is important to maintain perceptions and procedures that do not treat nuclear weapons as normal usable weapons.[53]

This "conventionalization" of small nuclear weapons could delude American leaders into thinking that a nuclear victory over a rogue power might be had without undue collateral damage. Such an operation might well be less costly in life and damage than a wider nuclear strike. There is no guarantee, however, that it will be successful, and the risk of failure raises yet another question about nuclear retaliation: what if the United States relies on small, tightly targeted weapons such as bunker-busters—and the enemy leadership survives the retaliatory strike anyway?

This is not a trivial possibility. As a 2010 RAND study pointed out, the late North Korean leader Kim Jong-Il had "a history of disappearing during high-end provocations, presumably so that he [could not] be targeted," and his son and the rest of the Kim coterie doubtless will take similar precautions.[54] Nuclear targeting is not a trial-and-error process: if the object is to kill or disable the enemy leadership with nuclear weapons, there will be no second chance if the attack fails. One nuclear salvo is going to be difficult enough to plan and execute, and a second will be impossible, politically if not militarily. Should some member of the Kim family and the rest of North Korea's high command emerge alive and defiant from the damage of a U.S. nuclear retaliatory strike, the United States will have taken its nuclear shot and missed, much like the conventional "shock and awe" operation that tried to kill Saddam Hussein—and didn't—on the eve of the 2003 invasion of Iraq. A nuclear blow against the enemy leadership must not fail the first rule of regicide: if one is to strike the king, one must kill the king.

All of these challenges undermine the credibility of nuclear threats against small states, not because they cannot be answered, but because the answers are unacceptable and the West's potential enemies surely know it. Some of these problems, such as a public panic about radiation, are unavoidable but might not present an ultimate barrier to the retaliatory use of nuclear weapons. Other concerns are far more daunting, chief among them that breaching the nuclear barrier will require policymakers to believe that they have been given nearly perfect intelligence, that there will be no mistakes in translating that information into meaningful nuclear targeting, and that the strikes themselves will never suffer some kind of operational failure or error. Meanwhile, the terrible consequences of collateral damage to innocent civilians have no solution at all. These choices, risks, and eventual costs will all have to be made and accepted if nuclear weapons are used in a regional conflict.

War is more than a series of immediate technical or political problems. It involves the taking of human life on a national scale. In the case of nuclear war, it also includes the possible destruction of cities and regions that are part of the common heritage of mankind. When thinking about a major war between peers such as the former Soviet Union and the United States, the moral anguish of these questions was often set aside in the name of maintaining the balance of terror. When considering nuclear war with small states, where U.S. national existence is not at stake, moral restrictions cannot be so easily dismissed.

The Moral Dimension of Nuclear Retaliation

A nuclear attack from a small state will create unprecedented moral dilemmas for U.S. policymakers. The arguments marshaled to defend the Cold

War deterrence of the Soviet Union cannot be reapplied to deterring rogues in the twenty-first century. The most immediate moral obstacle to nuclear retaliation is asymmetry: nuclear retaliation from a superpower against a much smaller nation will unavoidably be disproportionate in its damage and collateral effects. Moreover, unless there is a need to destroy an identified second-strike force, there will be no military requirement for the United States to respond immediately, and the Americans and their allies will have to decide whether they are willing to engage in nuclear retaliation as a *choice* rather than a necessity. They will have to decide whether, in George Kennan's words, to demand a "nuclear eye for a nuclear eye."[55]

This dilemma is especially painful because rogue regimes are dictatorships, and the consequences of nuclear retaliation will therefore inevitably fall on people who had no say in whether to go to war in the first place. Ordinary citizens—perhaps it is more realistic simply to call them subjects or even slaves—in prison-states such as North Korea play no part in the decisions of their government. Should war come, these dominated populations will be placed in harm's way with no understanding of why they are about to die. Fighting these hapless North Koreans in self-defense, as the United States and South Korea may be forced to do if Pyongyang ever sends them across the 38th parallel, is one thing; choosing to exact nuclear payment for the actions of the sadistic Kim family by incinerating thousands of them is another entirely.

The moral equation was different during the Cold War. The United States and NATO had no choice but to treat the USSR and its satellites as fully culpable combatants whose populations, whatever their feelings about their governments, were unavoidable targets in a war. This was due to the deterrent symmetry of Mutual Assured Destruction. Still, this was not done lightly: as scholars Russell Hardin and John Mearsheimer noted in a 1985 overview of nuclear ethics, the notion of retaliation against Soviet cities and "the wholesale killing of innocents" for the destruction of American cities was regarded at the time by most Western moral philosophers as "incoherent" on the grounds that ordinary residents of Soviet cities, especially young children, could not possibly be held responsible for whatever happened to millions of Americans.[56] Still, theorists of Mutual Assured Destruction argued that both sides were left with no choice but to target those populations, because in the end, war meant extinction, and so the moral imperative of peace outweighed the moral evil of making deterrent threats against civilians.

In a conflict with a smaller rogue regime, this already thin moral reasoning evaporates. If an aggressive dictatorship uses nuclear weapons against the United States, no argument based on national survival will justify immediate nuclear retaliation. Nothing will be excusable by any appeal to reciprocity, since it is a bedrock principle of international custom and law that the sins of one side do not justify their repetition by the other. The argument of *tu quoque* (Latin for "you did it, too") has never been an acceptable defense for engaging in atrocities. In these circumstances, the choice to retaliate will seem like revenge, no matter how it is phrased.

After the rogue use of a nuclear weapon, the American people might well be in full-throated cry for such revenge. Indulging that desire, however, will focus global attention thereafter on the consequences of later U.S. nuclear strikes, which will unavoidably seem not only discretionary but disproportionate. Whatever started the war will soon be forgotten; all that will matter then and forever will be the deaths and lasting damage brought by America's nuclear punishment. Conflicts that once tortured the American conscience, such as Vietnam or Iraq, will seem minor by comparison.

Time will be a crucial factor in deciding whether to engage in retaliation. If there is any significant amount of time to consider whether to respond with nuclear weapons, doubts will grow in Washington and elsewhere. In the wake of a nuclear attack on the United States, the Oval Office will be inundated with expressions of sympathy and support, but if there is no need for immediate preemption of another strike, it will also be buried under a torrent of calls for restraint, mercy, and entreaties to resist further poisoning of the planet. The moral burden—again, no matter how the war started—will shift to the United States. The more time that elapses after the shock of the initial attack passes, the greater the moral onus and political damage to the Americans should they strike back. Australian nuclear thinker Andrew Newman has put it plainly: "Time works against nuclear retaliation."[57]

While all of these are obvious moral considerations, do they affect deterrence in any way, and if so, how? If deterrent threats keep the peace, as they seem to have done during the Cold War, why not make them? The answer here is necessarily speculative, but the moral consequences of nuclear retaliation themselves may corrode the credibility of nuclear threats, since the enemy might not believe that U.S. leaders will transgress their own traditions and values by engaging in deliberate nuclear revenge. The leaders of rogue regimes might count on the moral complexity of these issues to generate doubts—the sort that apparently never disturb their own sleep—among their Western counterparts, which would consequently undermine the willingness of presidents and prime ministers to follow through on their nuclear threats.

In 1996, U.S. Air Force Colonel Charles Dunlap (later Major General, and the senior legal officer in the USAF before his retirement) offered a thought experiment along these lines. Dunlap tried to imagine the United States fighting—and losing—a militarily and morally asymmetrical war against a cunning and brutal theocracy. The United States is defeated, in part, because it cannot cope with the moral challenges involved in asymmetrical warfare. The enemy regime's imagined "Holy Leader" later attributes victory to his willingness to ignore U.S. technological advantages and instead to shock the Americans with sheer barbarism and a series of atrocities. As this notional "Holy Leader" explains, the West's "so-called 'laws of wars' were conceived by the First World to keep our people oppressed. Furthermore, their 'law' presented no deterrent because the West demonstrated over and over that it lacked the conviction to enforce it."[58]

The moral crisis reaches a breaking point when nuclear weapons are introduced into the conflict. In Dunlap's scenario, final victory is achieved when the enemy detonates a nuclear weapon in one of its *own* cities, and then blames the Americans for a nuclear first-strike: "The world reaction to what was thought to be an American first use of nuclear weapons was universal condemnation. The Japanese were especially appalled. . . . Other important members of the world community turned against America as well. Of course, the United States vigorously claimed innocence. But few believed its government, even among the nation's own people. Clearly, Americans had grown so cynical of their government that they were quite willing to believe it capable of anything." This moral revulsion produces a dissolution of the U.S. military coalition, a plunge in America's international prestige, and the collapse of the domestic economy as world markets shun the United States. Of course, Dunlap was describing the outrage over the *first* use of nuclear weapons, but is difficult to see how a discretionary retaliation, aimed only at revenge and the killing of tens or hundreds of thousands of the enemy's population, would fare much better, even if the United States or Europe were attacked first.

Nearly two decades after General Dunlap's excursion into alternate future history, the question still remains whether enemy leaders will believe that the Americans will have the moral stomach for a nuclear conflict with a small nation. The kind of debate that Dunlap described over the morality and necessity of the nuclear bombing of Japan, for example, continues today, with many Western scholars still leading vigorous charges against President Harry Truman's decision to use nuclear arms and retroactively convicting Americans of the wartime 1940s for not behaving by the peacetime standards of the 2000s.[59] The American public itself is less certain year by year that Truman made the right call: by 2010, only 59 percent of Americans approved of the destruction of Hiroshima and Nagasaki.[60] This fact is revealing, because by comparison to choices U.S. leaders would have to make in the twenty-first century, the bombing of Japan is a model of relative moral clarity: it took place after a sneak attack, four grinding years of war, hundreds of thousands of U.S. casualties, and against a fanatical enemy who refused multiple chances to surrender.

Even the Soviets, more rational and less inclined to run risk than the mercurial leaders of North Korea and Iran, had their doubts about whether the Americans were really tough enough to follow through on Robert Mc-Namara's famous promise to kill 120 million Soviets in retaliation for an all-out attack on the United States. It is possible that an ordinary person, as presidents are, gripped by panic and rage, might have chosen to see the deterrent suicide pact to its conclusion by releasing all remaining U.S. nuclear forces while committing the whole matter to the hands of God. Thankfully, we will never know.

The more important point, however, is that if there could be any doubts about whether the president would have avenged the entire American nation with nuclear weapons under the worst possible circumstances, how much more doubt might there be about retaliating over anything less? In a conflict with a small nation, the president will be issuing orders from the White House, not from a bunker under a mountain. There will be no dilemma over whether to use or to lose the American strategic deterrent, or between surrender and a tragic last stand in the face of an overwhelming surprise attack. There will be no argument—as grandiose, existential, and wrong as it might be—that the American government must use the last minutes of its existence to save its allies and future generations by taking the enemy into the same nuclear oblivion that is about to engulf the United States. An increasing number of civilian and military policymakers have begun to question whether they themselves, or any other U.S. leaders, would really resort to the use of nuclear weapons in any circumstance, much less over far less desperate straits than global war.

Interestingly, these doubts have been expressed not by the usual array of academics and activists who have always opposed nuclear weapons, but by the very people who have had the responsibility for planning, maintaining, and commanding the U.S. nuclear arsenal. This list is not limited to the more well-known advocates of nuclear reductions such as Henry Kissinger or William Perry. General Butler, for example, tried to scale back the U.S. strategic deterrent after being named to head the U.S. Strategic Command in 1992. Butler reduced the list of nuclear targets by 20 percent, a relatively modest paring of a U.S. war plan that at the time envisioned striking Russia with massive and repeated nuclear blows in the event of war. No sooner was Butler gone, however, than his successors actually *increased* the targeting requirements, restoring Butler's cuts and adding yet more targets. Two years after his retirement from the Air Force, Butler joined the call for the complete elimination of all nuclear weapons.[61]

Some critics call these post-career conversions part of a "retirement syndrome," a phrase coined decades ago by psychiatrist and antinuclear activist Robert Jay Lifton to describe people who feel free to change their views once they are no longer captured by the requirements of their career. Conservatives and liberals alike distrust these changes, arguing that they are the luxury of old men who no longer bear responsibility (either for good or ill) for the national defense and now seek only to assuage their consciences.[62] There is some justice to this criticism: it is no act of bravery to oppose official policy from the safe distance of a pension.

People have the right, however, to change their minds. Some embrace change after retirement not because they are cowards, but because they are finally removed from the torrent of quotidian decisions and pressures that can undermine reflection and reconsideration. They have been, literally, too busy implementing policy to change it. And in some cases, the charge of "retirement syndrome" is flatly unfair, since dramatic turns in the international system, such as the Soviet collapse, came too late to play a role in the policy positions of senior leaders who did not think they would see such revolutionary changes in their lifetimes.

In addition, some policymakers and military leaders have advocated rethinking important concepts about the use of nuclear force while still playing an active role in policy. U.S. Marine Corps General James Cartwright was one of General Butler's successors at U.S. Strategic Command, and like Butler, he did not wait until retirement to express his views. A

2008 profile of Cartwright noted: "Before his first year as commander of STRATCOM was up, Cartwright began publicly questioning the role of the nuclear arsenal in a way that none of his predecessors ever had. He did not go so far as to call for the elimination of nuclear weapons. . . . [W]hile still in uniform, Cartwright has sufficiently broken with years of tradition to make some nuclear strategists nervous. Critics allege that the general naively ventured into an area outside his expertise and contend that he has no idea how much harm he is doing to U.S. national security."[63]

Cartwright, however, was pointedly dismissive of policy analysts who advocated nuclear use, noting that "none of them have had the responsibility or the accountability" to launch a nuclear weapon.[64] In the end, Cartwright said, "I will do what I am told, obviously. But I think people ought to understand at least what a commander perceives as sometimes a mismatch for what it is we have as a threat out there and what we have as an arsenal."[65] After retirement, Cartwright continued to advocate for reform on nuclear issues while at Harvard's Kennedy School of Government, and later as the Harold Brown Chair of Defense Policy Studies at the Center for Strategic and International Affairs.

Air Force General Charles Horner, commander of U.S. air forces in the 1991 Gulf War and later the head of U.S. Space Command, also questioned whether any U.S. leader would use nuclear weapons. "The nuclear weapon is obsolete," he said in 1994. "I want to get rid of them all. . . . What are nuclear weapons good for? Busting cities. What President of the United States is going to take out Pyongyang?" Like many advocates of reductions, he also noted that deep nuclear cuts will seize "the high moral ground" of nonproliferation efforts against regimes such as North Korea.[66] Horner's position on unilateral reductions directly contradicted Clinton administration policy at the time, and he retired soon after making his remarks.

Ironically, none of these debates over whether to use nuclear weapons may matter very much in the twenty-first century, because the Americans may have already removed any deterrent effect of the policy of "ambiguity" by talking so much about it. Former U.S. leaders have made it clear that while in office, they spent a great deal of time thinking about, and then rejecting, the use of nuclear weapons. The repeated abandonment of nuclear options from Korea to the Gulf has been well documented, and the cat is now out of the bag; America's potential enemies can read, and so U.S. officials must from now on assume that they have done their homework.

"It's hard to make credible threats," former Defense Department official Clark Murdock wrote in 2008, "when you tell the world (including future adversaries) that you were bluffing the last time you made one."[67]

A word is in order here about missile defense, because some U.S. and other Western thinkers maintain that one way to solve the problem of a nuclear stand-off with a small state is to invest in enhanced theater missile defenses. Instead of relying on deterrence by nuclear punishment, the argument goes, where rogues are concerned the West should attack the enemy's strategy at its foundations by injecting a major element of uncertainty into whether their small launches can succeed at all. This uncertainty, the reasoning goes, will deter a rogue regime from risking its small arsenal at all.

It is possible that under the best conditions, defenses could save some lives by making a successful intercept should all else fail and a desperate regime tries to strike U.S. forces or neighboring countries with a ballistic weapon, nuclear or otherwise. Missile defenses, however, will not play a part in resolving a nuclear crisis between the United States and a small aggressor. The irrelevance of missile defenses in a crisis has nothing to do with technological and operational obstacles, although it bears repeating that no evidence exists that those problems will be solved any time soon.

Rather, the flaw in the concept is the human element. Relying on missile defenses in a conflict with an unstable or fanatical nation is a cosmic gamble that would be wagered with the lives of millions of people. This level of risk will create a psychological barrier that policymakers, so long as they are human beings, are unlikely ever to overcome. Missile defense advocates might argue if the enemy has only one or two missiles, they may not want to place only a 50/50 bet on a successful hit. The real issue, however, is whether any Western leader will gamble on a 50 percent—or 20 percent, or even 1 percent—chance of a successful nuclear hit on a city.[68] To assume that a U.S. president would run such a risk based on a complicated and unproven system is the kind of modeling that only goes on in the arid world of theory. It does not reflect what will likely happen in the urgent meetings of political leaders and their advisors during a crisis, where mathematical acrobatics will quickly give way to far more seductive arguments for the immediate destruction of the enemy force rather reliance on a system that has never been used in battle.

What, then, is left? If the United States cannot threaten the rogues with nuclear force, and missile defenses are in reality no defense at all, what could deter small nuclear regimes from engaging in adventurism under their own nuclear shield? Here, advocates of traditional deterrence have a point when they argue that there is no reason to take nuclear threats off the table if there is any chance at all that they are doing any good. Indeed, some have argued that even talking about a reticence to use nuclear arms is dangerous. Retired U.S. Air Force Colonel Tom Ehrhard, for example, charged in 2008 that General Cartwright's comments about the low probability that the United States would ever resort to nuclear force were irresponsible: "Any senior official who diminishes in any way the perception that the U.S. might use nuclear weapons effectively denuclearizes us. It amounts to unilateral arms control by fiat."[69]

Deterrence traditionalists, however, must contend with the risk that empty bluster is the most hazardous strategy of all. Dark vows to inflict inconceivable amounts of damage, and perhaps even to approach genocide, are dreadful in themselves, but if they amount only to a gaudy bluff, they are worse than immoral: they are stupid beyond reckoning. Once such threats are made, the results will be disastrous regardless no matter what the outcome. If these nuclear promises are fulfilled, countless people will perish. If they turn out to be empty talk, however, the long-term outcome could be just as bad, with previously weak regimes enjoying a new status as untouchable nuclear states, uranium-empowered Davids taunting a handful of muscle-bound Goliaths.

The answer, as difficult as it might be to accept, is to abandon threats of nuclear retaliation completely. Deterrence will not be strengthened by creating smaller or more accurate nuclear bombs or by drawing up militarily senseless campaigns of desultory nuclear strikes. In the end, the search for a way out of the nuclear dead-end inevitably leads back to large-scale conventional options, and the United States and its allies must therefore replace pointless threats of nuclear attack with new and more credible promises.

Facing the Inevitable: Conventional War and Regime Change

To strengthen deterrence with rising nuclear states, the United States needs a new doctrine that does not rely on inherently incredible threats to use nuclear weapons in crowded regions. Minimum deterrence is the best option for improving the stability of the U.S. nuclear relationship with Russia and China, but there is little point in trying to tailor a nuclear minimum deterrent to far smaller nations. The policy of ambiguity—which was always less a strategy than an improvisation—is now more than twenty years old. It has lost whatever deterrent value it once had, not least because successive U.S. leaders and policymakers have for more than two decades repeatedly ruled out nuclear use against small states and thus made it clear that "calculated ambiguity" in fact involves no ambiguity at all.

The United States should therefore replace ambiguity with certainty. The first steps would be for American leaders to affirm that the United States will never be the first to use strategic nuclear weapons, and that it will never use nuclear weapons at all except in defense of its own existence. This assurance, however, needs to be coupled to a warning to smaller states or lesser powers: WMD attacks, including the use of even a single nuclear weapon of any kind in any region, will precipitate major conventional war *with the explicit goal of regime change and the apprehension or death of the enemy leadership.*

If this recommendation seems like a conventional version of the nuclear "countervailing strategy" of the 1980s, the resemblance is intentional. Whatever the practical flaws of the "countervailing strategy" in its day as a plan of nuclear attack, it attempted to respond to an essential truth: dictators and autocrats value their continued reign and their privileged lives as rulers far more than they value anything else. Threats to do huge amounts of damage to their nation and to take the lives of millions of their people may not mean very much to leaders who will gladly move their operations to their bunkers, let their helpless subjects suffer the consequences of their actions, and ride out the storm of war so long as it is they who control whatever is left after the ashes cool.

How would this new policy enhance deterrence? Wouldn't giving up the ultimate nuclear threat simply embolden rogue leaders to take even greater risks—especially those who may not have a firm grasp on reality in the first place? Even worse, what about the risk that threats of regime change would only strengthen the belief among rogue leaders that the only way to prevent such a fate would be to acquire nuclear weapons yet more quickly? When Moammar Qaddafi was deposed and killed with NATO assistance in 2011, for example, the North Koreans crowed that the hapless Libyan, by giving up his nuclear program, had negotiated away the only protection he might have had against the military might of the West.[70]

The problem with this argument is that there is no evidence that nuclear threats matter much to rogue states or to their terrorist clients. The U.S. nuclear deterrent, representing billions of dollars of research and production on everything from stealth bombers to missile defenses, so far seems to have deterred exactly nothing among rogue states. Indeed, the United States, Britain, France, and Russia have all learned the limits of nuclear power in recent years. Nuclear arsenals, and ambiguity about their purpose, have not prevented terrorist attacks, internal rebellions, hostage-takings, territorial disputes, or the advancement of rogue nuclear arsenals.

In the years before the final invasion of Iraq, for example, U.S. and NATO nuclear weapons did not deter Saddam Hussein from firing on U.S. and British aircraft more than 700 times in the decade after his ejection from Kuwait. The North Koreans not only risked war with the United States over their nuclear program in 1994, but then defied Western pressure and sanctions for years until they managed to detonate two nuclear weapons in 2006 and 2009. They then successfully launched a rudimentary ICBM in 2012. Iran, according to then-U.S. Defense Secretary Leon Panetta in 2012, could construct a nuclear weapon within a year of a decision to process enough uranium, despite years of diplomatic conflict, sanctions and open threats of an Israeli preventive attack. Even established members of the international system mock the nuclear powers: thirty years after losing a war to the United Kingdom, Argentina again pressed its claim to the Falkland Islands, and turned the tables on London by accusing the British of trying to "nuclearize" the dispute.[71]

It is especially galling that outlaw states use the circular reasoning that the West's hostility should be accepted as explanation of their nuclear ambitions, thus reversing the relationship between cause and effect. Rogue regimes do not need nuclear weapons because they are in danger; they are in danger because they are rogue regimes and they seek nuclear weapons. Historically, states such as revolutionary Iran, Baathist Iraq, Syria, North Korea, and Qaddafi's Libya most often found themselves in conflict with the United States and other Western nations mainly over two issues: support for international terrorism, and attempts to gain weapons of mass destruction. Such regimes feel besieged by the rest of the world, and rightly so: dictators who train terrorists, use chemical weapons against their enemies as well as their own people, and show pure contempt for the norms of the international order cannot expect to be overburdened with friends and admirers. If such regimes feel the pressure of a security dilemma among their neighbors or with the great powers, it is only because they have labored so hard to create one.

American foreign policy should not fall prey to this fallacy.[72] Rogue states such as Iran and North Korea have engaged in nuclear programs for their own reasons. They have remained as constant as the Northern Star in their fixation on nuclear weapons through many years and many changes of U.S. presidents and policies. It is superpower vanity to believe that smaller nations care what the United States wants or hopes, or that U.S. hostility to odious regimes is the key determinant of whether their leaders will try to travel the nuclear road.

It is pointless to try to replicate Cold War deterrence with these small states. Worse, it is dangerous: rogues and dictators must never be encouraged to play the complicated game of great power nuclear deterrence. They cannot be allowed to believe that their small arsenals have placed them on an equal footing with the United States or NATO—or for that matter, with Russia, which is a regular target of Islamist wrath—or that they have recreated some form of Mutual Assured Destruction in which they may threaten or even use nuclear weapons while the United States and its allies are left without any retaliatory options.

A promise to engage in conventional war, no matter how long it takes, reduces the quandary of deterring small states to a simple equation: a nuclear attack on the United States or its allies will produce no other outcome but the end of the enemy regime and the death or capture of its leaders. A doctrine of conventional retaliation thus resolves several problems at once. First, it removes the danger of Scott Sagan's "commitment trap," in which Western leaders find themselves forced to make, or are boxed in by, threats they secretly have no intention of carrying out. The public desire for revenge will be satisfied, and the offending regime will be destroyed, but U.S. leaders will have a broader range of means available to them if they have not staked America's credibility and prestige on a promise to go nuclear.

Second, conventional retaliation provides an alternative to extended deterrence. North Korea or Iran might well doubt whether the United States would launch a nuclear attack on either of them should Japan or Turkey be struck, especially if the consequences and risks are great. It is far less doubtful, however, that the United States and its allies will go to war with overwhelming conventional superiority should close American allies be attacked in any way, nuclear or otherwise.

Perhaps the strongest argument in favor of conventional retaliation is that it is rooted in history. Commitments to capture or kill rogue leaders have an actual track record by which they can be judged, and thus are far more believable than idle threats to use nuclear weapons. The United States has not engaged in a nuclear strike since 1945. But from Panama in 1990 onward through Kosovo in 1999, Iraq in 2003, and Libya in 2011, the United States and its allies have attacked or outright invaded other nations, and imprisoned or killed their leaders. While the late British Prime Minister Margaret Thatcher may have had a point that "there is a monument to the failure of conventional deterrence [before World War II] in every French village," it is equally true that there are more than a few prison cells and cemetery plots that now serve as testimony to the fate of enemy leaders who thought they were invulnerable.[73]

There is one more reason to forego nuclear retaliation, and it has to do with the traditions and taboos about nuclear use. This taboo may not be as strong as it has been described by social scientists and historians. It may be, as scholar T. V. Paul has noted, less a taboo than a tradition, held in place so far by culture, history, and contingency.[74] Nonetheless, something has kept the nuclear peace now for almost seven decades, including among the smaller and newer nuclear powers. Whether by taboo or tradition, the nuclear world has been more stable than deterrence theory, circumstance, or pure luck might have otherwise allowed. While the prohibition on using nuclear weapons seems inviolable, however, it will continue to appear so only up until the moment it is violated. Should a nuclear weapon be used in anger in the twenty-first century, the eventual question will be: How can the major powers restore the status quo ante, a world in which the use of nuclear weapons is again effectively unthinkable?

Nuclear traditionalists might answer that the most effective way to reestablish the taboo is to follow through on the logic of deterrence. A retaliatory nuclear attack would demonstrate to the aggressor—but more importantly, perhaps, to the world—the full consequences of violating the taboo. If it takes the horror of a nuclear exchange to cauterize the wound opened by a rogue nuclear launch, then it would be a small price to pay if measured against the possibility of further nuclear anarchy.

If the nuclear taboo is violated, however, it makes no sense to try to reestablish it by violating it *again*. The argument for engaging in nuclear retaliation as punishment for breaking the nuclear taboo is short-term thinking that makes little sense as a long-term strategy for the restoration of peace and the future protection of the United States. Retaliation in kind is also an approach that civilized nations, including the United States, no longer take with regard to any other form of prohibited weaponry. There is no serious argument, for example, that the United States or NATO should respond to a first use of chemical or biological weapons with a reciprocal use of chemicals or germs, even though it would save Allied lives. After all, chemical retaliation would do far less damage to surrounding areas than a nuclear counterattack. So why not threaten to do it?

And yet, Western nations consider no such thing, because they long ago decided that chemical and biological agents are both impractical and immoral. Their effects are unpredictable—the wind is a fickle ally—and they are a burden to any state that stocks them. Whatever the short-term tactical gain (if any), a chemical exchange with a smaller power would do nothing to reestablish any prohibitions, legal or moral, on using such agents. This realization is why U.S. leaders in the 1991 Gulf War warned Iraqi leaders and generals that they, personally, would be held responsible at the war's end for any use of chemical arms, and that if they did not disobey orders to employ them, they would be hunted down and either killed or brought to justice through conventional military means—which is exactly the policy the United States should embrace with regard to nuclear weapons as well.

Waging Postnuclear War

Assuming the worst, and that no threat of any kind keeps a smaller nuclear power from using a nuclear weapon, how would the deterrent threat of conventional retaliation actually be fulfilled? The 2010 Nuclear Posture Review, perhaps anticipating this question, already speaks of holding open the option of a "devastating conventional military response" to a WMD attack, and holding "responsible" anyone involved, "whether national leaders or military commanders."[75] Bold language, to be sure, but what exactly does it mean to "hold someone responsible"? A rain of cruise missiles? A series of embargoes? Indictments in The Hague? A series of toothless excoriations in the UN Security Council?

The problem with the 2010 NPR, as well as with other proposals for conventional strikes, is that they all evade the central question of deterrence: what would such conventional strikes *do* that an enemy would fear so much? Saddam Hussein endured several rounds of conventional bombing before the 2003 invasion of Iraq. The Chinese and North Koreans sacrificed thousands upon thousands of men during the mad scheme to seize the Korean peninsula in 1950. In fact, the Chinese were apparently ready to go for another round in Indochina had the United States invaded North Vietnam in the 1960s.[76]

Today, Pyongyang invests millions of precious dollars in trying to make nuclear weapons and ICBMs while the starving North Korean people are left literally eating the bark off the trees. In 1998, a North Korean defector warned: "Which is better prepared for nuclear exchange, North Korea or the USA? The DPRK can be aptly described as an underground fortress. . . . For their part, the North Koreans are highly motivated candidate martyrs well prepared to run the risk of having the whole country exploding in nuclear attacks from the USA by annihilating a target population center."[77] This level of preparation for a nuclear attack not only raises once again the uncomfortable problem of what to do next should the leadership survive the first nuclear retaliatory strike, but suggests that the North's leaders are willing to sustain considerable damage to their nation.

This kind of readiness to sacrifice the lives of their subjects is one of the reasons that the goal of conventional retaliation should be *war*, rather than "strikes" or "raids" or "enforcement of UN decisions."[78] If the United States is attacked with nuclear weapons, the U.S. Congress should do no less than to issue an actual declaration of war, with all of the powers of mobilization that go with it. A declaration of war—the first since 1941—would not be difficult to obtain in the wake of a rogue nuclear attack or a state-supported act of nuclear terrorism. A formal state of war would also involve the American people in the conflict on a daily basis. Americans in the twenty-first century have become too accustomed to their government fighting multiple wars without much impact on their lives, but a war against a nuclear aggressor will, and must, be a different matter entirely.

Even without a declaration of war, an explicit strategy of conventional retaliation would represent a public American commitment to depose rogue regimes, find their leaders, and eliminate their terrorist clients in the event of the use of a nuclear weapon. America's allies, for their part, have already demonstrated that they would not need a declaration of war to render assistance. After 9/11, both NATO and ANZUS activated their common defense provisions with the United States, decisions that were largely ignored by the U.S. government because of the diplomatic ineptitude of the Bush 43 administration.[79] Whatever the occasionally disorderly state of America's alliances, dozens of countries would come to the aid of the United States and the American people after a nuclear attack, and the enemy regime would find itself at war, literally, with most of the developed world. The biggest danger to such a united front would be if the Americans, in a fit of rage, engaged in a precipitous act of nuclear retaliation and horrified allies and neutrals alike, which is one more reason to engage in a conventional campaign rather than nuclear revenge.

Conventional war and regime change are momentous decisions. Conventional retaliation is a less drastic alternative than nuclear attack, but it is still a proposition that will entail huge expenses, take a great deal of time (months or years, instead of days or weeks), involve serious casualties, and court grave domestic political risk. The American people will have to support a long campaign of air and sea operations of various kinds, and even an invasion if necessary. Retaliation need not be the spasmodic and unrestrained demolition of a foreign nation; the United States has a full range of conventional options that can be used to peel an enemy regime like an onion, stripping it layer by layer of its defenses, infrastructure, communications, military capacity, and finally of any sanctuary for its leaders.

It is possible, as in the wake of the NATO air campaigns in Serbia in 1999 and in Libya in 2011, that an outraged population could eventually turn on its own leaders and effect regime change on their own initiative. This good fortune cannot be counted upon, but that does not in turn mean that the removal of the enemy regime requires a long-term occupation of the kind that took place in Iraq and Afghanistan. Destroying an outlaw regime is not the same thing as pledging to create a liberal democracy in its place. Afghanistan, for example, is still a completely dysfunctional country, but with Al-Qaeda there largely destroyed, it is no longer incubating sweeping terrorist plots against the United States. If the outcome of the Western project to create a better life for the Afghan people is still uncertain, the effort to prevent more threats against Western lives has nonetheless succeeded, at least for the foreseeable future.

Moreover, once a campaign against the enemy regime has begun—that is, once the war has entered its post-nuclear phase—there is no immediate need to invade. The United States waited more than a month to strike Afghanistan after 9/11 even though there was no way of knowing at the time whether more terrorist attacks were in the offing. Once a nuclear attack has already taken place, there will be no pressing need to neutralize a specific military threat. Rather, the goal will shift to the removal and capture of the enemy leadership after the methodical and relentless destruction of its means of political control. In this, the luxury of time will accrue to the Americans and their allies, who can plan the dismantling of the enemy regime piece by piece rather than overreacting or attacking indiscriminately.

Justice may come slowly in such a campaign, but there is significant and recent historical experience to remind rogues and terrorists that justice does come sooner or later. Saddam Hussein was captured by U.S. forces nine months after the fall of Baghdad in 2003, about the same amount of time it took to find and apprehend Moammar Qaddafi once NATO began assisting the Libyan rebels in 2011. Osama Bin Laden was not a state leader, and he was therefore more difficult to locate, but he was finally killed by a U.S. Navy SEAL team—in sovereign Pakistan, no less—nearly ten years after the American-led invasion of Afghanistan. Most of his subordinates in that time were either captured or killed as well. Other war criminals and wanted men have been hunted down after conventional military campaigns of varying sizes have wound down. The murderous Bosnian Serb commander General Ratko Mladic, for example, was finally arrested in 2011 after staying on the run for more than fifteen years from his indictment by a tribunal at The Hague for war crimes, and a year after his family's 2010 request that he be declared dead after being missing so long.[80]

This kind of sure retribution, no matter how long it takes, is a far more credible threat than nuclear retaliation, and probably one that the pitiless men who control rogue states fear more. The Kim clan may shrug and retreat to a bunker, but North Korea's generals may not be so complacent while their nation's defenses are slowly being being cut to pieces and plans for their inevitable trials are being drawn up. And while Iran's Revolutionary Guards and their followers shout defiance and a willingness to die, one cannot help but notice that few of terrorism's top leaders personally embrace suicidal jihadism, a practice that seems reserved for Islamist foot soldiers but from which the governing elites are apparently exempt. Experiences from Afghanistan to Serbia and elsewhere suggest that when war arrives on its red horse, brave promises of resistance vanish quickly.

Washington will have to match deeds to words and reconfigure U.S. conventional and nuclear forces to this new strategy of conventional retaliation. The United States will have to make major investments in conventional forces, a long-term project that must enhance America's already considerable conventional capabilities. The Americans have already taken steps in this direction by seeking to create rapid conventional capabilities that can strike with the speed and force of nuclear weapons. Initially, these plans were part of the confused and confusing "Prompt Global Strike" concept described in Chapter 3. The program has since been retooled as "*Conventional* Prompt Global Strike" (C-PGS). The eventual mix of forces, however, is less important than giving national leaders more options than the employment of nuclear weapons.

Finally, the issue of regime change is intimately bound to the option of preventive war, a subject that raises hackles, both for and against, among people of every political persuasion. To some extent, this is a political, rather than strategic, debate. Much like "counterinsurgency" was once a synonym for "Vietnam," so too has "preventive war" become inextricably bound with the 2003–2011 war in Iraq and the presidency of George W. Bush.

To think of preventive war only in the context of Bush 43 and the war in Iraq, however, is to take a short view of history. Preventive war might not be a good idea, but it is not new; unfortunately, it is a practice as old as war itself. Preventive attack has appeared in conflicts ranging from the ancient contest between Athens and Sparta to World Wars I and II, and onward through Kosovo and Iraq. It is not a peculiarly American concept, although as a French diplomat wryly noted in 2006, the American-led invasion of Iraq *did* manage to give preventive war a worse name than it already had.[81] This debate is too large to open here, but in an earlier work, I showed that preventive war not only predated the invasion of Iraq, but that it now has a new face and is here to stay, whether we like it or not. Since I titled that book *Eve of Destruction*, I hope it is clear that I regard the advent of an age of unrestrained preventive warfare with great trepidation.

The salient point about preventive war with regard to conventional retaliation is that as more states acquire nuclear weapons and the means to deliver them, policymakers will be haunted by the terrible logic that the only sure way to avoid a nuclear attack is to destroy rogue nuclear systems before they become operational. The fearsome implications of this truth have gripped U.S. presidents from Harry Truman and John F. Kennedy to Barack Obama.[82] Preventive attack is a strong temptation to nations faced not just with nuclear threats, but with threats to their security of any kind that may emanate from failed or rogue states.[83] Thus, an unemotional appraisal of preventive strikes will have to be part of the larger discussion about nuclear reductions, minimum deterrence, and conventional retaliation. The subject is unavoidable: there can be no meaningful change in U.S. policy on any of these questions without reassurances to the American people and to their Congressional representatives about what would replace the current reliance on classical notions of nuclear deterrence.

For the United States and NATO to engage in preventive strikes as a matter of policy would unleash chaos and danger beyond repair in the international system. Like all difficult policy choices, however, preventive options must be weighed against the costs of inaction. The most stabilizing approach is likely to lie, paradoxically, in coupling unilateral changes in U.S. nuclear doctrine and forces on one hand to more concrete warnings to the international community about the new rules of nuclear war and peace on the other. For example, if the United States is going to abandon missile defenses—and much good, domestically and internationally, could come from doing so—then the political reality is that the American people will want some sort of assurance that defenses are no longer needed. The strongest assurance to U.S. citizens and their allies would be for Washington to vow that the United States never need missile defenses because it will never tolerate the existence of rogue missile programs.

This is not an idea from the political fringe, nor is it new. In 2006, William Perry (Bill Clinton's defense secretary) and Ashton Carter (who under Obama later became deputy secretary of defense, the number two job at the Pentagon) reluctantly accepted a need for preventive action—with conventional weapons—in a *Washington Post* editorial discussing the North Korean ICBM program. At the time, Pyongyang was readying a test of its *Taepodong* ICBM prototype, and Perry and Carter were clear that the entire enterprise had to be stopped, by force if necessary.

> Should the United States allow a country openly hostile to it and armed with nuclear weapons to perfect an intercontinental ballistic missile capable of delivering nuclear weapons to U.S. soil? We believe not. The Bush administration has unwisely ballyhooed the doctrine of "preemption," which all previous presidents have sustained as an option rather than a dogma. . . . But intervening before mortal threats to U.S. security can develop is surely a prudent policy. *Therefore, if North Korea persists in its launch preparations, the United States should immediately make clear its intention to strike and destroy*

the North Korean Taepodong missile before it can be launched. [emphasis added][84]

Critics could argue that taking out a missile on its launch pad raises the specter of unbridled American unilateralism. It is also an outright act of war. Advocates of preventive action could counter that the North Korean regime thinks *everything* is an act of war anyway, and rightly ask what purpose a three-stage North Korean missile could have other than nuclear blackmail—especially since the North Koreans have already admitted that they fully intend to aim such weapons at the United States.

Both choices, either to wait or to strike, are dangerous. War in Korea would be a tragedy, but the only thing that might be worse would be an unstable Korean regime armed with a nuclear ICBM and determined at some point to make war on its own terms anyway. The world may yet be saved from having to make a decision by the eventual implosion of the Kim regime, but whatever the final act of the Korean drama, choices such as these will increasingly be part of the debate over how to deter or defang rogue nuclear programs.

Likewise, there is the continuing question of whether the United States or Israel—or both—will strike the Iranian nuclear program. In early 2012, rumors of an impending Israeli attack began to accumulate as Israeli defense minister Ehud Barak argued that the Iranian program would enter a "zone of immunity" if the Iranians succeeded in moving components for a bomb deep into bunkers and mountain retreats where they would be far more difficult to strike. The Americans and Israelis disagree on what constitutes such a "zone," but as a report in the *New York Times* noted, "if the Israeli argument is right, the question of how fast the Iranians can assemble a weapon becomes less important than whether there is any way to stop them."[85]

U.S. thinkers and policy experts are sharply divided on whether the United States itself should strike Iran. Scholar Matthew Kroenig set off a debate in the pages of *Foreign Affairs* in 2011 with a piece arguing for attacking Iran, an article blasted by Harvard professor Stephen Walt as "a textbook example of war-mongering disguised as 'analysis'," and derided by Georgetown scholar and former Obama administration defense official Colin Kahl as just another "page out of the decade-old playbook used by advocates of the Iraq war."[86] The public is likewise conflicted, with an early 2012 poll showing that nearly half of the American public was inclined to support the use of military force should all else fail to stop the Iranian program.[87] The Obama administration, for its part, said only that the United States would not tolerate a nuclear-armed Iran and that Washington would use "all elements" of U.S. power to prevent such an outcome, a statement that could mean almost anything.[88]

Politics, like nature, abhors a vacuum. Absent a firm American threat of conventional retaliation, something else from the nuclear inventory will fill the intellectual void that now exists with regard to deterring small nuclear states. Sooner or later, this lack of clarity will produce a disaster. Should the United States remain in denial about the incredibility of its own nuclear threats against small states, every crisis with a rogue proliferator will devolve into a farce: the Americans will make threats they cannot or will not fulfill, and America's enemies will pretend to care while they try to run out the clock in the race to explode a nuclear device.

The paths to nuclear war with small states are so numerous that it is fruitless to try to trace each one of them. Preventive measures to stop rogue nuclear programs may end up being either too difficult or too morally distasteful, as preventive attacks so often are. In such cases, Washington and its allies must be willing to affirm a new deterrent, one that spares innocent millions from nuclear disaster and places the people and regimes who threaten global peace squarely in the crosshairs of conventional retaliation. Potential enemies must know that no matter how many lives are lost, the tally will always include their own. The threat of conventional war, with all the horror it will bring if that threat must be fulfilled, is the only hope of a road toward a real deterrent, and away from a reliance on fantasies of limited nuclear wars that are outdated, dangerous, and immoral.

The Price of Nuclear Peace

> The enemy's an age—a nuclear age. It happens to have killed man's faith in his ability to influence what happens to him. And out of this comes a sickness, and out of sickness a frustration, a feeling of impotence, helplessness, weakness.
>
> —From *Seven Days in May*, 1965

> One nuclear war is going to be the last war, frankly, if it really gets out of hand. And I just don't think we ought to be prepared to accept that sort of thing. But I'm not at all sure that there are very many people who look on this as being as terribly dangerous as I do, so I may be exaggerating the whole thing. But I just don't think we can tolerate it.
>
> —Lawrence Eagleburger, 2009

The Nuclear Legacy: From Fear to Apathy

The subject of nuclear weapons breeds both apathy and dread at the same time. During the Cold War, most people did not want to think about the realities of the nuclear age, especially since there was nothing that the average American (or Soviet) could have done about nuclear arms. The nuclear standoff of the late twentieth century was unavoidable, the alchemic result of a collision between a technological discovery and an ideological conflict, and it could not be exited with any sense of safety until the Cold War itself was somehow settled.

Then as now, people cannot be blamed for feeling helpless about nuclear arms. The human imagination fails when confronted with the idea of a war in which a hundred cities or more cease to exist within hours of the outbreak of hostilities. While it is possible to write words like "40 million casualties," no one really has any idea what those words mean, or what 40 million people killed and injured in less than a day would actually look like. Thinking about it at all seems a futile and tiring expenditure of emotion and intellect.

People cannot live in a state of perpetual anxiety. Accordingly, each succeeding generation of Americans since the end of World War II found its own way to reach an accommodation with the nuclear age. Many of the veterans of World War II felt their lives were saved by the use of nuclear weapons, especially those (like a young George Shultz at the time) who were getting ready to ship out for the invasion of Japan in 1945.[1] Later, the men and women who fought the Cold War during the 1960s and 1970s grimly accepted the "balance of terror" as the price of global peace. In the 1980s, the Americans gambled on an escalation of the arms race against a failing Soviet opponent, a huge risk whose wisdom will be debated for years to come but whose outcome seemed to vindicate its supporters. Today, younger people untouched by the Cold War see more nuclear danger in the meltdown of one power plant in Japan than in thousands of nuclear bombs.

The end of the Cold War, however, resolved nothing about nuclear weapons. There will never be a way to define with any precision the role that nuclear deterrence played in the peaceful end of the East-West conflict, since partisans of every school of thought, from MAD theorists to antinuclear activists, are all convinced that the peaceful end of the Cold War confirmed their preexisting beliefs. It was humanity's salvation that a Soviet-American nuclear war never took place, but we will never really know why it did not happen. It is impossible to prove a negative. And so at the outset of the twenty-first century, there is still no agreement about the ultimate meaning or purpose of nuclear weapons.

All sides in this debate, however, are right about one thing: the costs of any one of them being wrong would be ghastly. If nuclear disarmament invites war, then the central tenet of nuclear deterrence will be proved in the most violent way possible. The nuclear abolitionists will have created the conditions for the outcomes they feared the most, as arms reductions lower the bar to conflict and a major war finally breaks out, perhaps even with the nuclear bombs they were hoping to eradicate. But if the advocates of traditional nuclear deterrence are wrong, and the costs and risks of using nuclear weapons are far greater than they calculated, then they, too, will bring upon themselves—and the rest of us—the misery they were hoping to prevent, and many thousands, maybe even millions, will be dead and the world changed beyond all recognition.

Unfortunately for everyone involved, the record of post–Cold War deterrence strategies has not done much to settle matters either. These strategies seem to have deterred very little, although their defenders might say that it is enough only that nuclear weapons have helped to maintain, beyond the end of the Soviet-American conflict, the "long peace" of a Cold War that stayed cold. After all, Russia and China are theoretically no more and no less a danger to the United States than they were a decade ago. And yet, while war with either of them is, by any analysis, highly improbable, debate goes on over whether that stability is a product of politics or plutonium.

If nuclear deterrence was meant to work on a global scale after the end of the Soviet-American confrontation, however, other countries do not seem to have received the news. Smaller proliferators have gone about their business heedless of U.S. plans or warnings. North Korea has exploded at least three nuclear weapons and likely has more in storage. The death of Kim Jong Il has produced no moderation in Pyongyang's rhetoric, which has actually become yet more unhinged since the newest Kim, the "Dear Leader's" son, took power. Iran, meanwhile, is entering its own nuclear endgame, despite explicit warnings from Israel and the United States that they will not tolerate the existence of an Iranian bomb. (Tehran might not believe the United States has the will to launch military action, but the Israelis have a proven history of preventive attacks.) So far, however, nothing seems to have worked in blunting Iran's determination to gain a nuclear weapon.

In the midst of this turbulence, debates within the United States over the size and role of the U.S. nuclear arsenal continue as though the Cold War never ended.[2] New threats to American security, however, cannot be deterred with little more than new variations on old concepts and the modernization of existing forces. For too many years, the United States and its allies have relied on nuclear weapons as a kind of backstop against the unforeseeable threats of the future, comforting themselves with the notion that any changes or new dangers in the international system can always, in the last instance, be countered with nuclear deterrence. A change in nuclear doctrine, strategies, and forces is inevitable if the United States is to have any hope of leading the rest of the world to a more stable nuclear future.

Nuclear reductions, minimum deterrence, and specific threats of conventional action all offer exits from this atavistic reliance on nuclear force, but the costs of adopting a new doctrine, and in turn reforming American security strategy itself, will be significant. The question is whether Americans will be willing to pay them.

The Price of Minimum Deterrence

Minimum deterrence is already America's unspoken nuclear doctrine in the wake of the Cold War, at least where Russia and China are concerned. In retrospect, it now seems that the deterrent power of only a few nuclear weapons has always been at the foundations of global nuclear peace since the mid-twentieth century. To what degree those weapons kept the peace, or how they did so, are questions whose answers will rest on further work and debate among Cold War historians. In the twenty-first century, however, the major nuclear contenders—Russia, China, and the United States—interact with each other in ways that show not only that they are fully aware of the disproportionate costs of nuclear conflict, but also that indicate how little a role the nuclear element plays in their daily affairs. The only thing left for the United States now is to admit publicly, and to elaborate in more detail, what it informally has already accepted in its thinking about deterrence.

The costs of declaring an explicit doctrine of minimum deterrence would largely be political, and all the more so in the domestic arena rather than at the international level. A U.S. president who declares a doctrine of minimum deterrence and undertakes the restructuring of U.S. strategic forces to reflect that doctrine will be subjected to charges that he or she is endangering the Republic. These criticisms will be especially sharp because there is virtually no chance that the Russians will reciprocate such a move, at least not any time soon. Some of these objections, like any political fight in Washington, will reflect pure partisanship. But some of them will also reflect deeply held, if outdated, beliefs in the Cold War assumptions about nuclear deterrence and MAD.

The debate over New START is instructive here. New START was a far less radical treaty than many of the reductions that preceded it, and yet it generated partisan divisions over nuclear policy not seen since the Cold War. Only SALT II, a doomed exercise that passed from Gerald Ford to

Jimmy Carter and was finally killed by Ronald Reagan, really produced the same kind of stormy opposition to a nuclear treaty seen during the New START debate. Dire warnings about nuclear dangers were aired about New START in the U.S. Senate as though America were still staring down the barrel of the Soviet nuclear buildup of the 1970s. And in a distorted but recognizable echo of the Cold War, American and Russian foreign policy conservatives once again traded the same tired charges about who was trying to intimidate whom, even though the nuclear numbers agreed upon by both sides in New START were, by any reckoning, only trivially different from existing levels.

Of course, much of the New START debate was really about many other things, including the poor state of relations between the Russian Federation and the United States. Perhaps most important, it was a surrogate debate about national missile defense. American conservatives in particular are averse to treaties with the Russians—although ironically, this aversion has not historically been shared by Republican presidents—and there were outraged charges in 2010, including from Republican presidential candidate Mitt Romney, that President Obama had allowed the Russians to write a prohibition on defenses into New START.[3] Obama disputed this claim, and in another irony, arms controllers tried to sell New START to its opponents by claiming it was actually "missile-defense friendly," an illustration in itself of how scrambled the nuclear and missile defense debates have become since the 1970s.[4]

Today, both U.S. political parties are on record in support of defenses, and the notion is now ingrained in U.S. security policy. As Robert Jervis noted in 2002, "no U.S. president since Jimmy Carter has been willing to renounce missile defense, despite the clear lack of foolproof technology."[5] Ten years later, that commitment was reaffirmed by President Obama and by all of his 2012 Republican challengers. There is no reason to expect any departure from this commitment by either U.S. political party in the coming decades.

Political pressure to maintain a national missile defense program will almost certainly increase if strategic nuclear arms are reduced further than the New START limits. In part, this is because defenses seem like a natural corollary to a doctrine of minimum deterrence. With fewer missiles, there is no way to interpret defenses as a screen for a disabling first strike, thus largely obviating Russian and Chinese complaints, sincere or otherwise. Trading offensive forces for defensive systems would seem to be an obvious improvement in strategic stability, and shifting resources from offensive systems to defensive programs could mollify missile defense advocates and cushion the shock of large nuclear reductions, politically and economically.

What might make a minimum deterrent more palatable on a domestic level, however, could make diplomacy and further progress at the international level more difficult. Other countries might wish to follow suit in reducing their nuclear arsenal, but while they can emulate a unilateral reduction, they cannot emulate the pairing of reductions to exotic high-technology defense programs. Moreover, a reduction in forces coupled to an increase in defenses sends a mixed message. If the declared reason for the existence of U.S. nuclear weapons is only to act as a deterrent of last resort against central nuclear war, then defenses will play no role in any case, since there is no hope in any foreseeable future of a missile shield that can protect the United States against a major ICBM attack. For Russia and China, with less capable or aging arsenals, defenses raise the question of whether the Americans are still harboring thoughts of fighting and winning a nuclear exchange. Even more unfortunate, a stubborn insistence on a program of national missile defense, especially one that includes space-based elements, will undercut much of the international political impact of a shift to a minimum deterrent.

This is unfortunate, because among the many benefits of unilateral U.S. strategic reductions, they would eviscerate one of the foundations of current Russian foreign policy. President Vladimir Putin's hollow and manipulative Russian nationalism has morphed over time from partnership with the West into a chest-thumping anti-Americanism based heavily on a mythical U.S. and NATO threat to Russia's treasured nuclear superpower status. Repeated instances of American diplomatic clumsiness, from NATO expansion in the 1990s to the fracas over European missile defenses a decade later, have only helped Putin, who is now set to rule the Russian Federation until at least 2018 and perhaps for the rest of his life. American strategic reductions and a shift toward theater-only defenses would put the lie to Putin's propaganda, and the Kremlin would be left trying to explain why the United States only fields hundreds of weapons while Russia needs thousands.

The Chinese, too, would find themselves in a political dilemma once the Americans moved to a minimum deterrent. They would be faced with a nuclear doctrine that matches their own, thus depriving them of any argument that the United States is seeking a nuclear advantage in Asia, or that the United States is planning for limited nuclear war in the region. A U.S. minimum deterrence doctrine would also upend Chinese assumptions—or what seems to be their assumptions—that they could engage in a localized nuclear exchange with U.S. forces at sea. If the Americans remove all the rungs of the escalatory ladder by renouncing the first use of nuclear weapons and maintaining only a small strategic deterrent, a nuclear strike on U.S. forces or bases in the area will leave Washington boxed into the corner of having to choose either a major conventional war or nuclear retaliation against China itself.

American critics of minimum deterrence would probably agree with this analysis, and argue that this kind of situation—in which the White House has no good choices—is exactly what U.S. strategy should strive to *avoid*. A strategy of minimum deterrence, however, is not a strategy of poor options; rather, it enhances nuclear deterrence by simply dispensing with the illusion that there can be "limited" nuclear exchanges between powers the size of the United States and China. Planners can generate options and trace out elaborate "limited nuclear doctrines" until the cows come home, but national leaders are not likely to take any of them, because they all lead to disaster. There is more danger in keeping such options, and possibly believing in them, than in finally dismissing them. As James Schlesinger said in 1974: "Doctrines control the minds of men only in periods of non-emergency. In the moment of truth, when the possibility of major devastation occurs, one is likely to discover sudden changes in doctrine."[6] Confronting the Chinese with a U.S. minimum deterrent would signal the end of any implied American willingness to join the PRC's generals in gaming out the use of nuclear weapons on a limited scale.

Finally, a doctrine of minimum deterrence might incur political costs with America's allies. Some of them will be uneasy about the subsequent renunciation of extended deterrence, while others have wanted to denuclearize their relationship with the United States for some time. In either case, extended deterrence is outdated. It was a gamble that worked—or seemed to work, anyway—in Europe during the Cold War, largely because Europe was the one place where the fighting between East and West was almost certainly going to spiral out of control once war started.[7] The same dynamic simply cannot be replicated in Asia or the Middle East, where the existence of the West is not at stake. It is dangerous nostalgia to hope that the security of America's allies can be guaranteed as though protecting South Korea in 2012 is somehow just like defending West Germany in 1962.

An American doctrine of minimum deterrence will not only bring U.S. declaratory policy into line with political reality, it will represent the final abandoning of both the pretense, and the burden, of adhering to Cold War nuclear maxims. Such a doctrine, coupled to a "no first use" pledge, would establish America's commitment to removing the threat of nuclear war from relations among the major powers. Embracing minimum deterrence as the foundation of the nuclear relationship with Russia and China, however, is the easy part. Abandoning the policy of ambiguity and replacing it with a stated threat of conventional retaliation against smaller threats will be much harder, and much costlier, by every metric.

The Price of Conventional Retaliation

Conventional retaliation would be the single largest change in U.S. security policy since the advent of the nuclear age. It will entail huge costs, and will almost certainly erase any savings to be found from scaling back the strategic deterrent to minimum levels. Ships, aircraft, and tanks are far more expensive than nuclear weapons, and nothing is more expensive than the care and welfare of the soldiers, sailors, and airmen who will command them. More than a half century ago, the United States responded to the asymmetric balance of power between NATO and the Soviet empire by replacing human beings with nuclear weapons, a move the Soviets later tried to emulate as well.[8] Whether seeking "more bang for the buck" or "more rubble for the ruble," the superpowers tried to find greater economy in nuclear deterrence, but in the end both failed in their efforts to substitute machines for men.[9]

The United States can no longer rely, however, on the crutch of nuclear threats to deter small nuclear powers. Neither nuclear force nor unproven (and unprovable) missile defenses will protect the United States or its allies against these new challengers. Nuclear counterattack is not a practical or moral option, and defenses are so unlikely to work that no U.S. leader can in good conscience rely on them, or even pretend to rely on them. Nor should the United States take the path of its European allies, who have reduced their conventional capabilities so dramatically that executing an air campaign against a bottom-rank power such as Libya, right on NATO's doorstep, strained the military resources of powers such as the United Kingdom and France. The painful fact of the matter is that there is only one threat that can be made against rogue states: war and regime change. And war is a slow and expensive proposition.

Preparing for conventional war means a commitment to significant levels of defense spending. Still, if large sums are to be spent on defense, then investing in people, training, and conventional arms makes more sense than plowing more money into the nuclear complex. During his inaugural address in 1989, President George H. W. Bush famously declared that America has "more will than wallet."[10] The elder Bush was wrong: America, even after the financial crisis of 2008, remains the largest economy in the world and still has plenty of wallet. Whether Americans are willing to strengthen their conventional forces is a political, not an economic, question.

At the least, the immediate budgetary goal should be a reallocation of defense spending, changing current priorities and reinvesting in weapons and systems U.S. troops can actually use.[11] Defense reforms since the end of the Cold War have emphasized smaller armies and complicated hardware. Countries such as North Korea and Iran, however, do not command even second-tier militaries, and dismantling their defenses and destroying their regime's forces will not require the kind of hyper-advanced systems meant for all-out war with a top competitor so often defended by the Pentagon's program managers. Moreover, the goal of a future war with a rogue state will not be to invade and control every inch of enemy territory, but to strip the regime of its defenses and eventually to dislodge, and then to capture or kill, its leadership. Western forces have already executed such operations at least three times in ten years in Serbia, Iraq, and Libya, which is three times more often than they have had to use nuclear weapons in the same period.

In the end, political commitment is more important than money. A prolonged war to remove a rogue regime will not resemble the relatively easy victories over Serbia or Libya, and if a potential nuclear-armed enemy senses anything less than a complete American commitment to regime change in the event of nuclear use, the resulting miscalculations and gambles could bear catastrophic consequences. A clear threat is only part of a credible deterrent, and will mean little without the willingness and capability to carry it out.

The price of conventional retaliation at the international level is difficult to gauge. U.S. allies, faced with a new policy that relies on conventional war, might be reluctant to sign on to an open obligation to come to America's aid. And yet, America's allies offered similar aid after 9/11. Moreover, a threat to go to war would not require the complete mobilization of NATO; indeed, a policy of conventional retaliation might be the one firm guarantee the United States could give to its allies without endangering international security by relying on the reckless promises of extended nuclear deterrence.

International organizations such as the United Nations would likewise find themselves arguing about conventional military actions, an area in which its members have at least some experience, rather than being forced into the terra incognita of nuclear exchanges. This might not make their deliberations any more productive than they usually are, but at least they would not take place in an atmosphere of nuclear crisis. They would also have been given warning in advance that their interference would be fruitless: they will know, from the stated goals of the policy itself, that any conflict will end when, and only when, the American people and their Congressional representatives say it will.

Still, a public vow to go to war represents a kind of "commitment trap" all its own. The only way to avoid such traps, however, is never to say anything at all. Even if the United States were to abandon all foreign alliances, commitments about U.S. security itself must be made, and some of those commitments must entail threats about what might happen if that security is violated. The "trap" of conventional retaliation is not as confining as it might seem, however, and it is far less of a dead end than the threat to use nuclear weapons. Once war is declared there is no requirement as to how it must be fought; neither the U.S. government nor the U.S. military will be forced to use particular weapons, or to adhere to any specific steps or goals other than the defeat of the enemy regime. Washington might be forced to backtrack from a threat to use a nuclear weapon, but the vow to remain at war as a political state of affairs for as long as it takes is far more credible, not just because it is more sustainable than nuclear use, but because rescinding it would effectively mean an American defeat. It would be a promise that no U.S. president could abandon.

Conventional retaliation also entails significant risk to U.S. military personnel. There will be casualties and deaths, as in every war, and there will be calls to use nuclear weapons rather than risk the lives of the men and women of the U.S. armed forces. Former Reagan administration official Kathleen Bailey argued in 1995 that the United States was under no requirement to offer its children's lives on the altar of the nuclear taboo, even during a conventional war: "Imagine that North Korea has attacked South Korea. The United States, bound by alliance to defend the South, must intervene. If you were to ask American parents whether they would rather sacrifice a son or daughter in a ground war, or use nuclear weapons to end the confrontation early, the answer might well be the latter."[12]

Unfortunately Bailey's example is so inflammatory that it offers nothing as a guide to policy. It is unfair ever to ask parents if they would refuse any step, no matter how awful, to save the life of their child. Very few military actions—including peripheral operations such as the invasion of Grenada that were taken under the president Bailey herself served—would pass such a test. Still, there is an important point here: it offends both strategic logic and common sense to argue that any country should take great casualties to its own forces in order to limit damage to the enemy.

This kind of reasoning, however, is based on the strategically mistaken notion that nuclear weapons can somehow clear the battlefield and solve intractable military problems through sheer force. A war in which the United States uses nuclear weapons against a small nation will not end after the strikes have been conducted and the damage assessed. The Americans and their allies will have to invade the stricken enemy, subdue what's left of its forces, and administer its affairs. The risks of conventional fighting remain, but they will be multiplied by a nuclear environment that will present unique and dangerous problems long after hostilities have ceased. The fallacy that nuclear weapons can replace the use of conventional force could result instead in the combined disasters of nuclear use *and* conventional war, and the soldiers who return from that next war will not only bear the scars of traditional combat, but will represent the first generation of "nuclear veterans" since the 1950s, when military men were used for U.S. nuclear warfare experiments.

In the end, rogue regimes may be undeterrable, at least in any way the West understands deterrence. They may be, as former U.S. Defense Secretary William Perry once said, "madder than MAD."[13] But if there is any hope of deterring them, it does not lie in empty nuclear threats. And if the day comes when deterrence fails, not only must the American people be avenged, but a durable peace must be reestablished. This will require removing the offending regime and its leaders. The United States and its allies should start considering the costs of such an eventuality and preparing for it now, and not when all is lost and war is imminent.

Conclusion: The Past Is Not Prologue

This book, like every other about nuclear weapons and deterrence, is a work of speculation. The world has never seen a fully realized nuclear conflict. No matter how scholars, strategists, and policymakers use the language of science to clothe their many assertions about how it would start, how it might be fought, and its effect on humanity, they (and we) are all gambling on elegant hunches. The physical properties of nuclear explosions are well understood; it is the political and social outcomes of nuclear use that are unknowable.

No matter what position they represent, however, the analysts, scholars, military officers, policymakers, and activists in this debate are intelligent and well-intentioned people who share a common goal. No one wants to see the use of a nuclear weapon, and if the world were not a dangerous place, all of them would likely be just as glad to see nuclear weapons (and the chemical, biological, incendiary, and other members of their extended family) consigned to museums and history books. Nuclear planners and nuclear protesters have the same goal—peace—even if they do not see their duty to serve it the same way.

Previous generations can say that they did their best. At the least, they can argue that whatever they did, it apparently worked: we're all still here. Cold Warriors can point out that Western leaders made a virtue of necessity, by building an entire intellectual and military establishment dedicated to figuring out how the most dangerous weapon ever invented could be harnessed to the cause of peace. Activists can say with honor that they tried to keep that establishment honest and constrained. If in retrospect the theories and strategies of the nuclear theologians seem unmoored from reality, perhaps they were. And if the protests of yesterday's demonstrators now seem too shrill or single-minded, that too has more than a little truth in it. All of this human activity took place under great duress and was the product as much of fear as of rational thought. But in the end, all of these efforts accomplished the only task that mattered: preventing the extinction of human civilization.

In the twenty-first century, however, we must now admit that our best has not been good enough. We no longer live under the crushing pressure of the Cold War, and yet we adhere to its formulas and maintain its weapons. We have succumbed to inertia. In part, this is because people still feel a kind of helplessness when confronted with the awesome power of nuclear arms.

But it is also the result of fatigue: Americans, especially, were so relieved to see the Cold War end that they chose to stop thinking about it the moment it was over, like exhausted students tearing up their notes after the end of an exam in a grueling subject they never want to study again. Perhaps worst of all, we have continued to accept the presence of huge numbers of nuclear weapons in our midst *because we have just gotten used to them.*

And yet we now declare ourselves shocked, after years of relying on nuclear weapons, that other nations want them too. We are bewildered that China wants to build more, that Russia will not live with fewer, and that North Korea and Iran are determined to have at least one. None of this should be surprising. Other nations value nuclear weapons precisely because the great powers have taught them to do so. The Cold War may have been a nuclear standoff that no one expected and no one wanted—the Bomb was invented, after all, in the struggle with Hitler, not Stalin—but when it was over, almost nothing changed. To this day, both Russia and the United States speak of their nuclear arsenals in the same terms they did a half century ago. Little wonder, then, that the commitments of public figures to a world without nuclear weapons sometimes seem like hypocrisy and empty rhetoric.

The world may never be free of nuclear weapons. Now that they exist, they will likely always exist; technological advances, and especially military innovations, are never forgotten even if they are sometimes abandoned.[14] Perhaps, at some essential level, they actually are the last barrier to major interstate conflict, or at least will remain so until humanity outgrows the instinct to make war, if it ever does. None of that, however, grants us a dispensation to surrender to the technology. A nuclear bomb, like every other weapon ever invented, is a servant, not a master. It will do as it is told and does not care whether it is used or ignored. Nothing about nuclear weapons is inevitable, and we must abandon a nuclear debate that so far has been framed by previous notions that make change impossible.

The people who lived through the Cold War felt they had no choice but to endure the dangers of nuclear deterrence. Maybe they were right, in their time. Today, we do have a choice. We no longer have to walk paths taken in the past merely because we are too fearful or too unimaginative to make new decisions. If disaster eventually strikes due to our inaction, we will not have the titanic ideological struggles of the twentieth century to blame. And so we must begin to create a more durable nuclear peace by reducing the number of nuclear arms and renouncing them as weapons of war. It is long past time, and we are out of excuses.

Notes

Introduction

1. "Text of Bush's Address to Nation on Gorbachev's Resignation," *New York Times* online archive, December 26, 1991.

2. George P. Shultz, William J. Perry, Henry A. Kissinger, and Sam Nunn, "Toward a Nuclear-Free World," *Wall Street Journal*, January 15, 2008.

3. Gareth Evans, "Bombs Away," *thedailynewsegypt.com*, May 27, 2011.

4. This number is a conservative estimate of how many nuclear arms are actually ready for use; by the terms of New START, the United States and Russia will reduce operational warheads to 1,550 each. In addition to this 3,100 weapons, France, Britain, China, and the smaller powers have arsenals that together total another estimated 2,000 bombs. See Steven E. Miller, "Nuclear Weapons 2011: Momentum Slows, Reality Returns," Bulletin of the Atomic Scientists 68, no. 1 (January-February 2012), and Jamshed Baruah, "Nuke-free World Optimism Fading Away," IDN-InDepthNews, indepthnews.info, October 3, 2011.

5. Oliver Bloom, "Defence Secretary Liam Fox Offers New Thoughts on Trident Replacement," Center for Strategic and International Studies, www.csis.org, July 10, 2010.

6. Exactly what kind of object the North Koreans launched into space was still unclear as of early 2013. Pyongyang, for its part, claims it was a satellite. See Robert Beckhusen, "One Small Step for Kim: North Korea Inches Closer to an ICBM," The Danger Room, Wired.com, December 12, 2012, and Joe Cirincione, "One Small Step for Kim Jong Un," CNN.com, December 13, 2012.

7. See, for example, Choe Sang-Hun, "North Korea Calls Hawaii and U.S. Mainland Targets," *New York Times*, March 26, 2013, and Eric Talmadge "North Korea Nuclear Threats Make Japan Increasingly Nervous," Associated Press, April 8, 2013.

8. Sharad Joshi, "Playing Politics: How the Regional Context Impedes Confronting Myanmar's Alleged Nuclear Program," *Nuclear Threat Initiative Issue Brief*, February 4, 2011.

9. The Chinese arsenal is so small it is not capable of a protracted or massive exchange, but the Chinese seem to have settled on a small force as a sufficient deterrent. See Jeffrey Lewis, *The Minimum Means of Reprisal: China's Search for Security in the Nuclear Age* (Cambridge, Mass.: American Academy of Arts and Sciences, 2007).

10. "Russia to Remain Nuclear Power Until Nukes Lose Their Deterring Role—General," ITAR-TASS, December 17, 2010. Also see Pavel Felgenhauer, "New Military Doctrine Underscores Kremlin's Aspirations to Become Regional Superpower," *Jamestown Report* 28, no. 7, February 10, 2010. The actual document, "Voennaia doktrina Rossiiskoi Federatsii," signed February 5, 2010, is available through the Russian president's office at kremlin.ru.

11. Quoted in Mary Beth Sheridan, Felicia Sonmez, and William Branigin, "New Arms Treaty with Russia Passes Key Hurdle," *Washington Post*, December 21, 2010.

12. See, for example, Barry Schweid, "Panel Faults Obama on Arms Reduction Treaty," Associated Press, May 5, 2010. Some of the negative reaction to New START also arose because the treaty quickly became a kind of exhibition of national security bona-fides by possible presidential challengers for the next election cycle. Former Massachusetts governor Mitt Romney, for example, weighed in against the treaty in late 2010; see Mitt Romney, "Stop START," *Boston Globe*, December 3, 2010.

13. U.S. Department of Defense, Office of the Undersecretary of Defense for Acquisition, Technology, and Logistics, "Report of the Defense Science Board Task Force on Nuclear Deterrence Skills," September 2008, v.

14. Quoted in Anna Mulrine, "START Treaty: Mullen Delivers Tough Speech on Nuclear Weapons Agreement," *Christian Science Monitor*, November 15, 2010.

15. Michael Krepon, "Numerology in the Second Nuclear Age," IFRI *Proliferation Papers* no. 30, Fall 2009, www.ifri.org, 10.

16. Bernard Gwertzman, "Confronting a Nuclear Tipping Point," an interview with George Shultz, Council on Foreign Relations, CFR.org, March 12, 2010.

17. George Lee Butler, "The General's Bombshell: What Happened When I Called for Phasing Out the U.S. Nuclear Arsenal," *Washington Post*, January 12 1997, C01.

18. Harold Feiveson, ed., *The Nuclear Tipping Point* (Washington, D.C.: Brookings Institution, 1999), 35.

19. "Nuclear Weapons in Twenty-first Century U.S. National Security: Report by the Joint Working Group of American Academy of Arts and Sciences, the American Physical Society, and the Center for Strategic and International Studies," Center for Strategic and International Studies, December 2008.

20. See Stephen Walt, "Nuclear Posture Review (or Nuclear Public Relations?)," *Foreign Policy*, April 6, 2010, and Bruce Blair, quoted in Jonathan Weisman and Peter Spiegel, "U.S. Keeps First-Strike Strategy," *Wall Street Journal*, April 6, 2010.

21. Lawrence Freedman, *The Evolution of Nuclear Strategy* (New York: St. Martin's, 1983), 395.

22. John Mueller, "The Essential Irrelevance of Nuclear Weapons: Stability in the Postwar World," *International Security* 2, no. 13 (Fall 1988): 56.

23. See John Mueller, *Atomic Obsession: Nuclear Alarmism from Hiroshima to Al-Qaeda* (New York: Oxford University Press, 2009).

24. "Author Warns 'Second Nuclear Age' Is Here," National Public Radio, "Talk of the Nation," November 8, 2012. For Bracken's discussion at length, see Paul

Bracken, *The Second Nuclear Age: Strategy, Danger, and the New Power Politics* (New York: Times Books, 2012)

25. For more on the nuclear "taboo," see Nina Tannenwald, *The Nuclear Taboo* (Cambridge: Cambridge University Press, 2007); T. V. Paul believes that "taboo" is too strong a term, and instead calls nuclear non-use a "tradition." See T. V. Paul, *The Tradition of Non-Use of Nuclear Weapons* (Stanford, Calif.: Stanford University Press, 2009).

26. Keith Payne, for example, argues that the concept of deterrence is inherently flawed, that the Soviet-American relationship was never all that stable, and that mostly, the world got lucky during the Cold War. See *The Fallacies of Cold War Deterrence and a New Direction* (Lexington: University Press of Kentucky, 2001).

27. Hans M. Kristensen, "U.S. Strategic War Planning After 9/11," *Nonproliferation Review* 14, no. 2 (July 2007).

28. The targets were not specified. See Michael R. Gordon, "Maneuvers Show Russian Reliance on Nuclear Arms," *New York Times,* July 10, 1999.

29. Matthew Day, "Russia 'Simulates' Nuclear Attack on Poland," *Telegraph,* November 1, 2009.

30. One of the problems with war games in general is that they are organized around what is convenient to the exercise, rather than the messy realities of what might actually happen. In 1988, I was invited to be an observer at one of the last of the Cold War iterations of the Naval War College's "Global War Games," and when I asked what would happen if the scenario reached strategic nuclear levels, a retired officer who was one of the referees told me that the hypothesized conflict would not get that far because at that point the game would no longer be useful or interesting. This was rationalized during the games as a conclusion, supposedly reached independently by both "Red" and "Blue," that nuclear use would be counterproductive. See Bud Hay and Bob Gile, "Global War Game: The First Five Years: 1979–1983," U.S. Naval War College Newport Papers no. 4, June 1993, and "Global War Game: Second Series, 1984–1988," Newport Papers no. 20, 2004, especially chapter 4, which covers the 1988 game.

31. Arkin described Vigilant Shield in his *Washington Post* blog, reproduced at William M. Arkin, "The Vigilant Shield 07 War Games: Scenario Opposing the U.S. to Russia, China, Iran and North Korea," www.globalresearch.ca, February 10, 2007.

32. Janne E. Nolan and James R. Holmes, "The Bureaucracy of Deterrence," *Bulletin of the Atomic Scientists* 64, no. 1 (March-April 2008): 40–41.

33. See Graham Allison, ed., *Hawks, Doves, and Owls* (New York: Norton, 1986).

34. Ivo Daalder and Jan Lodal, "Toward a World Without Nuclear Weapons," *Foreign Affairs* 87, no. 6 (November-December 2008): 83, Nolan and Holmes, "The Bureaucracy of Deterrence," 41.

Chapter 1. Nuclear Strategy, 1950–1990

1. See Bernard Brodie, *The Absolute Weapon: Atomic Power and World Order* (New York: Harcourt Brace, 1946).

2. Robert Jervis, *The Illogic of American Nuclear Strategy* (Ithaca, N.Y.: Cornell University Press, 1984), 19.

3. Colin Gray, "Nuclear Strategy: The Case for Theory of Victory," in Steven Miller, ed., *Strategy and Nuclear Deterrence* (Princeton, N.J.: Princeton University Press, 1984), 24.

4. Fred Kaplan, *The Wizards of Armageddon* (Stanford, Calif.: Stanford University Press, 1983).

5. Lawrence Freedman, *The Evolution of Nuclear Strategy* (New York: St. Martin's, 1983), 76.

6. See William Burr and Svetlana Savranskaya, "Previously Classified Interviews with Former Soviet Officials Reveal U.S. Strategic Intelligence Failure over Decades: 1995 Contractor Study Finds that U.S. Analysts Exaggerated Soviet Aggressiveness and Understated Moscow's Fears of a U.S. First Strike," National Security Archive online, September 11, 2009, www.gwu.edu/~nsarchiv.

7. Many historians have argued that Stalin's risk-taking in Korea illustrated his indifference to the U.S. nuclear monopoly. More recent revelations, however, show that Stalin was in fact deeply concerned about war with the West coming before the USSR was ready for it, and was operating on calculations that the West did not want a wider war any more than he did. He had previously turned down North Korean leader Kim Il Sung's entreaties to allow him to invade the South in 1950, and he essentially abandoned the North Koreans as soon as the operation went poorly and a quick victory was out of reach. See John Gaddis, *We Now Know* (New York: Oxford University Press, 1998), 81–84, and Thomas Nichols, *Winning the World: Lessons for America's Future from the Cold War* (Westport, Conn.: Praeger, 2003), chapter 2.

8. Quoted in John Newhouse, *War and Peace in the Nuclear Age* (New York: Knopf, 1988), 95.

9. Quoted in Newhouse, *War and Peace in the Nuclear Age,* 95; for the full article, see J. F. Dulles, "Policy for Security and Peace," *Foreign Affairs*, April 1954.

10. Quoted in Harriet Fast Scott and William Scott, eds., *The Soviet Art of War* (Boulder, Colo.: Westview Press, 1982), 157. See also M. Kozlov, "Iz istorii razvitiia voenno-strategicheskikh kontseptsii SShA," *Voenno-Istoricheskii Zhurnal* 10, 1983, 72, and V. Sokolovskii, *Soviet Military Strategy* (Englewood Cliffs, N.J.: Prentice-Hall, 1963), 153–59.

11. Newhouse, *War and Peace in the Nuclear Age,* 162. In 1958, the Strategic Air Command produced a classified motion picture for internal use, *The Power of Decision*, that simulated a Soviet sneak attack; at the end, both the United States and the Soviet Union are in ruins, but the script implies that the Americans have the upper hand and will dictate the cease-fire. See National Security Archive, "Nobody Wins a Nuclear War but 'Success' Is Possible: Mixed Message of 1950s Air Force Film on a U.S.-Soviet Conflict," National Security Archive Electronic Briefing Book No. 336, available at the National Security Archive online, http://www.gwu.edu/~nsarchiv/nukevault/.

12. See Newhouse, *War and Peace in the Nuclear Age*, 162–64, and Freedman, *The Evolution of Nuclear Strategy*, 228.

13. Desmond Ball, "U.S. Strategic Forces," in Steven Miller, ed., *Strategy and Nuclear Deterrence* (Princeton, N.J.: Princeton University Press, 1984), 220.

14. Kaplan, *The Wizards of Armageddon*, 391.

15. See Sharon Ghamari-Tabrizi, *The Worlds of Herman Kahn: The Intuitive Science of Thermonuclear War* (Cambridge, Mass.: Harvard University Press, 2005), for a discussion of Kahn's life and work.

16. Kaplan, *The Wizards of Armageddon*, 390–91.

17. Quoted in David Hoffman, *The Dead Hand: The Untold Story of the Cold War Arms Race and Its Dangerous Legacy* (New York: Doubleday, 2009), 381–82.

18. Kaplan recounts that General David Shoup objected to the 1962 nuclear war plan, which called for striking Communist China no matter what started the war. "Sir," Shoup said to the secretary of defense, "this is not the American way." Kaplan, *The Wizards of Armageddon*, 270.

19. See Henry Kissinger, *Nuclear Weapons and Foreign Policy* (New York: Council on Foreign Relations, 1957), and Herman Kahn, *On Thermonuclear War* (Princeton, N.J.: Princeton University Press, 1960).

20. See Freedman, *The Evolution of Nuclear Strategy*, chapter 15.

21. Quoted in Freedman, *The Evolution of Nuclear Strategy*, 285.

22. The late Jeremy Azrael called the buildup an "all-azimuth" increase, taken in part to remedy Nikita Khrushchev's efforts to cut corners in defense spending. See Jeremy Azrael, "The Soviet Civilian Leadership and the Military High Command, 1976–1986" RAND R-3251-AF, June 1987.

23. George H. W. Bush said something similar to this during the 1980 presidential campaign, but later denied he was endorsing a "winnable" war. See Robert Scheer, *With Enough Shovels: Reagan, Bush and Nuclear War* (New York: Random House, 1982).

24. For a discussion of the Soviet civil-military debate over the concept of "nuclear victory," see Thomas Nichols, *The Sacred Cause: Civil-Military Conflict over Soviet National Security, 1917–1992* (Ithaca, N.Y.: Cornell University Press, 1993), 156–60.

25. Empirical work on the attitude of the Soviet generals and marshals, most of whom are now dead, is inconclusive and too large a subject to cover fully here. Some of them, as in the 1995 interview project discussed by Burr and Savranskaya, showed a clear reluctance to think about nuclear war. Others (including some that I personally interviewed at the General Staff level) were convinced that the USSR would have survived a nuclear war. Even after the Soviet demise, hard-liners such as Soviet Ground Forces commander Valentin Varennikov intimated that they might have preferred war with the West over what they saw as Mikhail Gorbachev's treasonous surrender. Valentin Varennikov, "My srazhalis' za Rodinu'," *Zavtra* 17, no. 22 (May 1994). Varennikov was the only man tried in court for the 1991 coup—at his own insistence. He was acquitted.

26. Robert Jervis, for one, identified at least four "MADs" during the late Cold War. See Robert Jervis, *The Meaning of the Nuclear Revolution: Statecraft and the Prospect of Armageddon* (Ithaca, N.Y.: Cornell University Press, 1989), chapter 3.

27. See Freedman, *The Evolution of Nuclear Strategy*, 247.

28. Quoted in Newhouse, *War and Peace in the Nuclear Age*, 202.

29. Kaplan, *The Wizards of Armageddon*, 315–21.

30. Spurgeon M. Keeny Jr., and Wolfgang K. H. Panofsky, "MAD Versus Nuts: Can Doctrine or Weaponry Remedy the Mutual Hostage Relationship of the Superpowers?" *Foreign Affairs* 60, no. 2 (Winter 1981).

31. Portions of this section are taken from Joan Johnson-Freese and Thomas M. Nichols, "Space, Stability and Nuclear Strategy: Rethinking Missile Defense," *China Security* 6, no. 2 (Summer 2010).

32. Kaplan, *The Wizards of Armageddon*, 346.

33. Kaplan, *The Wizards of Armageddon*, 347.

34. This is the "stability-instability paradox," the irony that frozen bipolarity at the strategic nuclear level, in which neither side would dare a direct Soviet-American war, could open the door to *more* instability at lower levels of violence, especially through the use of proxies and client states. For a short synopsis of this concept, including Glenn Snyder's 1961 discussion of the concept in *Deterrence and Defense*, see Michael Krepon's discussion at Arms Control Wonk online: "The Stability and Instability Paradox," November 2, 2010, available at http://krepon.armscontrolwonk .com/archive/2911/the-stability-instability-paradox.

35. Anatolii Dobrynin, *In Confidence* (Seattle: University of Washington Press), 405.

36. See William Burr, "The Nixon Administration, the 'Horror Strategy,' and the Search for Limited Nuclear Options, 1969–1972," *Journal of Cold War Studies* 7, no. 3 (Summer 2005): 47.

37. National Security Council, "Minutes of the Verification Panel Meeting Held August 9, 1973," August 9, 1973, 4. Available at the National Security Archive, http:// www.gwu.edu/~nsarchiv/.

38. "Minutes of the Verification Panel Meeting Held August 9, 1973," 2.

39. Burr, "The Nixon Administration and the 'Horror' Strategy," 47.

40. "Minutes of the Verification Panel Meeting Held August 9, 1973," 4.

41. The White House, Henry Kissinger, "Memorandum for the President," January 7, 1974, 2. Available at http://www.gwu.edu/~nsarchiv/.

42. The story of the interagency battle over NDSM-242 is worthwhile, if unsettling, reading. See Kaplan, *The Wizards of Armageddon*, 372–78.

43. This story is told more completely in Burr, "The Nixon Administration and the 'Horror' Strategy."

44. Newhouse, *War and Peace in the Nuclear Age*, 284.

45. Freedman, *The Evolution of Nuclear Strategy*, 376.

46. The next plan had just two small nuclear strikes on the roads from the Soviet Union into Iran, an equally useless option, which suggests that the JCS was sending Kissinger the message that it wanted to draft its own nuclear plans without meddling from civilians. Quoted in Kaplan, *The Wizards of Armageddon,* 370–71.

47. See James Goodby, *At the Borderline of Armageddon: How American Presidents Managed the Atom Bomb* (Lanham, Md.: Rowman and Littlefield, 2006), 110.

48. Carter used the expression in a May 22, 1977, speech at Notre Dame University. It is archived in several places, including the Miller Center at the University of Virginia: http://millercenter.org/president/speeches/detail/3399.

49. Newhouse, *War and Peace in the Nuclear Age,* 294.

50. For a longer discussion of this period, see Thomas Nichols, "Carter and the Soviets: The Origins of the U.S. Return to a Strategy of Confrontation," *Diplomacy and Statecraft,* June 2002.

51. See Nichols, *Winning the World,* chapter 6, for more discussion on this point.

52. For more on the rationale behind the countervailing strategy, see Walter Slocombe, "The Countervailing Strategy," *International Security* 5, no. 4 (Spring 1981).

53. Jervis dissects the flaws of PD-59 in detail in *The Illogic of American Nuclear Strategy.*

54. Georgii Arbatov, *Zatianuvsheesia vyzdorovlenie* (Moscow: Mezhdunarodnye Otnosheniia, 1991), 237–38, 241.

55. Gray, "Nuclear Strategy: The Case for Theory of Victory," in Miller, ed., *Strategy and Nuclear Deterrence,* 36.

56. As Soviet Ambassador Anatolii Dobrynin later recalled, "[I]t had been quite impossible for me to imagine anything much worse than Carter." Quoted in Nichols, *Winning the World,* 143.

57. John Newhouse, "The Abolitionist," *New Yorker,* January 2, 1989.

58. Quoted in Newhouse, *War and Peace in the Nuclear Age,* 297.

59. Ronald Reagan, "Address to the Nation on Defense and National Security," March 23, 1983.

60. The U.S. public's fascination with missile defense is discussed in Johnson-Freese and Nichols, "Space, Stability, and Nuclear Strategy," 4–7.

61. See Nichols, *Winning the World,* 190–95.

62. Reagan's change of heart, the cumulative effect of a series of scares during 1983, was detailed by Beth Fischer in *The Reagan Reversal* (Columbia: University of Missouri Press, 1997).

63. While outside the scope of this book, there was a significant link to progress on the Conventional Forces in Europe (CFE) negotiations that opened the door for the Americans to think more seriously about nuclear reductions. The CFE talks were eventually overtaken by events and finally collapsed in 2011. My thanks to James Graham Wilson for clarifying this point.

64. Hoffman, *The Dead Hand,* 381–82.

65. Fukuyama meant only that the intellectual history of the West, as a struggle between individual freedom and collectivist tyranny, had been resolved by the Soviet collapse in favor of freedom and markets. See Francis Fukuyama, *The End of History and the Last Man* (New York: Free Press, 1992).

Chapter 2. Nuclear Weapons After the Cold War

1. "Nuclear inertia" is Belgian scholar Tom Sauer's phrase. See Tom Sauer, "The Role of Nuclear Weapons in Strategic Thinking and Military Doctrines in the 1990s: The United States," in Joachim Krause and Andreas Wenger, eds., *The Role of Nuclear Weapons into the Twenty-First Century*, Studies in Contemporary History and Security Policy 8 (Bern: Peter Lang, 2001).

2. Stephen M. Meyer, "Testimony Before the Senate Foreign Relations Committee," in Theodore Karasik, ed., *Russia and Eurasia Armed Forces Review Annual,* vol. 15, 1991 (Gulf Breeze, Fla.: Academic International Press, 1999), 348. Other Sovietologists made similarly bold, but wrong, statements during the immediate years before the Soviet collapse. See Nikolas Gvosdev, ed., *The Strange Death of Soviet Communism: A Postscript* (Piscataway, N.J.: Transaction, 2008).

3. The National Defense Strategy was inserted into the national security process by then–Secretary of Defense Donald Rumsfeld in 2005 and 2008, presumably because the secretary did not like the communication between Congress and the Joint Chiefs taking place without his input. However, this document had no basis in legislation, and in 2010 it was eliminated by Rumsfeld's successors.

4. I arrived at the Naval War College in 1997, and until then, despite years as an adjunct and as a Secretary of the Navy Fellow, I'd never seen a copy of the National Security Strategy, and I don't recall ever having had to teach it. (I noticed it one day when a glossy stack of them were left on a table in the hallway of one of the War College departments with a sign that said, "Take One.") It is now a required part of the curriculum in the National Security Affairs Department.

5. Richard Weitz, "Global Insights: The Many Messages of National Strategy Documents," *World Politics Review*, February 22, 2011.

6. Quoted in David Hoffman, *The Dead Hand: The Untold Story of the Cold War Arms Race and Its Dangerous Legacy* (New York: Doubleday, 2009), 382.

7. See Thomas Nichols, "The Soviet Legacy: Nationalism, Ideology and the New CIS Militaries," in Theodore Karasik, ed., *Russia and Eurasia Military Review Annual,* vol. 15, 1991 (Gulf Breeze, Fla.: Academic International Press, 1999).

8. Attempts to pressure Pyongyang were derailed, much to the Clinton administration's anger, by the ubiquitous Jimmy Carter, whose intervention only delayed, but did not avert, the emergence of the North Korean bomb; an unnamed Clinton cabinet official later referred to Carter as "a treasonous prick" for his involvement in the 1994 fiasco. See Chris Suellentrop, "Jimmy Carter: He Would Have Gotten Away with It If It Weren't for Those Meddling Voters," *Slate.com*, May 17, 2002.

9. Quoted in Tom Sauer, *Nuclear Inertia: U.S. Weapons Policy After the Cold War* (New York: I. B. Tauris, 2005), 104.

10. Quoted in Harold Feiveson, ed., *The Nuclear Turning Point: A Blueprint for Deep Cuts and De-Alerting of Nuclear Weapons* (Washington, D.C.: Brookings Institution, 1999), 148.

11. Quoted in Thomas Nichols, *The Sacred Cause: Civil-Military Conflict over Soviet National Security, 1917–1992* (Ithaca, N.Y.: Cornell University Press, 1993), 1.

12. Feiveson, ed., *Nuclear Turning Point,* 148.

13. Janne E. Nolan and James R. Holmes, "The Bureaucracy of Deterrence," *Bulletin of the Atomic Scientists* 64, no. 1 (March–April 2008): 42–43.

14. Janne Nolan, *An Elusive Consensus* (Washington, D.C.: Brookings Institution, 1999), 45.

15. Quoted in Feiveson, ed., *Nuclear Turning Point,* 250, and Nolan, *An Elusive Consensus,* 42.

16. Nolan and Holmes, "The Bureaucracy of Deterrence," 42–43.

17. See Nolan, *An Elusive Consensus,* 57, and Feiveson, ed., *Nuclear Turning Point,* 262–64.

18. Nolan, *An Elusive Consensus,* 52.

19. Hans M. Kristensen, *U.S. Nuclear Strategy Reform in the 1990s,* working paper, Nautilus Institute, March 2000.

20. Sauer, *Nuclear Inertia,* 95.

21. Nolan, *An Elusive Consensus,* 57.

22. See Bill Gertz, "The New Nuclear Policy: Lead but Hedge," *Air Force Magazine,* January 1995.

23. See Hans M. Kristensen, *Global Strike: A Chronology of the Pentagon's New Offensive Strike Plan,* Federation of American Scientists, March 15, 2006.

24. Kristensen, *Global Strike,* 151.

25. Quoted in "Clinton Issues New Guidelines on U.S. Nuclear Weapons Doctrine," *Arms Control Today,* November–December, 1997.

26. Nolan and Holmes, "The Bureaucracy of Deterrence," 41.

27. John Deutch, "A Nuclear Posture for Today," *Foreign Affairs* 84, no. 1 (January–February 2005): 49.

28. Dana Priest and Walter Pincus, "U.S. Rejects 'No First Use' Atomic Policy: NATO Needs Strategic Option, Germany Told," *Washington Post,* November 24, 1998, A24.

29. Thomas Schelling, *Arms and Influence* (New Haven, CT: Yale University Press, 1966), 93.

30. Scott D. Sagan, "The Commitment Trap: Why the United States Should Not Use Nuclear Threats to Deter Biological and Chemical Weapons Attacks," *International Security* 24, no. 4 (Spring 2000): 86.

31. Quoted in John Barry and Evan Thomas, "Dropping the Bomb," *Newsweek,* June 24, 2001.

32. In keeping with the notion of nuclear "hedging," the Pentagon wanted to keep the warheads in reserve, rather than destroy them. Bush's negotiators wanted to store the weapons in case of unnamed possible future threats, and saw no reason the Russians should object. The Russians, whose arsenal was aging and who would have to dismantle their outdated weapons in any case, saw this move as evidence of bad faith and were understandably nonplussed. See Tom Nichols, "Scrap 'Em," *National Review Online*, January 16, 2002.

33. Bush claimed he had reached an understanding with Putin on the matter. Putin quickly distanced himself from Bush's comments, but agreed that junking the ABM Treaty posed no threat to Russia. See Terence Neilan, "Bush Pulls Out of ABM Treaty; Putin Calls Move a Mistake," *New York Times*, December 13, 2001.

34. See, for example, Pavel Felgenhauer, "Russian Military Weakness Increases Importance of Strategic Nuclear Forces," *Eurasia Daily Monitor* 6, no. 112 (June 11, 2009), and Pavel Felgenhauer, "Military Doctrine Consolidates Xenophobia of the Russian Elites," *Eurasian Daily Monitor* 7, no. 28 (February 10, 2010), both at www.jamestown.org.

35. I am grateful to Robert Lieber, Oliver Thraenert, and other colleagues for their assistance with this general description of the political debate.

36. See Joan Johnson-Freese and Thomas Nichols, "Space, Stability, and Nuclear Strategy: Rethinking Missile Defense," *China Security* 6, no. 2 (Fall 2010).

37. A 1998 Claremont Institute poll (a pro-defense group) found that 54 percent of registered voters believed the United States could destroy an enemy missile in flight, the same number who reported themselves from "surprised" to "shocked and angry" to find out no such capability exists. "1998 Missile Defense Poll," http://www.clare mont.org/ballmiss/bmd_poll.cfm.

38. Barry and Thomas, "Dropping the Bomb."

39. See Beth Fischer, *The Reagan Reversal* (Columbia: University of Missouri Press, 1999), 120–21.

40. Quoted in Hoffman, *The Dead Hand*, 16.

41. U.S. Department of Defense, "Findings of the Nuclear Posture Review," slide presentation, January 9, 2002.

42. William M. Arkin, "Secret Plan Outlines the Unthinkable: A Secret Policy Review of the Nation's Nuclear Policy Puts Forth Chilling New Contingencies for Nuclear War," *Los Angeles Times*, March 9, 2002.

43. Richard Betts, "Suicide from Fear of Death," *Foreign Affairs*, January-February 2003, 41.

44. I discuss this collapse of faith in deterrence in detail in Thomas Nichols, *Eve of Destruction* (Philadelphia: University of Pennsylvania Press, 2008), chapter 4.

45. See Arkin, "Secret Plan Outlines the Unthinkable."

46. See M. Elaine Bunn, "Can Deterrence Be Tailored?" Institute for National Strategic Studies, National Defense University, 2007.

47. Conservative organizations such as the Heritage Foundation still argue that the traditional triad is essential to U.S. nuclear security. In 2012 a Heritage analyst castigated U.S. STRATCOM chief General Robert Kehler for being insufficiently energetic in his testimony before Congress on the need for the Cold War triad. See Bryan DeWinter, "U.S. Nuclear Triad Essential for National Security," Heritage Foundation, "The Foundry" blog (heritage.org/blog), July 12, 2012.

48. See Dave Majumdar, "Prompt Global Strike Won't Use ICBMs," *Defense News*, March 1, 2011, and "Conventional ICBM Still an Option: Schwartz," March 2, 2011; for a recap of the discussion, see David Axe, "Air Force Waffles on Nutty 'ICBMs Vs. Terrorists' Plan," Danger Room, wired.com, March 3, 2011.

49. See Emi Kolawole, "Hypersonic Craft X-51A Fails Latest Test," *Washington Post* online blog, August 15, 2012, and Guy Norris, "X-51A Waverider Achieves Hypersonic Goal On Final Flight," *Aviation Week*, May 3, 2013.

50. Kristensen, *Global Strike*, 6.

51. T. V. Paul, *The Tradition of Non-Use of Nuclear Weapons* (Stanford, Calif.: Stanford University Press, 2009), 182.

52. Michael Gordon, "Nuclear Arms: For Deterrence or Fighting?" *New York Times*, March 11, 2002, A1.

53. Quoted in William Arkin, "Not Just a Last Resort?" *Washington Post*, May 15, 2005.

54. Walter Pincus, "Pentagon Revises Nuclear Strike Plan," *Washington Post*, September 11, 2005.

55. Cartwright was voted the 2012 "Arms Control Person of the Year" in a poll of arms control groups led by the Arms Control Association. See "Retired General James Cartwright Voted 2012 Arms Control Person of the Year," Arms Control Association online press release, January 8, 2013.

56. For a dissection of the draft, see Jeffrey Lewis, Doctrine for Joint Nuclear Operations (Joint Publication 3–12), ArmsControlWonk.com, April 4, 2005, archived at http://lewis.armscontrolwonk.com/archive/512/doctrine-for-joint-nuclear-opera t ions-joint-publication-3–12. Lewis notes that the Defense Department took the documents off the public Defense Technical Information Center (DTIC) after Lewis found them (by using, as he snarkily put it, the "noted hacking tool 'Google'"). See also "Pentagon Cancels Controversial Nuclear Doctrine," February 2, 2006, *The Nuclear Information Project*, http://www.nukestrat.com/us/jcs/canceled.htm.

57. Kristensen, *Global Strike*, 3.

58. Keith Payne, "The Nuclear Posture Review: Setting the Record Straight," *Washington Quarterly* 28, no. 3 (Summer 2005): 147.

59. Quoted in Keith Payne, *The Fallacies of Cold War Deterrence and a New Direction* (Lexington: University of Kentucky Press, 2001), 79.

60. For a good example of the pointless Cold War fixation on things like "throw-weight," see James J. Tritten, "Throw-Weight and Arms Control," *Air University Review*, November-December 1982. This article was unearthed by Jeffrey Lewis in his article "It's Not You, It's Me," *Foreign Policy* online, March 8, 2013.

61. It is surprising that Payne defended the Bush NPR on such grounds, because his 2001 book is an excellent exploration of the problem of irrationality—and even of wild cards such as drug and alcohol abuse, prescription medication, and insanity—in thinking about deterrence. See Payne, *The Fallacies of Cold War Deterrence.*

62. Quoted in H. Josef Hebert, "Bush Orders Cuts in Nuclear Stockpiles," Associated Press, December 18, 2007.

63. Charles D. Ferguson, "Nuclear Posture Review," *Nuclear Threat Initiative Issue Brief,* Nuclear Threat Initiative, www.nti.org, August 2002.

64. Thom Shanker and Marc Landler, "Putin's Accusation Draws Cool Riposte from Gates," *International Herald Tribune,* February 11, 2007.

65. Elizabeth Bryant, "Paris Denies Ending Deterrence Strategy," United Press International wire, October 27, 2003.

66. *Nuclear Weapons in Twenty-first Century U.S. National Security: Report by a Joint Working Group of AAAS, the American Physical Society, and the Center for Strategic and International Studies* (Boston: AAAS, December 2008), i.

67. U.S. Department of Defense, "Report of the Secretary of Defense Task Force on DoD Nuclear Weapons Management," September 2008, 3.

68. U.S. Department of the Defense, "Report of The Defense Science Board Task Force on Nuclear Deterrence Skills," September 2008.

69. "Report of the Secretary of Defense Task Force on DoD Nuclear Weapons Management," 1–2. When I arrived at the Naval War College in 1997, the core curriculum contained almost nothing about nuclear strategy. For a brief time the Strategy Department (which is essentially a course in military history and strategic theory) included a section on the Cold War and nuclear weapons, but it was taken out, put back, and taken out again. It was not until 2010 that a specific section on nuclear strategy was added to the National Security Affairs department's curriculum.

70. Among its recommendations, the Science Board asked the Secretary of Defense to probe the nation's war colleges to find out what they were doing to stem the loss of nuclear expertise. The Naval War College was subsequently called and asked that same question about a year later, by which time it had already returned nuclear strategy to its curriculum. The Air Force, for its part, has tried to revitalize a "nuclear weapons school" it established in New Mexico by adding a five-day course called "Nuclear 300," which "explores nuclear deterrence theory and application, nuclear operations policy and strategy, nuclear incident response and nuclear surety and effects"—in five days. See Mark Thompson, "Up in the Mushroom Clouds Somewhere, Curtis LeMay Is Smiling," *Time* online "Battleblog," March 19, 2012.

71. The British "gang of four" was Douglas Hurd, Malcolm Rifkind, David Owen, and George Robertson, who published "Start Worrying and Learn to Ditch the Bomb" in *The Times* (London), June 30, 2008. See also Bruce Blair, Victor Esin, Matthew McKinzie, Valery Yarynich, and Pavel Zolotarev, "Smaller and Safer: A New Plan for Nuclear Postures," *Foreign Affairs* 89, no. 5 (September–October 2010).

72. The best arguments that scientists and antinuclear activists played a critical role in ending the Cold War arms race can be found in Matthew Evangelista's highly influential book, *Unarmed Forces: The Transnational Movement to End the Cold War* (Ithaca, N.Y.: Cornell University Press, 2002). The most comprehensive account of the nuclear arms movement is Lawrence Wittner's magisterial three-volume study, *The Struggle Against the Bomb*, vol. 1, 1993, vol. 2, 1997, and *Toward Nuclear Abolition*, vol. 3, 2003, all from Stanford University Press. Whether the various antinuclear movements were as important as Evangelista and Wittner claim is a reasonable and debatable question. I do not believe these movements were nearly as influential as these studies depict them, but that is a discussion for a different study.

73. Quoted in Drake Bennett, "No Nukes: Once a Quixotic Slogan, the Idea of Actually Dismantling Every Nuclear Weapon Is Attracting Mainstream Policy Thinkers," *Boston Globe*, November 23, 2008.

74. Office of the Press Secretary, White House, "Remarks by President Barack Obama, Hradcany Square, Prague, Czech Republic" (as delivered), April 5, 2009.

75. Jeffrey Lewis, "Forget the Posture Commission, OK?" ArmsControlWonk .com, August 11, 2009.

76. See David E. Sanger and Peter Baker, "Obama Limits When U.S. Would Use Nuclear Arms," *New York Times*, April 5, 2010.

77. The 2010 Posture Review is available at http://www.defense.gov/npr/.

78. Peter Eisler, "U.S. Warhead Disposal in 15-year Backlog," *USA Today*, May 13, 2009.

79. The Obama administration had to sweeten the original $80 billion with $4.1 billion more before the whole business was over and the treaty ratified. See Barron Young Smith, "START to Finish? The Fate of Obama's Nuclear Treaty," *New Republic*, November 13, 2010.

80. See George Bunn, "The Legal Status of U.S. Negative Security Assurances to Non-Nuclear Weapon States," *Nonproliferation Review*, Spring–Summer 1997.

81. R. James Woolsey, "Too Much Mr. Nice Guy," *New York Times* online, May 6, 2010.

82. Quoted in Matt Negrin, "Gates: 'All Options Are on the Table'," Politico.com, April 6, 2010.

83. U.S. Department of Defense, *2010 Nuclear Posture Review Report*, April 2010, viii.

84. *2010 Nuclear Posture Review Report*, x.

85. See, for example, Ruth Conniff, "Obama Shifts Away from Mutually Assured Destruction," *The Progressive*, April 6, 2010.

86. See John Vandiver, "U.S. Missile Defense Plans Likely Topic During Obama, Medvedev Talks," *Stars and Stripes*, May 25, 2011.

87. Stephen Walt, "Nuclear Posture Review (or Nuclear Public Relations?)," *Foreign Policy*, April 6, 2010.

88. Quoted in Jonathan Weisman and Peter Spiegel, "U.S. Keeps First-Strike Strategy," *Wall Street Journal*, April 6, 2010.

89. *2010 Nuclear Posture Review Report*, 16.

90. Scott D. Sagan, "The Case for No First Use," *Survival* 51, no. 3 (2009): 177.

91. *2010 Nuclear Posture Review Report*, 26.

Chapter 3. The Return of Minimum Deterrence

1. The description of the postwar period as "the long peace" was put forward by John Gaddis in 1986. See John Gaddis, "The Long Peace: Elements of Stability in the Postwar International System," *International Security* 10, no. 4 (Spring 1986).

2. McGeorge Bundy, "To Cap the Volcano," *Foreign Affairs* 48, no. 1 (October 1969): 9–10.

3. After the crisis over the Yom Kippur War in 1973, Nixon called Soviet Ambassador Anatoly Dobrynin to Camp David and described the "previous week as just an unpleasant episode in our relations," and asked him to "please inform [Leonid Brezhnev] that as long as I live and hold the office of president I will never allow a real confrontation with the Soviet Union." Quoted in Anatoly Dobrynin, *In Confidence: Moscow's Ambassador to Six Cold War Presidents* (Seattle: University of Washington Press, 2001), 300. For the Brezhnev incident, see David Hoffman, *The Dead Hand* (New York: Doubleday, 2009), 20.

4. Paul H. Nitze, "A Threat Mostly to Ourselves," *New York Times*, October 28, 1999.

5. James Goodby related this story in 2009, and suggests Nitze's advice "went back to his thinking about protracted nuclear war, which had to do with [Nitze's] ideas about how to deter the use of nuclear weapons. But of course deterrence easily blends into the idea of using these weapons in warfighting situations, and that's what we had gotten ourselves into." See James Goodby, "Arms Control Since the Cold War," *Footnotes: The Newsletter of FPRI's Wachman Center* 14, no. 9 (May 2009).

6. In March 2012, the National Security Archive at George Washington University published documents that added more context to a story first related by former CIA chief and later Defense Secretary Robert Gates in 1996 about a series of false alarms issued by NORAD (North American Aerospace Defense Command) in 1979 and 1980—one of which resulted in National Security Advisor Zbigniew Brzezinski being awakened in the middle of the night and told that the United States was under a massive Soviet ICBM attack. This alarmed Soviet leaders so much that Politburo chief Leonid Brezhnev privately reached out to President Jimmy Carter for reassurance that the U.S. command and control system was secure. See "The 3 A.M. Phone Call: False Warnings of Soviet Missile Attacks During 1979–80 Led to Alert Actions for U.S. Strategic Forces," National Security Archive, March 1, 2012 (www.gwu.edu/~ns archiv).

7. Kissinger made the comment during a panel held on the Public Broadcasting System after a showing of the British motion picture *Threads* in March 1985.

8. James Wood Forsyth Jr., B. Chance Saltzman, and Gary Schaub Jr., "Minimum Deterrence and Its Critics," *Strategic Studies Quarterly*, Winter 2010, 3.

9. Jeffrey G. Lewis, "Minimum Deterrence," *Bulletin of the Atomic Scientists*, July–August 2008.

10. A list of these accidents (known as "Broken Arrows" in U.S. military parlance), some of which are not acknowledged by the U.S. government, may be found at Michael Krepon, "Broken Arrows," ArmsControlWonk.com, December 26, 2011.

11. See Lewis's discussion in "Minimum Deterrence."

12. Oskar Morgenstern, *The Question of National Defense* (New York: Random House, 1959), 153. I thank Andrew Ross for pointing out this citation.

13. See Jeffrey Lewis, *The Minimum Means of Reprisal: China's Search for Security in the Nuclear Age* (Cambridge, Mass.: MIT Press, 2007), 4.

14. The idea that arms races might substitute for war was pioneered by Samuel Huntington as early as 1958. See Charles Glaser, "When Are Arms Races Dangerous? Rational Versus Suboptimal Arming," *International Security* 28, no. 4 (Spring 2004).

15. Stephen Walt, "All the Nukes That You Can Use," *Foreign Policy*, foreign policy.com, May 24, 2010.

16. Quoted in Luis Martinez, "Russia, China Major Threats? Intel Director Clapper's Comments Perplex Senators," ABC News online, March 10, 2011.

17. See, for example, Jacob Kipp, "Russia's Military Doctrine: New Dangers Appear," *Eurasia Daily Monitor* 7, no. 35 (February 22, 2010), and Mikhail Tsypkin, "What's New in Russia's New Military Doctrine," *Radio Free Europe/ Radio Liberty Commentary*, February 27, 2010. The actual document, "Voennaia doktrina Rossiiskoi Federatsii," signed February 5, 2010, is available through the Russian President's office at http://news.kremlin.ru/ref_notes/461.

18. See "Lavrov Says RF Sees No Threat in NATO," *Itar-TASS*, July 4, 2011.

19. Mikhail Rostovskii, "Disappointment in Sochi: Why Russia is Failing to Impose Its Will on West Regarding Missile Defense," *Moskovskii Komsomolets*, July 5, 2011, reproduced and translated in *Johnson's Russia List* no. 121, June 8, 2011.

20. "Russia, U.S. Ink Uranium Enrichment Pact for 2013–2022," *RIA-Novosti*, December 21, 2011.

21. U.S. Department of Defense, "Sustaining U.S. Global Leadership: Priorities for Twenty-First Century Defense," January 2012.

22. A panel of experts, for example, criticized the Obama administration for accepting New START's terms. While some were recent members of the Bush 43 administration, the panel's chair was James Schlesinger—the former Secretary of Defense who tried to find a way out of the all-or-nothing SIOP of the 1970s—who said that he could "support ratification only if the Senate provides for new U.S. weapons not prohibited by the treaty." Barry Schweid, "Panel Faults Obama on Arms Reduction Treaty," Associated Press, May 5, 2010.

23. Bruce Blair, Victor Esin, Matthew McKinzie, Valery Yarynich, and Pavel Zolotarev, "Smaller and Safer: A New Plan for Nuclear Postures," *Foreign Affairs* 89, no. 5 (September–October 2010): 20.

24. Hans M. Kristensen, Robert S. Norris, and Ivan Oelrich, *From Counterforce to Minimal Deterrence: A New Nuclear Policy on the Path Toward Eliminating Nuclear Weapons*, Natural Resources Defense Council and Federation of American Scientists Occasional Paper No. 7, April 2009, p. 15.

25. Blair et al., "Smaller and Safer," 20.

26. George Lee Butler, speech at the University of Pittsburgh, May 13, 1999, archived at www.wagingpeace.org.

27. Until the mid-1960s, the U.S. war plan called for an all-out attack on the USSR and China if the president were killed or could not be found during an attack on the United States, even if the strike turned out to be an accident. Lyndon Johnson, with the support of the Joint Chiefs, changed the policy in 1968. See William Burr, "U.S. Had Plans for 'Full Nuclear Response' in Event President Killed or Disappeared During an Attack on the United States," National Security Archive online, National Security Archive Electronic Briefing Book No. 406, December 12, 2012, www.gwu.edu/nukevault.

28. Quoted in John Newhouse, *War and Peace in the Nuclear* Age (New York: Random House, 1988), 120.

29. Rear Admiral Roy M. Johnson, "Adaptation of the National Military Posture to the Era of Nuclear Parity; a Suggested Navy Position," memo to Distribution List, December 3, 1957, available at the National Security Archive, www.gwu.edu/~ns archiv/.

30. The precision of the number was a function of how many weapons were dispersed among how many weapons systems, not the number of enemy targets.

31. Quoted in David Alan Rosenberg, "U.S. Nuclear War Planning, 1945–1960," in Desmond Ball and Jeffrey Richelson, eds., *Strategic Nuclear Targeting* (Ithaca, N.Y.: Cornell University Press, 1986), 51.

32. See Stephen Younger, *The Bomb: A New History* (New York: Harper Collins, 2009), 212, and U.S. Senate, Committee on Governmental Affairs, Subcommittee on International Security, Proliferation, and Federal Services, "Hearing on The Future Of Nuclear Deterrence," February 12, 1997.

33. C. A. Haskins, National Security Council staff, "Polaris," February 10, 1960, available at the National Security Archive, www.gwu.edu/~nsarchiv/.

34. Quoted in Fred Kaplan, *The Wizards of Armageddon* (Stanford, Calif.: Stanford University Press, 1983), 259–60.

35. For more on this period, see David Alan Rosenberg, "The Origins of Overkill: Nuclear Weapons and American Strategy, 1945–1960," *International Security* 7, no. 4 (Spring 1983).

36. "They're Smart and Ruthless . . . It's the Same Way as the Communists; It's Exactly the Same Techniques," "Admiral Burke's Conversation with Secretary Franke, August 12, 1960," available at the National Security Archive, http://www.gwu.edu/~nsarchiv.

37. Memorandum to President Kennedy from Secretary of Defense Robert S. Mc-Namara, "Recommended Long Range Nuclear Delivery Forces, 1963–67," September 23, 1961, available at the National Security Archive, http://www.gwu.edu/~nsarchiv/.

38. Memorandum from Secretary of Defense McNamara to President Johnson, "Recommended FY 1966–1970 Programs for Strategic Offensive Forces, Continental Air and Missile Defense Forces, and Civil Defense," December 3, 1964, available at the National Security Archive, http://www.gwu.edu/~nsarchiv/.

39. Desmond Ball, "The Development of the SIOP, 1960–1983," in Ball and Richelson, eds., *Strategic Nuclear Targeting,* 61.

40. Kristensen et al., *From Counterforce to Minimal Deterrence,* 30.

41. I discuss the Soviet debate over World War II and its applicability to the nuclear age in more detail in Thomas Nichols, *The Sacred Cause: Civil-Military Conflict over Soviet National Security, 1917–1992* (Ithaca, N.Y.: Cornell University Press, 1993), chapter 3.

42. Younger, *The Bomb,* 213.

43. Kenneth Waltz and Scott Sagan have debated this issue for a decade with considerable wisdom and persuasiveness on both sides. See Scott Sagan and Kenneth Waltz, *The Spread of Nuclear Weapons: A Debate Renewed* (New York: Norton, 2003).

44. "It would be best," Mearsheimer wrote, "if proliferation were extended to Germany but not beyond." John Mearsheimer, "Back to the Future: Instability in Europe After the Cold War," *International Security* 15, no. 1 (Summer 1990): 38.

45. For more on U.S. thinking about attacking the Soviet arsenal, see Thomas Nichols, *Eve of Destruction: The Coming Age of Preventive War* (Philadelphia: University of Pennsylvania Press, 2008), 19–21. For an account of the debate over the Chinese program, see William Burr and Jeffrey Richelson, "Whether to 'Strangle the Baby in the Cradle'," *International Security* 25, no. 3 (Winter 2000–2001).

46. See Nichols, *Eve of Destruction,* chapter 4.

47. Bruce Russett's examination of the position of the Catholic bishops in 1984 is a good example of the way the moral dilemmas of targeting were discussed during the Cold War. See Bruce Russett, "Ethical Dilemmas of Nuclear Deterrence," *International Security* 8, no. 4 (Spring 1984).

48. Michael Walzer, *Just and Unjust Wars,* 3rd ed. (New York: Basic Books, 2000), 251–62.

49. Quoted in John Barry and Even Thomas, "Dropping the Bomb," *Newsweek,* June 24, 2001, archived online at www.thedailybeast.com/newsweek/2001/06/24/dropping-the-bomb.html.

50. See Robert Jervis, Richard Ned Lebow, and Janice Gross Stein, eds., *Psychology and Deterrence* (Baltimore: Johns Hopkins University Press, 1989).

51. Vladimir Isachenkov, "Nikolai Makarov, Russia Military Chief, Sees Rising Risk of Nuclear Conflicts," Associated Press, November 17, 2011.

52. Even the former Chief of Staff of the Russian Strategic Rocket Forces admitted in 2009 that "the Russian military is not going to abandon its reliance on nuclear

weapons to ensure national security . . . when the Russian general purpose forces are significantly less powerful than the armed forces of the countries competing with Russia on the world stage." Viktor Esin, "Possible Attributes of a New Russian-American Treaty on Strategic Offensive Weapons: The View from Russia," Carnegie Council on Ethic and International Affairs, Global Engagement program series, July 21, 2009.

53. Patrick Tyler, "As China Threatens Taiwan, It Makes Sure U.S. Listens," *New York Times*, January 24, 1996, A3.

54. Thomas Fingar, "How China Views U.S. Nuclear Policy," *Bulletin of the Atomic Scientists,* May 20, 2011.

55. Michael Howard, "On Fighting a Nuclear War," *International Security* 5, no. 4 (Spring 1981): 9.

56. Kristensen et al., *From Counterforce to Minimal Deterrence*, 41.

57. See Peter Carlson, "Raiding the Icebox," *Washington Post*, December 30, 2005. There was a variety of other so-called "color" plans, including "Green" against Mexico and "Orange" for Japan.

58. See George Kennan, *The Nuclear Delusion* (New York: Pantheon, 1982).

59. I am grateful to Paul Smith for his comments on this question.

60. Hans Kristensen, Robert Norris, and Matthew McKinzie, *Chinese Nuclear Forces and U.S. War Planning* (Washington, D.C.: Federation of American Scientists, 2006), 180–86.

61. Kristensen et al., *Chinese Nuclear Forces*, 190.

62. Keir A. Lieber and Daryl G. Press, "The End of MAD? The Nuclear Dimension of U.S. Primacy," *International Security* 30, no. 4 (Spring 2006): 9.

63. Keir A. Lieber and Daryl G. Press, "The Nukes We Need," *Foreign Affairs* 88, no. 2 (November–December 2009): 50.

64. See Ivan Safranchuk, "Beyond MAD," *China Security*, Autumn 2006.

65. Tom Sauer, "Correspondence: The Short Shadow of U.S. Primacy?" *International Security* 31, no. 3 (Winter 2006–7): 179.

66. James Wirtz, "Correspondence: The Short Shadow of U.S. Primacy?" 183.

67. Keir A. Lieber and Daryl G. Press, "Correspondence: The Short Shadow of U.S. Primacy?" 190.

68. Scholars Robert Jervis and John Mueller conducted a debate on this issue as the Cold War was winding down more than twenty years ago. Jervis argued that World War III had not taken place (or at least not *yet*) because policymakers found the prospect of nuclear conflict uniquely frightening, while Mueller countered that the memory of World War II was just as likely to have deterred Soviet and American leaders as the prospect of World War III, a comparison that Jervis (rightly in my view) saw as unacceptably flawed. See John Mueller, "The Essential Irrelevance of Nuclear Weapons: Stability in the Postwar World," *International Security* 13, no. 2 (Autumn 1988), and Robert Jervis, "The Political Effects of Nuclear Weapons: A Comment," *International Security* 13, no. 2 (Autumn 1988).

69. Lieber and Press, "The Nukes We Need," 47.

70. Lieber and Press, "The Nukes We Need," 50.

71. See Keir Lieber and Daryl Press, "Superiority Complex," *Atlantic Online*, July–August 2007.

72. The U.S. Congress's Office of Technology Assessment study on nuclear war warned in a famous study more than thirty years ago that it would be virtually impossible to make such calculations, a conclusion used in many studies since. See U.S. Congress, Office of Technology Assessment, *The Effects of Nuclear War* (Washington, D.C.: Government Printing Office, 1979), and Michael Riordan, *The Day After Midnight* (Cheshire, Conn.: Cheshire Books, 1982).

73. Recriminations over Hurricane Katrina have since been replaced with bickering over the reconstruction required by Hurricane Sandy, which struck the mid-Atlantic states in 2012. Nerves are raw over both disasters: when Senate Majority Leader Harry Reid (D-NV) claimed that Sandy was a far worse catastrophe than Katrina, Senator David Vitter (R-LA) took to Twitter to call Reid an "idiot." Reid later apologized and said he "misspoke." See Rachel Weiner, "Vitter: Reid 'an Idiot' for Sandy Comments," *Washington Post* Politics blog online, January 7, 2013.

74. Jan Lodal, "The Counterforce Fantasy," *Foreign Affairs* 89(2), March–April 2010, 146. Lodal was Kissinger's assistant when the JCS was planning "limited" nuclear strikes with hundreds of weapons. See Kaplan, *The Wizards of Armageddon,* 371.

75. Oliver Bloom, "Defence Secretary Liam Fox Offers New Thoughts on Trident Replacement," Center for Strategic and International Studies, July 15, 2010, www.csis.org.

76. Bruno Tertrais, "The Last to Disarm? The Future of France's Nuclear Weapons," *Nonproliferation Review* 14, no. 2 (July 2007): 251.

77. See Lewis, *The Minimum Means of Reprisal.*

78. Rajat Pandit, "Nuclear Weapons Only for Strategic Deterrence: Army Chief," *Economic Times of India,* January 16, 2012.

79. Among the many people who capably delegimitized the antinuclear movement, few had more impact than an Australian pediatrician named Helen Caldicott. During the 1980s, she made bizarre statements about how, as a doctor, she could negotiate better than U.S. diplomats with Soviet leaders, and how reelecting President Reagan would make nuclear war a "mathematical certainty." She also wrote books such as her 1985 opus *Missile Envy*, whose explanation of the Cold War nuclear arms race should be evident from its unfortunate title. When Reagan agreed to slash an entire class of nuclear weapons from Europe in 1987, Caldicott (at least according to some who knew her) was deeply confounded, and eventually she went home to Australia. The damage she did to serious notions of nuclear disarmament, however, lingered for some time.

80. How this group of statesmen came together on the issue of nuclear disarmament is a fascinating story in itself. See Philip Taubman, *The Partnership: Five Cold Warriors and Their Quest to Ban the Bomb* (New York: Harper, 2011).

81. See, for example, Gerson, "No First Use: The Next Step for U.S. Nuclear Policy," *International Security* 35, no. 2 (Fall 2010): 33.

82. See Scott D. Sagan, "The Case for No First Use," *Survival* 51, no. 3 (2009).

83. Morton Halperin, Bruno Tertrais, Keith Payne, K. Subrahmanyam, and Scott Sagan, "Forum: The Case for No First Use: An Exchange," *Survival* 51, no. 5 (April–May 2010): 22–25.

84. For a detailed discussion of de-alerting, see Bruce Blair, Victor Esin, Matthew McKinzie, Valery Yarynich, and Pavel Zolotarev, "Smaller and Safer: A New Plan For Nuclear Postures," *Foreign Affairs* 89, no. 5 (September–October 2010).

85. Kristensen et al., *From Counterforce to Minimal Deterrence*, 31.

86. Kristensen et al., *From Counterforce to Minimal Deterrence*, 22.

87. Kristensen et al., *From Counterforce to Minimal Deterrence*, 39.

88. Quoted in Peter Baker, "Arms Control May Be Different Things on Paper and on the Ground," *New York Times*, March 31, 2010.

89. Joan Johnson-Freese and I have argued that this unilateral approach could be applied to a number of international agreements where the Americans are ready to move ahead but where progress is hindered by endless legal and political barriers even among states with whom Washington is in agreement. The United States should take a page from the Nike Corporation's popular slogan and "just do it." See Joan Johnson Freese and Thomas Nichols, "The Nike Doctrine: A New American Security Policy," AOL Defense, October 20, 2011.

90. See Baker, "Arms Control May Be Different Things on Paper and on the Ground."

91. See James Wood Forsyth Jr., B. Chance Saltzman, and Gary Schaub Jr., "Remembrance of Things Past: The Enduring Value of Nuclear Weapons," *Strategic Studies Quarterly* 4, no. 1 (Spring 2010).

92. Gary Schaub Jr., and James Forsyth Jr., "An Arsenal We Can All Live With," *New York Times* online, May 23, 2010.

93. Forsyth et al., "Remembrance of Things Past," 5–7.

94. Kristensen et al., *From Counterforce to Minimal Deterrence*, 44.

95. James Goodby, "Arms Control Since the Cold War," Wachman Center, Foreign Policy Research Institute newsletter online 14, no. 9 (May 2009).

96. "Scrap Nuclear Arsenal, General Says: Military: Air Force Officer's Comments Run Counter to the Clinton Administration View that the Stockpile Can Be Reduced, But Not Eliminated," *Los Angeles Times* online, July 17, 1994.

97. Quoted in Bennet, "No Nukes."

98. Elbridge Colby and Paul Lettow, "In Defense of the Triad," *Weekly Standard*, October 28, 2011.

99. Younger, *The Bomb*, 217.

100. Hans Kristensen estimated the number of remaining weapons in Europe at 180 in 2012. See Hans Kristensen, "Non-Strategic Nuclear Weapons," Federation of American Scientists Special Report No. 3, May 2012.

101. Tom Sauer, "NATO's Nuclear Policy Review: Saying Goodbye to Tactical Nukes," *World Politics Review*, June 9, 2011.

102. See, for example, Pavel Felgenhauer, "Russian Military Weakness Increases Importance of Strategic Nuclear Forces," *Eurasia Daily Monitor* 6, no. 112 (June 11, 2009), and Pavel Felgenhauer, "Military Doctrine Consolidates Xenophobia of the Russian Elites," *Eurasian Daily Monitor* 7, no. 28 (February 10, 2010), both at www.jamestown.org.

103. See Tom Sauer and Bob van der Zwaan, "U.S. Tactical Nuclear Weapons in Europe After NATO's Lisbon Summit: Why Their Withdrawal Is Desirable and Feasible," Belfer Center Discussion Paper, No. 2011–05, Harvard Kennedy School, May 2011; Steve Andreasen and Isabelle Williams, *Reducing Nuclear Risks in Europe: A Framework for Action*, Nuclear Threat Initiative, November 2011.

104. Schaub et al., "Minimum Deterrence and Its Critics," 8.

105. My Naval War College colleague Steven Ross and I objected to this development as it was taking place. See Thomas Nichols and Steven Ross, "Don't Use NATO to Fence Russia In," *Boston Globe*, December 19, 1997.

106. See Ralph A. Cossa and Brad Glosserman, "Japan and the New U.S. Nuclear Posture," *Nonproliferation Review* 18, no. 1 (March 2011): 141.

107. Clark Murdock, "The Department of Defense and the Nuclear Mission in the Twenty-first Century," Center for Strategic and International Studies, March 2008, 17; Evan Ramstad, "U.S. Plans No Nuclear Weapons in South Korea," *Wall Street Journal*, March 2, 2011.

108. Bruce W. Bennett, *Uncertainties in the North Korean Nuclear Threat* (Santa Monica, Calif.: RAND Corporation, 2010), 32.

109. "Hillary Strangelove," *Boston Globe*, April 27, 2008.

110. Matthew Lee, "Hillary Clinton's 'Defense Umbrella' Remarks Echo Her Campaign and Washington Think Tanks," Associated Press, July 25, 2009.

111. See the comments by Polish officials cited in John Warden, "Under the New Missile Defense Plan There Are Still Options for Assurance," Center for Strategic and International Studies, "Warden's Blog," www.csis.org, September 2009.

112. Tom Sauer lays out these competing arguments in much greater detail in *Eliminating Nuclear Weapons: The Role of Missile Defense* (New York: Columbia University Press, 2011).

113. See The White House, "Fact Sheet on U.S. Missile Defense Policy: A 'Phased, Adaptive Approach' for Missile Defense in Europe," September 17, 2009.

114. See Frederik Dahl, "Missile Shield May Spark China Nuclear Upgrade: Officer," Reuters online, July 18, 2012. Of course, the Chinese first claimed the need for better ICBMs years ago: they unveiled the long-range DF-31 in 1999 and fielded the first brigade of them in 2003. Thus, China has always "needed" to pursue post–Cold War ICBM modernization, whether the U.S. administration in power is headed by Bill Clinton, George Bush, or Barack Obama. See Lyle Goldstein, ed., *China's Nuclear Force Modernization*, Naval War College Newport Papers No. 22, 2005, 2–3.

115. See "Russia Says Destroyed 9 ICBMs in 2009 Under START 1 Arms Pact," *RIA/Novosti*, December 16, 2009; in 2010, top Russian defense thinker Sergei Rogov admitted that there was "no need to panic" over NATO missile defenses, not least because Russia had endorsed similar defenses in the past. See Pavel Felgenhauer, "Moscow Finds U.S. Non-Strategic BMD Plans Threatening," *Eurasia Daily Monitor* 7, no. 38 (February 25, 2010.)

116. See, for example, Martha Raddatz, "U.S. Ready to Respond to N. Korea Missile," ABC News online, February 26, 2009.

117. Max Boot, "Reagan Vindicated: Missile Defense Works," *Commentary* online, November 18, 2012.

118. William J. Broad, "Weapons Experts Raise Doubts About Israel's Antimissile System," *New York Times*, March 20, 2013.

119. David Talbot, "Why Israel's 'Iron Dome' Missile-Defense System Actually Works," *MIT Technology Review* online, November 26, 2012. These numbers are from Ted Postal of MIT, a dedicated missile defense critic whose opposition to missile defenses is, to say the least, extreme. But Postal's eccentricities have nothing to do with whether his numbers are correct, or whether stopping a rocket between Gaza and Tel Aviv is the same problem as stopping a space-faring nuclear warhead traveling fourteen times faster.

120. Inbal Orpaz, "How Does the Iron Dome Work?" *Haaretz* online, November 19, 2012.

121. Cirincione made the comment on Twitter on November 26, 2012.

Chapter 4. Small States and Nuclear War

1. Jim Gomez, "North Korea Threatens 'Nuclear Deterrence' over Drills," Associated Press, July 23, 2010.

2. Choe Sang-Hun and David E. Sanger, "North Koreans Launch Rocket in Defiant Act," *New York Times* online, December 11, 2012.

3. Ju-min Park and Choonsik Yoo, "North Korea to Target U.S. with Nuclear, Rocket Tests," Reuters online, January 24, 2013.

4. Lake listed five major outlaws: North Korea, Iran, Iraq, Cuba, and Libya. See Anthony Lake, "Confronting Backlash States," *Foreign Affairs* 73, no. 2 (March–April 1994): 45.

5. On the erosion of deterrence, see Richard Betts, "Suicide from Fear of Death," *Foreign Affairs* (January–February 2003), and Thomas Nichols, *Eve of Destruction* (Philadelphia: University of Pennsylvania Press, 2008), 56–71.

6. The International Institute of Strategic Studies believed as of 2010 that Iran could marry a nuclear bomb to a long-range missile within 24 months of making a decision to go forward; U.S. intelligence estimates were a bit more cautious. Damien McElroy, "Iran Could Fire Nuclear Missile Within Two Years, Say Think Tank," *Daily Telegraph*, May 10, 2010. For the U.S. estimate, see United States Senate, Committee

on Armed Services, "Hearing to Receive Testimony on U.S. Policy Towards the Islamic Republic of Iran," Washington, April 14, 2010.

7. Various reports since the 2007 attack claim the bombing was code-named "Operation Orchard" by the Israelis, with theories ranging from the possibility that Syria was working with the North Koreans to an Israeli "dry-run" for a later Iranian operation. See Erich Follath and Holger Stark, "The Story of 'Operation Orchard': How Israel Destroyed Syria's Al Kibar Nuclear Reactor," *Der Spiegel Online International*, November 2, 2009, and Bret Stephens, "Osirak II?" *Wall Street Journal*, September 18, 2007.

8. Edith Lederer, "UN Experts Say North Korea Is Exporting Nuke Technology," Associated Press, May 28, 2008.

9. Henry Kissinger, "The Rules on Preventive Force," *Washington Post*, April 9, 2006, B7.

10. Rupert Smith, *The Utility of Force: The Art of War in the Modern World* (London: Penguin, 2005), 1.

11. Richard K. Betts, "What Will It Take to Deter the United States?" *Parameters* 25, no. 4 (Winter 1995–96): 72.

12. George Quester, "The Response to Renegade Use of Weapons of Mass Destruction," in Victor Utgoff, ed., *The Coming Crisis: Nuclear Proliferation, U.S. Interests, and World Order* (Cambridge, Mass.: MIT Press, 2000), 241, 244. See also George Quester, *Nuclear First Strike: Consequences of a Broken Taboo* (Baltimore: Johns Hopkins University Press, 2006), 101.

13. Quester, "The Response to Renegade Use," 238–39.

14. See Stephen Krasner, "The Day After," *Foreign Policy*, January–February 2005, 68–69.

15. Stephen Younger, *The Bomb: A New History* (New York: Harper Collins, 2009), 208.

16. U.S. Department of Defense, "Information Paper: Iraq's Scud Ballistic Missiles," July 25, 2000.

17. James Acton, "Managing Vulnerability," *Foreign Affairs* 89, no. 2 (March–April 2010): 147.

18. George Lee Butler, "Speech at the University of Pittsburgh," May 13, 1999, available at www.wagingpeace.org.

19. Quoted in Scott D. Sagan, "The Commitment Trap: Why the United States Should Not Use Nuclear Threats to Deter Biological and Chemical Weapons Attacks," *International Security* 24, no. 4 (Spring 2000): 92.

20. Quoted in Murdock, *The Department of Defense and the Nuclear Mission*, 18.

21. See Butler, "Speech at the University of Pittsburgh," and Keith Payne's comments and Sagan's response in Halperin et al., "Forum," 5.

22. Former G. W. Bush administration official Michael Anton claims that nuclear threats kept Saddam Hussein from using WMD in the 1991 Gulf War, but Sagan

disputes this specific claim, and the only person who can definitively answer the question – Saddam Hussein – is dead. See Michael Anton, "Our Nuclear Posture," *Weekly Standard*, April 19, 2010.

23. Quoted in Derek Smith, *Deterring America: Rogue States and the Proliferation of Weapons of Mass Destruction* (Cambridge: Cambridge University Press, 2006), 110.

24. Robert Wampler, "How Do You Solve a Problem like Korea? New Archive Document Collection Sheds Light on Nixon's Frustrating Search for Military Options," National Security Archive Electronic Briefing Book No. 322, June 23, 2010, available at the National Security Archive, www.gwu.nsa/~nsarchiv/.

25. Quoted in Wampler, "How Do You Solve a Problem like Korea?"

26. This and following data from Wampler, "How Do You Solve a Problem like Korea?"

27. "Clinton's Warning Irks North Korea," *New York Times*, July 13, 1993.

28. McCain made the remark on ABC's *This Week*; Chris Suellentrop quoted it years later in his December 19, 2006, "Opinionator" blog in the *New York Times* online.

29. Quoted in Douglas Jehl, "The Struggle for Iraq: Policy; Wary Powell Said to Have Warned Bush on War," *New York Times* online, April 17, 2004.

30. For a study of nuclear effects on urban areas, see William Bell and Cham Dallas, "Vulnerability of Populations and the Urban Health Care Systems to Nuclear Weapon Attack—Examples from Four American Cities," *International Journal of Health Geographics*, February 28, 2007.

31. Stephen Flynn, "Nightmare in a Nightclub: The Scary Truth Behind a Rhode Island Tragedy," *U.S. News and World Report*, February 11, 2007.

32. See O. B. Toon et al., "Atmospheric Effects and Societal Consequences of Regional Scale Nuclear Conflicts and Acts of Individual Nuclear Terrorism," *Atmospheric Chemistry and Physics*, April 2007, and Alan Robock and Owen Brian Toon, "South Asian Threat? Local Nuclear War = Global Suffering," *Scientific American*, January 2009.

33. Bruce W. Bennett, *Uncertainties in the North Korean Nuclear Threat* (Santa Monica, Calif.: RAND Corporation, 2010), 53–54.

34. Martin Fackler, "Nuclear Crisis Set Off Fears Over Tokyo, Report Says," *New York Times*, February 27, 2012.

35. Frank N. von Hippel, "The Radiological and Psychological Consequences of the Fukushima Daiichi Accident," *Bulletin of the Atomic Scientists* 67, no. 5 (September–October 2011): 28.

36. William J. Broad, "Scientists Project Path of Radiation Plume," *New York Times*, March 16, 2011.

37. Jon Rabiroff, "Military Monitors Radiation as Troops Deliver Humanitarian Aid," *Stars and Stripes*, March 16, 2011.

38. *Fox News Sunday* broadcast, Fox television network, March 13, 2011.

39. Molly Hennessy-Fiske, "Japan Radiation Risk to California Is Downplayed," *Los Angeles Times* online, March 16, 2011.

40. Mark Duell, "'It's Getting like 9/11': Rising Fear over Radiation Threat as Panicked Americans Buy More Gas Masks, Tablets and even Pet Shelters," *Daily Mail*, March 17, 2011.

41. Hiroko Tabuchi, "Radioactivity in Japan Rice Raises Worries," *New York Times*, September 24, 2011; "Radioactive Beef Found in Japan," United Press International, July 10, 2011; Naoko Fujimura and Chris Cooper, "Mushrooms Join Growing List of Radioactive Threats to Japan's Food Chain," Bloomberg News, August 14, 2011.

42. "Thousands Protest Against Nuclear Power in Japan," *Agence France Presse*, January 14, 2012.

43. "No Big Fukushima Health Impact Seen: U.N. Body Chairman," Reuters, January 31, 2012.

44. Victoria Kim, "Radioactive Particles from Japan Detected in California Kelp," *Los Angeles Times* online, April 9, 2012.

45. The UN found that the collective "thyroid dose" of radioactive contaminants in the Japanese population was about three percent of the dose received by the victims of Chernobyl and would cause no appreciable increase in cancer. "Post-Fukushima Collective Thyroid Dose About 3.3% the Dose from Chernobyl," *Asahi Shimbun* online, May 27, 2013.

46. For a more detailed discussion of the physical effects of earth-penetrating weapons, see Bryan L. Fearey, Paul C. White, John St. Ledger, and John D. Immele, "An Analysis of Reduced Collateral Damage Nuclear Weapons," *Comparative Strategy* 22, October 2003.

47. Thomas W. Dowler and Joseph S. Howard II, "Countering the Threat of the Well-Armed Tyrant: A Modest Proposal for Small Nuclear Weapons," *Strategic Review*, Fall 1991, 39.

48. Elbridge A. Colby, "Why We Should Study Developing Nuclear Earth Penetrators—And Why They Are Actually Stabilizing," *Foreign Policy Research Institute E-Notes*, www.fpri.com, May 2011.

49. Gerson also notes that a weapon even thirty times smaller, at ten kilotons, could still cause 100,000 casualties in an urban area, "and detonations in less populated areas could still cause substantial casualties if a high-yield weapon is used in unfavorable winds." Michael Gerson, "No First Use: The Next Step for U.S. Nuclear Policy," *International Security* 35, no. 2 (Fall 2010): 31.

50. Smith, *Deterring America*, 109.

51. I personally witnessed this phenomenon repeatedly as a senior personal aide to a U.S. senator during the 1991 Gulf War, when even senators with military experience would lose their patience (and sometimes their tempers) as briefings devolved into highly technical matters. Even the most intellectually capable political leaders can absorb only so much detail at any given moment, especially during a war.

52. For a good synopsis of this problem, see Eric Mlyn, "U.S. Policy and the End of the Cold War," in T. V. Paul, Richard J. Harknett, and James J. Wirtz, eds., *The Absolute Weapon Revisited: Nuclear Arms and the Emerging International Order* (Ann Arbor: University of Michigan Press, 1989), 191.

53. Joseph Nye, *Nuclear Ethics* (New York: Free Press, 1986), 104–5.

54. Bennett, *Uncertainties in the North Korean Nuclear Threat*, 32.

55. Quoted in Michael Walzer, *Just and Unjust Wars*, 3rd ed. (New York: Basic Books, 1977), 275.

56. Russell Hardin and John Mearsheimer, "Introduction," *Ethics* 95, April 1985, 414.

57. Newman is an analyst at the Nuclear Threat Initiative in Washington, D.C. I am grateful to him for his comments on this section.

58. This and all references to Dunlap are from Charles J. Dunlap Jr., "How We Lost the High-Tech War of 2007," *Weekly Standard,* January 29, 1996.

59. Scholar Joan Hoff, for example, argued in 2008 that Truman knew that invading Japan would be less costly that estimated—only 50,000 casualties, perhaps—and that to defend the bombing of Japan is "unsophisticated." See Joan Hoff, *A Faustian Foreign Policy from Woodrow Wilson to George W. Bush: Dreams of Perfectibility* (New York: Cambridge University Press, 2008), 97, and my discussion in my review of the book on H-NET online, in H-Diplo Roundtable Review IX (23), 2008.

60. The poll was taken by the Rasmussen organization. Rasmussen Reports, "59% Say A-Bombing of Hiroshima, Nagasaki Was a Good Decision," August 10, 2010, http://www.rasmussenreports.com/.

61. Butler, speech at the University of Pittsburgh.

62. See, for example, James Carroll, "Retirement Syndrome," *Boston Globe*, February 5, 2007.

63. Elaine Grossman, "A Former Nuclear Commander Not Wild About Nukes," *Global Security Newswire*, May 28, 2008.

64. Elaine M. Grossman, "Senior U.S. General Sees High Nuclear Threshold," *Global Security Newswire*, October 22, 2007.

65. Wade Boese and Miles A. Pomper, "Strategic Decisions: An Interview with STRATCOM Commander General James E. Cartwright," *Arms Control Today*, June 2006.

66. John Diamond, "Air Force General Calls for End to Atomic Arms," *Boston Globe*, July 16, 1994, A3. See also Steven Watkins, "Let's 'Go to Zero': How a General Developed His Anti-Nuclear Philosophy," *Air Force Times* 54, no. 6 (August 1, 1994).

67. Clark Murdock, *The Department of Defense and the Nuclear Mission in the Twenty-first Century* (Washington, D.C.: Center for Strategic and International Studies, March 2008), 18.

68. This, as journalist Ron Suskind wrote in a 2006 book, is the "one percent doctrine" of U.S. security, in which the very smallest chance of disaster is too much.

Ron Suskind, *The One Percent Doctrine: Deep Inside America's Pursuit of Its Enemies Since 9/11* (New York: Simon and Schuster, 2006).

69. Grossman, "A Former Nuclear Commander Not Wild About Nukes."

70. Mark McDonald, "North Korea Suggests Libya Should Have Kept Nuclear Program," *New York Times*, March 24, 2011.

71. Gerard Couzens, "Head of UN Calls on Britain and Argentina to Avoid Escalation of Row over Falklands as Buenos Aires Says Dispute Has Turned 'Nuclear,'" *Daily Mail* online, February 10, 2012.

72. This view has had prominent advocates in the United States, including retired U.S. Congressman and former presidential candidate Ron Paul, who shrugged off Iran's nuclear program by arguing that if he were Iran, living so close to a nuclear Israel, he would want a nuclear bomb too. He added that sanctions against Iran were "just going to cause more trouble." Paul West, "Ron Paul: Sanctions Against Iran Are 'Acts of War'," *Los Angeles Times* online, December 29, 2011.

73. Quoted in Morton Halperin, Bruno Tertrais, Keith Payne, K. Subrahmanyam, and Scott Sagan, "Forum: The Case for No First Use: An Exchange," *Survival* 51, no. 5 (April–May 2010): 25.

74. See T. V. Paul, *The Tradition of Non-Use of Nuclear Weapons* (Stanford, Calif.: Stanford University Press, 2009).

75. U.S. Department of Defense, *2010 Nuclear Posture Review Report*, April 2010, viii.

76. See Qiang Zhai, *China and the Vietnam Wars, 1950–1975* (Chapel Hill: University of North Carolina Press, 2000), 156.

77. Bennett, *Uncertainties in the North Korean Nuclear Threat*, 40.

78. Future CIA Director John Deutch argued in 1992 for a multilateral policy that would simply state that almost any use of a nuclear weapon by anyone, anywhere, "would be considered a casus belli," and while he did not go so far as to argue for regime change as a policy, he advocated that violators of the Nuclear Non-Proliferation Treaty should face not only sanctions but also "the possibility of multilateral, and in exceptional cases, unilateral military action." John M. Deutch, "The New Nuclear Threat," *Foreign Affairs* 71, no. 4 (Fall 1992): 133.

79. See James Mann, *Rise of the Vulcans: The History of Bush's War Cabinet* (New York: Viking, 2004), 304–5.

80. "Ratko Mladic Family Files Request for Him to Be Declared Dead," Reuters, June 16, 2010.

81. The comment was made by Philippe Errera, then the deputy director for disarmament and nuclear nonproliferation at the Quai d'Orsay. Interview with Philippe Errera, Paris, October 20, 2006.

82. See Nichols, *Eve of Destruction*, 20–24.

83. As British scholar Lord Robert Skidelsky has noted, rogue states by their nature "produce a demand for preventive war." Robert Skidelsky, "The Just War Tradition," *Prospect*, December 2004, 31.

84. Ashton Carter and William Perry, "If Necessary, Strike and Destroy," *Washington Post*, June 22, 2006, A29.

85. Mark Landler and David E. Sanger, "U.S. and Israel Split on Speed of Iran Threat," *New York Times*, February 8, 2012.

86. See Matthew Kroenig, "Time to Attack Iran: Why a Strike Is the Least Bad Option," *Foreign Affairs* 91, no. 1 (January–February 2012); Stephen Walt, "The Worst Case for War with Iran," *Foreignpolicy.com*, December 21, 2011, and Colin Kahl, "Not Time to Attack Iran," *Foreign Affairs*, January 17, 2012.

87. Jonathan Easely, "Hill Poll: Voters Willing to See U.S. Attack Iran over Nuclear Weapons," *The Hill*, February 6, 2012.

88. See, for example, Helene Cooper, " 'Loose Talk of War' Only Helps Iran, President Says," *New York Times*, March 4, 2012. In 2013, Congressman Mo Brooks (R-AL) tried to press Undersecretary of State Wendy Sherman for a more specific commitment to an attack on Iran, and decided that her adherence to ambiguity meant—as he announced in a press release—that President Obama had "left the door open" to an invasion of Iran or a nuclear attack on Iran's nuclear infrastructure. See Tom Nichols, "Iran and the Dangers of Ambiguity," *The War Room* blog, www.tomnichols.net/blog, May 21, 2013.

Conclusion

1. Shultz recalls his feelings at the time in a 2010 documentary produced by the Nuclear Security Project called *The Tipping Point*. Another young infantryman awaiting the same orders, as I note in the preface, was Nick J. Nichols, who fifteen years later would become my father.

2. As Jeffrey Lewis of the blog *ArmsControlWonk* wryly noted in a December 27, 2012, tweet, the President can use secret drone strikes at will, but nuclear weapons cuts still require an all-out fight in the Senate? See John Yoo, and John R. Bolton, "The Senate Should Block an End Run on Nuclear Arms: President Obama Needs Congressional Approval If He Wishes to Further Diminish America's Arsenal," *Wall Street Journal* online, December 27, 2012.

3. Mitt Romney, "Obama's Worst Foreign Policy Mistake," *Washington Post* online, July 6, 2010.

4. See, for example, the online *Newsletter of the Arms Control Association* 1 (31), "New START: A Missile-Defense-Friendly Treaty," November 16, 2010.

5. Robert Jervis, "Mutual Assured Destruction," *Foreign Policy* 133 (November–December 2002): 41.

6. Quoted in Desmond Ball and Jeffrey Richelson, eds., *Strategic Nuclear Targeting* (Ithaca, N.Y.: Cornell University Press, 1986), 179.

7. As Jervis put it, Soviet and American leaders "were never convinced of the utility of MAD," and took every precaution to avoid an all-out exchange, but "it is highly probable that a conventional war, or even more likely, the limited use of nuclear

weapons, would have prompted a full-scale nuclear war that would have resulted in mutual destruction." Jervis, "Mutual Assured Destruction," 41.

8. NATO set manpower goals in its 1952 Lisbon meeting, and soon realized it had no hope of meeting them; Khrushchev in 1959 hoped to cut 1.5 million men from the Soviet military and replace them with a mirror-image of the U.S. "massive retaliation" strategy, a move the *New York Times* editors correctly understood at the time as the "sincerest form of flattery." See "Khrushchev Adopts NATO Strategy," *New York Times*, February 6, 1960, 18.

9. The Soviets abandoned Nikita Khrushchev's nuclear-heavy strategy shortly after abandoning Nikita Khrushchev in the mid-1960s; NATO, for its part, reinvigorated its conventional forces after the damage done to the U.S. Army by Vietnam finally dissipated in the early 1980s. This led John Mearsheimer to argue in 1983 that conventional forces could act as a deterrent as long as neither side could launch a successful blitzkrieg in Europe. See John J. Mearsheimer, *Conventional Deterrence* (Ithaca, N.Y.: Cornell University Press, 1983). In a more mischievous vein, Samuel Huntington the same year proposed not conventional *deterrence*, but a conventional counterinvasion of Europe should the Soviets advance. It was militarily unsustainable, but it had the virtue of infuriating the Soviets, which Huntington later admitted to his students was one of his goals in publishing it. Samuel P. Huntington, "Conventional Deterrence and Conventional Retaliation in Europe," *International Security* 8, no. 3 (Winter 1983–1984).

10. Bernard Weinraub, "The 41st President; Bush Takes Office Asking Bipartisan Help in Fighting Social Ills Despite the Deficit," *New York Times* online, January 21, 1989.

11. The United States currently has 187 F-22 "Raptor" fighters, for example, and yet, not one of them has ever flown in combat, not only because they are plagued with unremedied problems, but because they are too costly to risk in places such as North Africa. The program was halted in 2009 and the last jet rolled out of production in late 2011.

12. Kathleen Bailey, "Why We Have to Keep the Bomb," *Bulletin of the Atomic Scientists*, January–February 1995, 35.

13. Kristiana Helmick, "Perry Puts Deterrence in Dustbin and Calls for Preventive Defense," *Christian Science Monitor*, May 15, 1996.

14. The desperate wish to forget the secrets of the nuclear bomb was a recurring theme in Cold War fiction, and likely motivated Walter Miller Jr., to write his classic 1959 novel, *A Canticle for Leibowitz*, where technology is guarded by a sect of monks for centuries after the nuclear devastation of the planet. They fail, and at the book's conclusion humanity destroys itself yet again, this time permanently. See Walter Miller Jr., *A Canticle for Leibowitz* (New York: Lippincott, 1960).

Index